Public order and private lives

The title of this book highlights the way in which legislation has impinged upon the private lives of British citizens during the last ten years. The twin results have been a curtailment of their civil liberties, and a greater surveillance upon both public order and private life.

'Freedom has replaced liberty in the Conservative lexicon, just as market democracy has replaced social democracy.'

Under Margaret Thatcher the Conservative party presented itself as the only political party taking the issues of law and order seriously. The party set its agenda around these issues, emphasising individual effort and endeavour, and advocating a return to 'Victorian values'. In this challenging critique of Conservative criminology, Michael Brake and Chris Hale contest the complacency of Conservative rhetoric about law and order, and record the abysmal failure of the Tories' hard line on crime and punishment. They argue that, ironically, Conservative policies have created the very social conditions in which crime has flourished.

Brake and Hale show that the rise in crime, rather than being stemmed by Conservative policy, actually increased. They link government economic and social policy to the increased militarisation of policing, the privatisation of law and order issues, the overcrowding of prisons, the rise in crime, fraud in business and industry, and the ignoring of health and safety regulations in industry and transport in favour of profit. They describe, for example, how the Conservative government was able to marshal the police and the courts to break organised working-class resistance to their economic and social programme, and show how a law and order society was created in Britain through the passing of a series of laws which, they argue, have undermined basic civil liberties.

Crime, like unemployment, remains a fact of life in Britain today. Both problems are here to stay, the authors believe, until a government is elected which is determined to tackle their root causes, embedded in poverty and exploitation.

Public order and private lives

The politics of law and order

Michael Brake and
Chris Hale

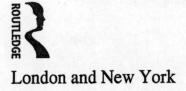

London and New York

First published in 1992
by Routledge
11 New Fetter Lane, London EC4P 4EE

Simultaneously published in the USA and Canada
by Routledge
a division of Routledge, Chapman and Hall, Inc.
29 West 35th Street, New York, NY 10001

Typeset by Michael Mepham, Frome, Somerset
Printed in Great Britain by
Biddles Ltd, Guildford and King's Lynn

British Library Cataloguing in Publication Data
Brake, Michael –
   Public order and private lives: the politics of law and order
   1. Great Britain. Public order. Role of government
   I. Title
   II. Chris Hale   364.941

Library of Congress Cataloging in Publication Data
Brake, Michael.
   Public order and private lives: the politics of law and
   order/ Michael Brake and Chris Hale
   p.   cm.
   Includes bibliographical references and index.
   1. Criminal justice, Administration of—Great Britain.   2. Great
   Britain—Social Policy—1979–   3. Criminology—Great Britain.
   I. Hale, Chris. II. Title.
   HV9960.G7B73   1992
   364.941—dc20   91–9034
                                                            CIP

ISBN 0–415–06830–4
      0–415–02567–2 (pbk)

Contents

List of tables	vi
Preface	vii
1 **Introduction**	1
2 **Economic liberalism and Conservative criminology**	13
3 **Private attitudes and public policy: control culture or the law and order society**	35
4 **The police as social workers: community and multi-agency policing**	69
5 **The failure of Conservative criminology under Thatcher**	94
6 **Fraud: white collars and grey areas**	116
7 **Inside the crisis and the crisis inside: prisons, punishment and Conservative criminology**	136
8 **Is Conservative criminology here to stay?**	158
Bibliography	174
Name index	184
Subject index	187

Tables

7.1 Sentencing trends (%) in England and Wales for
adult male convicted of indictable offences 1968–88   144

7.2 Prison overcrowding: the ten worst prisons on
31 March 1990   146

Preface

The original project for this book was suggested by Dr Steven Box, Reader in Criminology at the University of Kent. For Steve the criminological enterprise involved uncovering the skulduggery of the great and the good, and the revelations of the peccadilloes and criminal endeavours of the privileged filled him with glee. Criminology was linked intimately with studies of the powerful and the dispossessed. He understood the material basis of working-class criminality and the board room greed which produced corporate and white-collar crime. For him the deviant world was summarised in the title of Jeffrey Reiman's book, 'The rich get richer and the poor get prison.' No one had a defter hand in delving through the quotations quarries or scavenging obscure articles to make political points. Steve was a committed scholar with a keen academic mind. He defended the poor, and emphasised the structural reasons why the powerless were projected on criminal careers. As a control theorist he was puzzled as to why so many failed to riot or rebel. He was an interactionist who delighted in the games people play, an exchange theorist who understood gambling for something better and a structuralist who recognised the influence of the political economy.

He died tragically from cancer in 1987. Towards the end of his life he struggled with the ideological influences of sexism, writing one of the best analyses of rape by a male sociologist. He was a gifted lecturer who delighted in performing during his addresses, spicing his discussions with music hall songs, anecdotes and limericks. He was a good friend to us both and we miss him and owe him much. This book is dedicated to him – thanks for the ideas Steve, the mistakes are ours.

ACKNOWLEDGEMENTS

We would like to thank Eugene McLaughlin, for a sympathetic but critical reading of an earlier draft, Talia Rodgers of Routledge for persevering with what must have seemed like a never-to-be-completed task and Delice Gambrill for her valiant help in typing the manuscript. Finally we must thank Nicola and Tom, and Fran, Jack, Kate, Jody and Seth for their encouragement.

1 Introduction

> The most disturbing threat to our freedom and security is the growing disrespect for the rule of law. In government as in opposition, Labour have undermined it.... The number of crimes in England and Wales is nearly half as much again as it was in 1973. The next Conservative government will spend more on fighting crime even while we economise elsewhere.... Britain needs strong, efficient police forces with high morale.
>
> (Conservative Party Election Manifesto 1979)

> The origins of crime lie deep in society: in families where parents do not support or control their children; in schools where discipline is poor; and in the wider world where violence is glamorised and traditional values are under attack.
>
> Government *alone* cannot tackle such deep-rooted problems easily or quickly.
>
> (Conservative Party Election Manifesto 1987)

In one sense, law and order can be seen as the Conservative confidence trick of the 1980s, yet, in another, it was an integral part of their success. The emphasis on strong policing and the need to deter by the use of incarceration were key planks in their 1979 election propaganda. They certainly did not fail to meet the pledges made during that campaign to increase expenditure on the institutions of the criminal justice system. While other spending departments came under the razor-edged scrutiny of the Treasury and the ideologues of the market, the Home Office managed to expand the resources at its proposal. The cost of policing England and Wales increased by 60 per cent in real terms between 1974–75 and 1989–90 from £2.58 billion to £4.12 billion (Graef 1990). A major prison building programme was planned and its implementation begun. However, the implicit promise to reduce crime has palpably failed, if the official figures used by the Tories themselves are to be believed. Between 1979 and 1988 there was a 45 per cent increase in the numbers of notifiable offences reported to the police (Criminal Statistics

1988). This figure includes a reduction in recorded offences of 5 per cent in 1988, a turndown greeted with much self-congratulation by Home Office ministers. Figures for 1989 (*Guardian* 30.3.1990), which showed an annual increase of 4.2 per cent, and the highest ever rise in recorded crime of 17 per cent in the second quarter of 1990 compared with the same period of 1989 (*Independent* 27.9.90), suggest that this fall was simply a transitory blip in the otherwise steady increase in recorded crime. The average annual change in serious crimes known to the police was 4.3 per cent between 1979 and 1988 compared to 4.2 per cent between 1974 and 1979. Furthermore, the national clear-up rate was 41 per cent in 1979 but had fallen to 35 per cent by 1988 and 34 per cent in 1989, a drop of 17 per cent. Clearly the idea that the Conservative Party has the answers to rising crime rates has become difficult to sustain. However, equally there can be no doubt, that it has successfully portrayed itself as the only political party which takes the issues of law and order seriously.

In this book we will explore the notion that the Conservative Government, first elected in 1979 developed, as part of its determined campaign to replace socialism with a market economy, a distinct project: to reduce State involvement in the field of welfare provision and to break the power of the trade unions. To succeed with either aim it felt it had to develop a strong State in the arena of law and order, a task in which it could rely upon traditional conservatism for support. This first emerged in Margaret Thatcher's 1979 notorious 'barrier of steel' speech, in which she set her agenda by referring disparagingly to the support given by Labour cabinet ministers to the pickets at the free enterprise inspired, non-unionised Grunwick plant, commenting that:

> Labour ministers do not seem to understand their own responsibilities in the unending task of upholding the law in a free society.... Do they not understand that when ministers go on the picket line and when Labour backbenchers attack the police for trying to do their difficult job, that gives the green light for lawless methods right throughout the industry?
>
> (Televised campaign meeting 19 May 1979.
> Quoted in Taylor 1987)

Clarke and Taylor (1980) neatly make the point that this occurred the night before the appearance of Police Federation-financed advertisements in the national press challenging the prospective parties for the 1979 election to tackle what they saw as the problem of law and order. The Conservatives' commitment to the strong State and the rule of law meant they became engaged in the most openly partisan defence of law and order in post-war politics. The Conservative Government was setting its agenda around the issues of law and order, welfare, shiftlessness and immorality. It intended to move societal responsibility back to the individual and morality back to the family.

In order to understand this Conservative agenda, and in particular the area of law and order, which is the focus of this book, it is necessary to consider the post-war history of the economy in Britain, since the crisis of hegemony in the 1970s occurred precisely because of the failure of earlier attempts to achieve the restructuring required by capital within a Keynesian welfare-oriented framework. The identification of the Labour Party and the trade unions with the failure of this corporatist approach was used by the radical right, which had gained influence within the Tory Party in the 1970s, to launch an attack on the consensus approach to economic and social problems which had developed since 1945.

THE BRITISH ECONOMY SINCE 1945

Here we can only sketch the post-war economic developments in Britain. The brief discussion which follows has benefited from the work to be found in the journal of the Conference of Socialist Economists, *Capital and Class* and in particular from reading Atkins (1986), Gamble (1983), Grahl (1983), Hymans (1987) and McDonnell (1978). Another useful, if more sympathetic, source of information on the economic performance under Mrs Thatcher may be found in Maynard (1988).

The major economic crises of the 1920s and 1930s resulted in greatly increased intervention by the State in the economy and the adoption of Keynesianism in an attempt to reconcile the interests of capital and labour. Through taxation and Government borrowing the State actively intervened in the economy to encourage economic growth by keeping consumption high. The Labour Government of 1945–51 was committed to full employment and improved living conditions for the working class. There was an increase in State involvement in social policy, an expansion of welfare benefits and the establishment of the National Health Service. The Tory Governments of the 1950s accepted this 'welfarism' and it became part of the consensus of British political life. The parties might argue over the details of policy but the commitment to the Welfare State itself was not in question. The trade unions had co-operated closely with the Labour Government and the Tories avoided any confrontation with them. Indeed McDonnell argues that:

Working class demands were allowed to become the motor of capitalist development. Wage rises were permitted with productivity increases and rises beyond them were covered with mild inflation.

(McDonnell 1978)

During this period, under the Tories, economic policy followed cycles of contractions followed by expansion. Because of the strength of the working class the Government attempted to control wages by a succession of incomes policies, each of which met with only limited success. Economic policy at this time consisted, according to McDonnell:

> of reactions to the consequences of the underlying problems of the economy (balance of payments deficits, currency crises) without any real attempt to tackle these problems (low investment, low productivity).
>
> (McDonnell 1978)

The end of the 1950s saw a faltering in the post-war expansion of the British economy. This was due in part to the independence, and subsequent actions to defend their interests, of many Third World countries and also to the rapid expansion of the Japanese and German economies. However, the main reason was the strength of the trade unions, and in particular that of the shop stewards' movement, which was able to keep wage bargaining and other negotiations at the plant level, and so prevent employers from keeping down wage costs. It became clear that the economic boom had been maintained by an expansion of credit which had protected inefficient firms. What was required was a radical restructuring of the economy. However, the commitment to full employment and the strong working-class organisations made this difficult if not impossible. Instead the trend towards corporatism was intensified and the solution to the problem sought through the institutionalisation of class conflict and a massive increase in State apparatuses. The Labour Government elected in 1964 oversaw a proliferation of new State structures and the inclusion of the trade unions in the process of economic and State planning. Following the balance of payments crisis of 1965–66 the full-employment policy was abandoned and replaced by an incomes policy, sterling devaluation and industrial rationalisations. Employers attempted to force increases in productivity, wage cuts and rising unemployment on the workers. The end of the 1960s saw a major upsurge of mainly unofficial strikes and the incomes policy was finally broken in 1969. This resistance to forced cuts in living standards led to poor industrial relations being perceived as the root of the British problem.

The Tory Government elected in 1970 was committed to a radical programme of economic reform which foreshadowed what was to come in 1979. Committed at the start to the desirability of free market forces it abandoned the interventionist strategy and began to dismantle the State bureaucracy. Economic crises were to be allowed to force 'lame duck' firms into bankruptcy. Incomes policy was renounced as unemployment and strict control of public sector expenditure were to ensure wage restraint. The Industrial Relations Act was passed to place legal restraints on the power of the unions in an attempt to alter the balance of class forces. However, a number of bankruptcies of major companies such as Rolls Royce and the Upper Clyde Shipbuilders forced the Tories to abandon their non-interventionist stance, and strong working-class resistance to the Industrial Relations Act meant it was rarely applied. The abandonment of this radical approach led to the crises of profitability between 1972 and 1974 again being tackled by statutory incomes policies and familiar Keynesian measures to raise total demand by increasing State expenditure or to hold down costs by cutting taxation. These measures failed and led to a growing State budget deficit and the fiscal crisis of the mid-1970s. There were increasing tensions in industrial relations with numerous strikes culminating in the miners' strike of 1974 which contributed to the Tories' defeat in the general election of the same year.

Initially the new Labour Government reasserted its interventionist strategy. It repealed the Industrial Relations Act and, since the experience of the previous administration had shown that a statutory incomes policy was unlikely to be successful against the wishes of the trade unions, it negotiated a voluntary agreement, the Social Contract, with them. To create a suitable climate for this the 1974 Budget contained several measures advocated by the Trades Union Congress including subsidies on housing and food and increased welfare and pension payments. By the end of the year, however, the Government was announcing limits on planned increases in public expenditure and, as it became clear that the Social Contract was failing, in 1975 they launched a major campaign, aided by the press, to set a definite limit on wage increases. Meanwhile in his Budget speech in March 1975, Denis Healey argued that high unemployment was part of the price to be paid for high levels of inflation. As the incomes policy creaked, the Government began to rely on restricting the money supply and cutting public expenditure in the hope that tight monetary policy linked to increasing unemployment would produce wage restraint.

By 1976 following yet another series of sterling crises and the visit of officials from the International Monetary Fund, major cuts in public expenditure were announced in February, July and December. At the same time a major ideological campaign against State expenditure was launched by the Labour Government. While they were at this time abandoning commitments to welfarism supposedly under the pressure of the IMF, the Tory Party and nearly all the national press were ahead of them. If for the Labour Party monetarism was presented as a pragmatic necessity, for the Tories it became part of an ideology. They had adopted a thorough-going monetarist position in which the huge Government borrowing requirement and the subsequent increases in the money supply were the major problems. To quote from their 1979 manifesto:

To master inflation, proper monetary discipline is essential with publicly stated targets for the rate of growth of the money supply. At the same time a gradual reduction in the size of the Government's borrowing requirement is also vital.... The State takes too much of the Nation's income; its share must be steadily reduced. When it spends and borrows too much, taxes, interest rates, prices and unemployment rise so that in the long run there is less wealth with which to improve our standard of living.

(Conservative Manifesto 1979, p.8)

Massive cuts in State expenditure were, they argued, the only answer to the crisis. In addition State welfare expenditure was seen as stifling individual initiative, individual enterprise, and as holding back industrial investment and exports. Whether or not in practice the Tories ever had strict monetary policy or indeed the previous Labour administration had been anything other than competent in its policy is at least debatable. At the level of policy or ideology, however, it is crucial since, in the words of Gamble:

monetarism represents an attempt to legitimate the abandonment of responsibility for levels of unemployment and rates of economic growth and to protect the essentials of market order.

(Gamble 1984, p.15)

In its first years in power the Tories were faced with a massive deepening of the world recession. By 1981 industrial production was 12 per cent below the 1979 level, itself a marginal recovery from the 1975 slump. The doubling of the oil price and sterling's role as a petro-currency had led to a massive rise in the exchange rate between 1979 and 1980 resulting in a 30 per cent decline in international competitiveness. Unemployment in England and Wales leapt from a daily average of 1.4 million in 1979 to 2.3 million in 1981. Ironically, of course, this led to an immediate increase in welfare payments and an increase in Government expenditure and borrowing. With hindsight the depth of the recession was a bonus for the Tories since the shakeout of labour led to a weakening of the unions and a sharp reduction in strikes and pay claims.

So the years 1974–76 marked a watershed in the post-war Keynesian welfarist consensus in the United Kingdom. The Labour Government embraced monetarism and implicitly by so doing abandoned any commitment to maintaining full employment. It pursued reductions in public expenditure which were to make it difficult for the following Tory administration to find easy targets for cuts. More importantly it laid the ideological foundation for the so-called Thatcherite revolution. By involving the unions in the decision-making procedure they contributed to the weakening of their strength within the working class. The Unions and Labour became identified with the existence of an overbearing State bureaucracy which stifled individual initiative and encouraged moral decline through the welfare system. For the Tory Party a central feature of this monetarist approach was an attack on the Welfare State. Gough argues that this is for two reasons. First:

> it allegedly generates even higher tax levels, budget deficits, disincentives to work and save, and a bloated class of unproductive workers. Second because it encourages 'soft' attitudes to crime, immigrants, the idle, the feckless, strikers, the sexually aberrant and so forth.

(Gough 1983)

Again by undermining the welfare system the power of trade unions is attacked: one of the Conservatives' first measures in the 1980 Budget was to cut the amount of welfare benefits to which families of strikers were entitled. And in addition it reaffirmed the virtues of self-reliance, individualism, family and personal responsibility. Individuals must be encouraged to take responsibility for their own destiny and those who are unable to cope, or who are morally deficient should not expect sympathy. In this populist ideology generous welfare provisions and soft criminal justice policies are entwined in their detrimental effect upon morality and responsibility for the increasing crime problem.

In many ways the key to the subsequent Tory economic success was their industrial relations strategy which had the simple aim of breaking the power of the unions. The Employment Acts of 1980 and 1982 and the Trade Union Act of 1984 substantially restricted the legal possibilities for collective action by trade unions. The 1980 Act introduced the use of secret ballots prior to strike action, and restricted immunity for secondary industrial action, such as the blacking of goods and sympathy strikes. A Code of Practice introduced at the same time recommended that picketing be restricted to the workplace and that a maximum of six people was consistent with peaceful picketing. The 1982 Act placed union funds at risk by allowing unions as well as their officials to be sued for damages where they were responsible for 'unlawful action'. Since it also restricted the definition of a lawful trade dispute to those between workers and their own employers it meant that any supportive action was likely to place union funds in jeopardy. Finally, the 1984 Act laid down that legal immunities for strike action could only be maintained if supported by a majority of the union members in a secret ballot held not more than 4 weeks prior to its commencement.

These policies for radical reform of the economy had to be supported in the ideological sphere. For the Conservative government elected in 1979, law and order meant new forms of social discipline, leading, they hoped, to self-discipline. The ideological aspect of what we see as Conservative criminology during this period emerges because it has resonance with their economic policies. Under Conservatism, law and order is a metaphor for certain forms of morality, emphasising individual effort and endeavour. Ironically Conservative policies created the very social conditions in which crime has flourished. They have undermined many structural features, such as full employment, job security and the belief that the State would make provision for housing, health care and income maintenance. In order to shift responsibility from these effects they have been obliged to conceptualise public disorder and rising crime as moral issues, the acts of bad people. Crime has been dislocated from any structural context. Young offenders may be seen as passing through a phase, but responsible adult law breakers are seen as wicked individuals, needing punishment not mollycoddling.

CONSERVATIVE CRIMINOLOGY

For us there are several distinctive features of a conservative criminology. First, social conditions are irrelevant to criminality; it is the individual who is basically evil. Second, punishment and retribution are central. Third, and this follows on from the first two, there is a pessimistic emphasis on crime prevention through greater vigilance and awareness of the individual citizen. There is an essentialist flavour to this which rejects both psychological maladjustment and economic conditions in the aetiology of crime. Criminals are basically evil and the responsibility for this lies with themselves and their families who failed to install basic decency and morality.

One can, however, see the contradictions inherent in this when comparing the sentences of between 1 and 5 years meted out to the defendants in the Guinness fraud case with the outcry over the Strangeways prison uprising. Some people are better than others even if they are criminal. Class and respectability prevail over criminal acts. We shall argue in this book that conservative criminology has been made Conservative criminology through the development of law and order policies. That is to say, a political and ideological rather than an academic discourse has informed law and order policies. It has been politicians with enjoinders from both senior and rank-and-file police officers who have set the agenda. Whilst there may have been a populist groundswell which contributed to notions of Conservative criminology, expertise has been contributed by the judiciary and journalist and moral entrepreneurs, rather than by academics. Professional criminologists in Britain, unlike, as we shall see later, their counterparts in the United States, have not been a serious voice in the law and order debate.

Part of the story to be told in this book will record the abysmal failure of the Tory Party's hard retributive line on law and order. Another will be to acknowledge their use of the issue to distinguish themselves from the Labour Party, with its supposedly soft approach to crime and industrial relations. We shall see, from the arguments developed here, that while simply looking at the crime figures shows just how dismal this failure has been, the Conservatives nevertheless have succeeded in two important aspects. First, they have used law and order as a central unifying theme in their hegemonic project. An important part of this achievement was their ability to label industrial action and public protests as inherently criminal. This laid the foundations for their second success, in that they were able to marshall the police and the courts to break organised working-class resistance to their economic and social programme.

Clearly the tough policies and increased expenditure did not have the desired effect upon crime rates themselves, and this did not escape notice within the Government, and there was a subtle shift in emphasis in ministerial utterances on law and order from 1983 onwards. It was no longer simply a matter of extolling the virtues of strong police powers and tougher sentencing to curb crime; the problem was seen as a steady rise in the crime rate, not just in Britain, but in most other countries, too, due to uncontrollable exogenous forces. As with inflation, while successes were seen to be due to correct policies, failures were the result of factors outside the Government's power or reflected general world trends. The causes of increasing crime levels were perceived to lie within the family, schools and the media. Exactly how the Government has helped support family life or maintained the schools with its policies on social welfare and education is an issue to which we will return later in this work. For the Conservatives, it is not their economic policies, which have resulted in levels of unemployment, which are, even after the falls of 1988–1990 extremely high by historical standards, and a sizeable proportion of the population living below the poverty line, that have caused crime to rise but rather it is due to 'indiscipline, slovenliness and warped social attitudes' (*Politics Today*, February 1988, p.48). The law and order issue thus has been removed from the political economy into the realms of individual morality and pathology. In her own inimitable style Mrs Thatcher reminded us that what was therefore needed was to:

restore a clear ethic of person responsibility – we need to establish that the main person responsible for each crime is the criminal.

(Speech to the Annual Conference of Conservative Officers,
March 1988)

If anyone else were to blame, she continued:

it is the professional progressives among broadcasters, social workers and politicians who have created a fog of excuses in which the mugger and the burglar operate.

Gradually, Government speakers, as well as reiterating continued commitment to the police and prison building programmes, were also raising the idea that the police could not continue without public support. The corollary to this was the need to involve the public and businesses in combatting crime. In Mrs Thatcher's words:

> Combating crime is everybody's business. It cannot be left solely to the police anymore than we can leave our health solely to doctors.
>
> (Speech to Conservative Women's Conference, May 1988)

The way forward, the Government suggested, was through crime prevention programmes argued for in a series of papers published by the Home Office Research and Planning unit. This campaign implicitly suggesed that not much could be done about the fact that people commit crimes, but focused instead on reducing the opportunity to do so. Of course, if criminals are born not bred, then this approach combined with a policy of incarceration to quarantine the worst offenders, is no doubt sensible. The fly in the ointment is that prisons are expensive but appear ineffective in deterring criminals. Consequently, not only had the community become the focus of crime prevention but increasingly it had become involved in the punishment of the offender.

In the following chapters we will examine the use made by the Conservative Party of the law and order issue before the 1979 election and how the emphasis it gave to the problem has changed both in practice and rhetoric since then. As we suggested above and will expand further, this will involve examining not only their policies towards the police and sentencing but also their economic and social policies, since we believe that these themselves have had profound implications and repercussions for their more obviously criminological strategies. We begin by considering the impact of academic writers, and in particular the doyen of the American New Right criminologists, James Q. Wilson on the development of the Tory Party's ideas on crime prevention. More generally, we will look at how the influential economic and philosophical ideas of Frederick von Hayek, on individual freedom in the economic sphere, have required the presence of a strong State in order to establish the conditions for this freedom to flourish.

Throughout this book we will consider the development of a control culture, which we argue is a necessary corollary to the enterprise culture so dear to the heart of Conservative free-market economics, and so antithetical to the culture of dependency they see as created by the post-war consensus on welfare policy. We will examine the creation of the law and order society in Britain in the 1980s and the passing of a series of laws which, we will argue, have undermined basic civil liberties. Just as collectivism has become unfashionable, so have civil rights, being reduced to yet another expression of permissiveness. Freedom has replaced liberty in the Conservative lexicon, just as market democracy has replaced social democracy. This was made easier by the reintroduction of the social deviant, of the wicked and evil criminal, for whom excuses could no longer be made by soft-hearted do-gooders. This legitimated changes in legislation for reasons of political expediency rather than as extensions of democracy. The development of the control culture gave a more central role to the police, particularly in the arena of public order. One result of this was to call into question their public accountability.

As well as examining the changing fortunes of the police we will discuss the implications of their adoption of a more social-work oriented role via the vehicle of multi-agency policing while developing the technological resources to aid their reactive involvement in fire-brigading public-order situations. In discussing the police we will need to consider the debates which surrounded the 1984 Police and Criminal Evidence (PACE) Act.

Key moments in policing are considered within the context of concern about the rise in crime figures. By retaining the argument about evil individuals, the Government managed to exclude criticism about the political economy and the social structure which became associated with Thatcherism. Unemployment, it was argued, had nothing to do with crime; urban rioting nothing to do with deteriorating public/police relations. We will also consider a spin-off from Conservative notions about criminology, by examining the crimes of private enterprise – fraud, tax evasion and the deterioration of public and industrial health and safety, as well as the crimes of poverty, such as welfare fraud.

The government was plainly faced with a distinct contradiction. On the one hand it favoured a firm hand concerning law and order, but on the other, this was limited by the overcrowding of the prisons, forcing it to rethink and disguise 'soft options' as punishment in the community. By the mid-1980s, there was resignation to the fact that crime was a fact of life, and its increase inevitable. There were the beginnings of a privatised crime prevention programme by encouraging private enterprise and self-help. Neighbourhood watch schemes, self-fitted window locks were all part of this, as was the suggestion of private security firms used for electronic surveillance and private prisons and remand centres. Taylor (1987) compares the crime figures in the mid-1980s for Britain with the USA, where crime figures actually declined under Reagan. This suggested something distinctive about the English situation. Law and order policies, as with Thatcherite economic policies, were declared above reproach; it was therefore individual morality and family socialisation which was at fault. That there might be a link between rising crime, and a divided and deteriorating society was excluded from the debate, even though in this period racism was rife (the Joint Campaign against Racism estimated 20,000 racist attacks on black people in

1985). These attacks were often murderous, and the longevity of these and their perennial nature have been shown by the fact that in 1989 Asian schoolchildren in East London had to be accompanied to school because of organised racist attacks upon them.

We are faced with a scenario where on the one hand, there are distinct signs of social discontent, with its disorder, violence and increase in crime, and on the other hand, the cynical self-advancement of the enterprise culture which prioritises individuality over social responsibility. If getting rich by any sharp means is legitimated at one end of society, then using petty crime to pay for a good time over and above the subsistence level of welfare benefits or low wages, is hardly surprising. Those marginalised in the enterprise culture are subject to the same consumer pressures as the upwardly mobile employed, yet are clearly locked out of the golden world of the advertisements.

The move from controlling crime to cynically accepting it, and then trying to economise by developing punishment in the community as an alternative to the cost of custody indicates the extent to which the Government has surrendered its law and order campaign in the 1990s. By this period crime figures, like unemployment figures, had risen steadily, and crime like unemployment, became rewritten as an unpleasant fact of life. Both problems are here to stay until a government is elected which is determined to tackle their root causes, embedded in poverty and exploitation.

2 Economic liberalism and Conservative criminology

> For my first 25 years in politics it was socialist ideas that were influencing Conservatives. But the world has seen Socialism now and it is not for free human beings, it is not for the British character. It produces neither prosperity nor human dignity.
>
> (Margaret Thatcher, *Independent* 14.9.87)

The election of the 1979 Conservative Government, under the leadership of Margaret Thatcher, and the remarkable series of political victories which followed led to a very particular form of government. At a structural level there was the implementation of a series of economic and social policies premised on encouraging the freeing of the market. At the level of social psychology these were supported by a distinct set of social values premised upon individual responsibility. The Conservatives declared war upon socialism, (whether of the Labour or Tory variety), seen as underpinning a set of ideas and policies responsible for Britain's moral and economic decline in the post-war period. The major factor behind this deconstruction of economic and political theory, and the creation of a cultural climate conducive to accepting the equating of collective responsibility with totalitarianism, was Mrs Thatcher. Her self-confident personality and dogmatic leadership was ideally suited to communicating the populist ideas which appeal so uncritically to 'common sense'. One major area in which this appeal was made was that of law and order. While the academic discipline, criminology, has been at least partially rooted in that Conservative anathema, sociology, we shall see that in the 1970s and 1980s there developed within it a body of opinion that was used to justify more repressive measures by an appeal to convenience.

The Tory Government's aim was to establish an enterprise culture aimed at reducing dependency on the Welfare State by substituting self-sufficiency and individualism. As part of its strategy to develop such specific social values as nationalism, thrift, self-help and the sanctity of the nuclear family, it declared war on those perceived as threatening this social order, whether they were the terrorist, the trade union militant, the football hooligan, the permissive teacher or the 'soft' social worker.

To sustain public confidence in its ideas of discipline and order, the Conservative Government has had an ongoing commitment to combat crime. It promised to make the public street, as well as the private household, safe. Faced with the rising crime rates in the 1970s it declared itself the party of social discipline, the architect of a safer Britain. Prior to the 1979 election as we indicated, it emphasised the importance of supporting the police, and of swift and sure punishment with incarceration as the centrepiece. However, its policy even then was not simply that of the 'hang 'em and flog 'em brigade'. As Norman Tebbit succinctly put it, the problems of inner city life will be solved by:

> bringing back personal responsibility (through ownership), security (through law and order) and stability (through strengthening a sense of personal obligation, most notably within families).

> (Tebbit 1985)

Here, neatly tied together, are the themes: individual responsibility, the strong involvement of the State in security and the importance of the (nuclear) family for the transmission of moral values, which were constantly restated in Conservative statements on crime. Notable for its absence is, as usual, any need for the redistribution of income or any societal responsibility for wrongdoing. Whether security implies reducing crime or maintaining public order is a moot point. This philosophy impinged on most areas of life in the Thatcher decade and criminology could not have been expected to be an exception. Indeed, probably no government has ever generated such a level of comment and criticism around the issues of law and order, crime rates, public order and civil rights. One can also trace a relationship between the emergence, both in this country and the United States, of New-Right views about the nature of crime and the drift of Conservative thinking on crime and justice. This could be seen most clearly in the introduction of ideas on crime control, through the advocacy of private crime prevention schemes such as 'Neighbourhood Watch', by environmental manipulation – 'designing out crime', and extending and intensifying social control in the forlorn hope of reducing crime through the processes of discipline, deterrence and incapacitation. The Conservatives knew that the root causes of crime lay within the individual and hence preventing it by programmes of social intervention, such as those favoured, for example, by the French (see King 1989) was ruled out a *priori*. Similar reasoning led to the abandonment of any notion of rehabilitation of offenders: punishment whether in prison or in the community was to deter, and workers in the Probation Service were to become community-based warders rather than social workers.

LAW AND ORDER AS A PARTY POLITICAL ISSUE

People have asked me whether I am going to make the fight against crime an issue at the next General Election. No I am not going to make it an issue. It is the People of Britain who are going to make it an issue.

(Margaret Thatcher, Conservative Party Conference 1977)

Whatever the truth of this claim, within 12 months of making it, Mrs Thatcher gave the go-ahead to an advertising campaign, which so distorted the criminal statistics it had to be withdrawn because of widespread protests (*Guardian* 8.10.80). In the run-up to the General Election of 1979 the Tory Party correctly identified 'law and order' as the crystallisation of a range of social anxieties, successfully distinguishing itself from the other political parties as alone having solutions which made sense to ordinary people; support for the beleaguered police force and swift and punitive punishments. It drew together into a compelling tapestry the threads of industrial relations, public order and street crimes intertwining for good measure racism by isolating young black men as the sources of, and inner cities as, the sites of danger. The mugger on the street became symbolic of the general moral and economic decline of the nation.

In their muddled but different ways, the vandals on the picket lines and the muggers in our streets have got the same confused message – 'we want our demands met or else' and 'get out of the way give us your handbag'.

(Margaret Thatcher 1979)

This imagery struck a chord in the popular consciousness suffering under the widespread malaise and demoralisation produced by the Labour Party's inability to cope with the economic decline of the 1970s. The Tories seized upon the industrial unrest of the period as a clear sign of Labour's lack of 'discipline' and moral fibre. Thus the *Daily Telegraph* of March 1979 quoted Mrs Thatcher as saying:

A Trade Union leader has advised his members to carry on picketing because they would act in such numbers that the authorities would need to use football stadiums as detention centres. That is the rule of the mob and not of law, and ought to be condemned by every institution and minister in the land. The demand in the country will be for two things: less tax and more law and order.

(Daily Telegraph March 1979)

While promising to loosen the restraining hand of government in the economic sphere there was a commitment to strengthen it in the law and order arena. As David Downes observed:

> it evidently occurred to the Tories at the time of the Grunwick dispute, if not before, that Labour were vulnerable to attack on the 'law and order' flank of their industrial relations record. From that point it was a short step to the association of Labour with rising crime rates and falling moral standards.
>
> (Downes 1981, p.1)

At the same time this apparent populism was inattentive to other areas of 'invisible victimisation' and the consequent marginality of the victimised groups. Little, if any, discussion of corporate crime, racist attacks on black people, domestic violence, child abuse (save in the context of strengthening the family), sexual assault, police discrimination or attacks on the gay community will be found in Tory statements on law and order. Concentration on the dramas of mugging, armed robbery and public disorder justified shifts towards 'reactive' or 'fire-brigade' policing while at the same time the supposed existence of apparently dangerous sub-populations was used to warrant both disproportionate surveillance and punitive sentencing. Ironically the continued growth in recorded crime since 1979 did not seem to have worked to the Conservatives' disadvantage, but, as noted earlier, it did necessitate a displacement of explanations of crime to essentialist categories such as personal responsibility, declining moral standards and indiscipline. We will return to this shift later concentrating upon the Conservatives' stance on policing, public order and penal policy.

In Conservative ideology, the reasons for Britain's economic decline are intimately related to those aspects of creeping socialism, which brought disorder to the streets. The election of the Conservative Government in May 1979 was a watershed which marked a distinct change in the rhetoric in which the casualties of society were discussed, and a sharp acceleration in existing trends in the way they were treated. In particular, the rehabilitative approach to offenders was abandoned in favour of punitiveness, social problems became private ills and personal defects and poverty came to be seen in a way reminiscent of the distinction in the previous century between deserving and undeserving poor. The particular focus of this book is how, within the framework of a broader social policy, Conservative philosophy and populist beliefs have interacted in practice to produce and change the law and order programme of the British Government since 1979.

In the remainder of this chapter we will examine the new Conservative criminology which arose in opposition to the liberal rehabilitative consensus of the late 1960s and early 1970s.

THE CONTEXT OF CONSERVATIVE CRIMINOLOGY

In the ideological battle waged by the Conservatives before and after 1979 the Conservative Party successfully projected itself as the party of law and order. Conversely, the Labour Party has been pilloried as the bastion of permissiveness which uncritically supports the poor, the deviant, the feckless and the idle regardless of individual worthiness. The Labour Party, dominated, it has been argued, by its militants finds excuses for inner city youth. Its 'loony left' local authorities (personified, prior to its dismemberment by the Government in 1985, by the Greater London Council) have been obsessed by their support for non-familial, non-British residents, by their promotion and support for anti-racist, anti-sexist education programmes, gay support groups, lesbian mothers and other marginalised groups. The Labour Party, this argument continues, has presided over and encouraged a lack of discipline and failure of individual responsibility which resulted in the general economic and social decline.

The New Conservatism, from which Mrs Thatcher drew intellectual sustenance, relies heavily upon the economic philosophy of Frederick von Hayek and Milton Friedman to criticise the Welfare State by arguing that democracy and, indeed, freedom can only be based upon free-market choices. Interestingly, Hayek argues that the State, apart from providing a safety net against common hazards of life such as accidents and unforeseeable illness, should be interventionist only in the area of law and order. Indeed, the maintenance of public order and the policing of crime is a prerequisite for the proper functioning of the market.

In the United States as in Britain there has been a similar reaction by the right against soft approaches to law and order. Permissive attitudes were held to blame for the increase in crime during the 1960s and 1970s. This led to a revival of the classical theory of criminal responsibility which echoed the individualism of the marketplace.

Crudely, this conservative criminology may be characterised as resting upon two intellectual positions, both of which have had important policy implications. The first argues that explanations seeking the causes of crime in social conditions are wrong; answers lie at the level of individual characteristics. Furthermore, governments should not in any case interfere in these conditions. Such a strategy is presented as futility itself on intellectual grounds but is merely a reflection of the conservative propensity for hands-off government. The second belief is grounded in that brand of neoclassical economics which sees criminals involved in a complex internal calculus of utilities before deciding whether or not to commit an offence. In the words of Gary Becker, an offender offends:

if the expected utility to him exceeds the utility he could get by using his time and other resources at other activities. Some persons become 'criminals', therefore not because their basic motivation differs from that of other persons, but because their benefits and costs differ.

(quoted in Thompson *et al.* 1981)

Given these premises conservatives generally hold to some variant of the notion that crime is caused by inadequate 'control'. Insufficient checks on the instinctive desires and proclivities which cause people to break the law have led to high levels of crime. Conservatives ignore the other side of the neoclassical coin. They emphasise making crime less attractive by increasing its cost, which, since increasing arrest and conviction rates have in practice proved difficult, means increasing punishment, and ignore the possibility of increasing the benefits from law-abiding behaviour by, for example, improving the quantity and quality of employment opportunity.

THE LIGHTING OF THE BONFIRE OF THE VANITIES

An influential example of this response within the academic community, but one which had a much wider impact, was the work of James Q. Wilson. Wilson, a highly respected academic who was Professor of Government at Harvard and is now Professor of Management at the University of California, Los Angeles, has published extensively in the criminological field. We will examine Wilson's work as being representative of the pragmatic, policy-oriented approach which developed during the 1970s. In 1975 in *Thinking about Crime* he summarised much of the academic and technical literature on crime. Wilson, as are most conservative criminologists, is mainly concerned with robbery, burglary, larceny and car theft and ignores white-collar crime since:

> it also reflects my conviction, which I believe is the conviction of most citizens that predatory street crime is a far more serious matter than consumer fraud, antitrust violations and prostitution and gambling

(Wilson 1975, p. xix)

Wilson's reasons for this belief, which are not, incidentally, borne out by the evidence from research into public attitudes on white-collar crime (see, for example, Braithwaite 1982), is that such crime:

> makes difficult or impossible the maintenance of meaningful human communities.

(Wilson 1975, p. xix)

For Wilson crime, rather than inadequate transportation, unemployment, declining retail sales, poor housing, pollution or rising taxes, is the major factor in urban decline. Crime is symbolic of the breakdown of community cohesiveness which has gone hand in hand with the flight to the suburbs of middle class 'community leaders', who traditionally maintained local, neighbourhood standards of decency.

Wilson is critical of what he calls the 'social science view' of crime which he considers dominated American Presidential Commissions of the 1960s. By this he means the view that:

> crime is the result of poverty, racial discrimination, and other privations, and that the only morally defensible and substantively efficacious strategy for reducing crime is to attack its 'root causes' with programmes that aid poverty, reduce discrimination and meliorate privation.
>
> (Wilson 1975, p.43)

Wilson, observing that American crime rates had continued to rise during the 1960s and 1970s, when, he suggests, great advances were made in the income, schooling and housing of almost all segments of American society argues vigorously against the very concept of root causes. These for him:

> cannot be the object of policy efforts precisely because, being ultimate, they cannot be changed.
>
> (Wilson 1975, p.50)

This statement is justified by the observation that while it is an accepted fact that men commit more crimes than women and younger men more than older ones, this is, for obvious reasons, of little use to policy makers concerned with crime prevention. Failure to understand the point that:

> human behaviour ultimately derives from human volition... (which are, in turn) either formed entirely by choice or are the product of biological or social processes that we cannot or will not change.
>
> (ibid p.50)

has led politicians and citizens to believe that no problem is adequately addressed unless its causes are eliminated. Concluding that by regarding:

> any crime prevention or crime reduction program as defective because it does not address the 'root causes' of crime, then we shall commit ourselves to futile acts that frustrate the citizen while they ignore the criminal.
>
> (ibid p.51)

Wilson calls instead for:

a sober view of man and his institutions that would permit reasonable things to be accomplished, foolish things abandoned and utopian things forgotten.

(Wilson 1975, p.198)

To reduce the crime rate by altering the mental state of citizens is expensive and hazardous and so Wilson returns to the classical utilitarian theories of Bentham and Beccaria to propose that the policy maker has more to gain by:

altering risks, benefits, alternatives and accessibility.

(ibid p.54)

Wilson assumes that, apart from an unstable minority, offenders act rationally and hence will not engage in criminal activities if:

the expected cost of crime goes up without a corresponding increase in the expected benefits.

(ibid p.175)

This shift in emphasis from attempts to explain and so understand and perhaps forgive crime, to the pragmatic task of ensuring that crime is not committed, leads to an increased 'technical' bias in criminological writing. If we cannot change human behaviour, we must ensure that the physical environment is such as to discourage criminals from plying their trade. Hence the interest in the criminological literature in 'designing out crime' and what Cressey sees as the turning of modern criminologists into 'technical assistant(s) to politicians bent on repressing crime' (Cressey 1982, p.4). Wilson's realistic solution is for policies which change behaviour, by affecting objective conditions. Since we cannot make people more honest, we must rely instead on making stealing more difficult, and increasing the likelihood of getting caught and punished. Forget any idea of progressive social change; concentrate instead on the management, control and surveillance of public places. Sheltered in the ordered environs of academe, Wilson's adoption of the classical belief in human rationality is perhaps understandable. It leads him inevitably to ally himself with the proponents of the back-to-justice model of punishment, rejecting the idea of rehabilitation and arguing for sentences appropriate to the crime committed. If rational individuals are still not persuaded by their own internal calculus of utilities, then their just desert is to be incarcerated for the simple reason that behind bars they can no longer harm the rest of us. Prison is as ineffective as community-based measures in rehabilitating offenders, and may, or may not, deter the criminal, but while behind bars they will at least be prevented from any further law breaking (Wilson 1975, p.173). Deterrence and incapacitation are the order of the day. The world for Wilson is uncomplicatedly free of privilege and power, 'wicked people exist' and 'nothing avails but to set them apart from innocent people'; or in the words of Ronald Reagan 'some men are prone to evil, and society has a right to be protected from them.' Social responsibility, exploitation and power are all non-issues; both the State and the political economy are absent. These lacunae mean that Wilson fails to take issue with why crime is worse both at particular historical moments and in particular societies. Instead he suggests that differences between crime rates are not important, arguing a convergence thesis not borne out by international comparison. But as Currie (1985) reminds us, Japan and Switzerland, for example, did not have rapidly rising crime rates in the 1960s and 1970s. In industrial societies where crimes did rise, these tended to be mainly property offences. America is in fact rather unique in its increase in crime, especially violent crime. The convergence thesis, Currie argues, allows Wilson to conclude that the causal agent is the 'ethos of self expression'. Currie points out that Americans who argue for more severe punishment have a problem in that their society is both one of the most punitive and the most criminal. Nor has Britain been able to reduce its crime rates despite having by 1988 the largest absolute and relative prison population in Europe. In that year in the United Kingdom there were 97.4 prisoners per 100,000 of the population compared to 95.6 for Turkey, 44.0 for Greece and 40.0 for Holland. We shall have more to say about British penal policy in Chapter Seven.

Wilson acknowledges this failure to some extent in his subsequent revision of *Thinking about Crime*. While still clinging to the idea that deterrence works, he has moved away from expecting much success by increasing penalties, and in words which are uncannily prescient of the 1987 Conservative Party Manifesto (see p.1 above), sees the deeper causes of crime as:

> discordant homes, secularized churches, intimidated schools, and an ethos of self-expression.
>
> (Wilson 1983, p.88)

This has been echoed by another conservative American criminologist, Travis Hirshi, who blames crime on the 'metaphysics of the age' which for him is characterised by its 'tolerance for natural tendencies', which has resulted in permissive child rearing and failure to punish children consistently (Hirshi 1983). The unanswered question, in Britain as in the United States, is to what extent if any the policies pursued by the Thatcher and Reagan Governments in the 1980s can in any way whatsoever have contributed to constructing social conditions in which the family and school might have played a more influential role. Of course if, as conservative thinkers would argue, family problems are largely independent of external conditions, then clearly changing such policies would be fruitless. But for us the idea that families worn down by unemployment, living on inadequate social security payments in dilapidated housing are responsible for failure to instil the necessary moral fibre in their children is laughable. To be charitable, the defence of individual responsibility and the need for social order are commendable conservative beliefs, but not at the expense of social justice. However, they are, more often than not, coupled with an ability to turn a blind eye to the difficult social circumstances endured by many members of society.

In a later work written in collaboration with experimental psychologist Richard Herrnstein, Wilson returned to the fray. The title of the work *Crime and Human Nature* betrays the tenor of the work, emphasising as it does the authors' arguments that individuals possessing certain physical characteristics are more predisposed to crime than others. Indeed over one quarter of the book deals with the influence of genetic and constitutional factors in crime causation. Continuing with Wilson's emphasis on 'conventional' street and predatory crime rather than white-collar offences they concentrate on the 'criminal' rather than the crime, and in searching for causes of crime they focus on individual differences between non-offenders and those who repeatedly offend. Their aim is to explain 'why some individuals are more likely than others to commit crimes' (Wilson and Herrnstein 1985, p.20). Explanation is sought primarily in 'constitutional factors' which are:

> usually present at or soon after birth, whose behavioral consequences appear gradually during the child's development.
>
> (Wilson and Herrnstein 1985, p.69)

The factors which they consider differentiate criminals from non-offenders are male sex, youthful age, mesomorphic body type, sluggish autonomic nervous systems, parents who were convicted criminals, low IQ, aggressiveness and impulsiveness. In addition to these, Wilson and Herrnstein are prepared to accept only the family, and questionably the school, as having any impact upon crime:

> In our view, most of the variation among individuals in criminality can be accounted for by personal traits, family socialization, and (perhaps) school experience.
>
> (Wilson and Herrnstein 1985, p.311)

The essentialist theory of Wilson and Herrnstein has been succinctly summarised by John Braithwaite as:

> one of crime as choice. Crime is a choice made by offenders when it is perceived as having consequences preferable to doing something else. The larger the ratio of the net rewards of crime to the net rewards of non-crime, the more likely is crime. The net rewards of crime include a balancing of

such things as the likely material gain from crime and social approval from peers against pangs of conscience or social disapproval of onlookers. The net rewards of non-crime brings in for example, the renumrativeness of legitimate work as an alternative way of using one's time to illegitimate work, and the desire to avoid future punishment.

(Braithwaite 1987, p.48)

Wilson and Herrnstein attempt to deal with Japan's low level of crime by suggesting the development of a national character, which operates against criminality. Character and constitution become important in Wilson's later work, as he moves from a right-wing liberal to a more conservative position. This prepares the ground for racist arguments. For example:

even allowing for the existence of discrimination of the criminal justice system, the higher rates of crime among black Americans cannot be denied.

(Wilson and Herrnstein 1985, p.461)

Pragmatism is the order of the day. If this state exists, and if constitutional features abound, then the issue must be honestly faced. Sociological theory is dismissed, in favour of a rather neglected form of psychology, which stresses the effects of constitutional differences on behaviour. They accept unquestioningly that the average black IQ score is 15 points lower than the average white, regardless of class, and that there is a necessary link between low IQ and criminality. In case one should conclude that a constitutional, and hence a genetic base to criminality, should be allowed as mitigating factors in criminal behaviour, Wilson and Herrnstein are clear about the relationship between punishment and personal responsibility. The courts and legislation must conform to a prevailing consensus to maintain legitimacy. The legal concept of personal responsibility (free will if you like) is part of our system of justice. Punishment is an essential part of inhibiting criminality:

If the legal system stopped punishing offenders, and no other institution took over its functions, criminal behaviour would rise because it was no longer deterred and no longer disapproved.

(Wilson and Herrnstein 1985, p.507)

Wilson and Herrnstein make a comparison between the legal system and a labour market with welfare provision. We see here an economic view originating with Hayek and Friedman. A welfare state discourages the law-abiding, conscientious citizen, because it pays the industrious and the skilled the same as the idle and incompetent. Exploitation, inequality, racism, injustice and power are notably absent from this model. There is, instead, only human nature developing in the intimate setting of family life, and arising from a complex interaction of constitutional and social factors. This in turn affects how people choose between the social consequences of crime and its alternatives. Voluntarism is brought in by the back door. We are reminded of Mrs Thatcher's comment that there are no societies, only individuals and their families.

Amongst philosophers of human nature, three only are considered worthy of discussion. These are Bentham and his utilitarian calculus; Rousseau ('hopelessly romantic') who Wilson sees as the originator of the model, albeit in a watered-down form, most commonly used by the majority of sociologists of crime; and Aristotle, with his view that we have a social nature which reflects inheritable traits. Marx, and more surprisingly, Freud, are ignored. The family is uncritically (and uncriticised) the central social institution, far more important than better education, improved employment prospects, social work intervention or rehabilitation, in strengthening cultural values. Religion is the only other major contributor to our social values. Public policy is castigated, it should be more tutelary, influencing personal responsibility and virtue, whilst discouraging hedonic calculators which make us think crime might pay. Popular culture is not surprisingly non-existent as an influence; we are ahistorical, acultural beings.

Wilson and Herrnstein (1985) appear to abandon suggestions for rehabilitative policies altogether, stating that their argument is not one 'from which many (possibly any) clear policy recommendations can be deduced'. This lets them off the hook in terms of the effects of their work on conservative government, right-wing criminology and repressive legislation. Instead of suggestions for public policy, there are private prescriptions for family life. Wilson's interest in moral example (which would have benefited from a reading of Durkheim), however, does not seem to have led him to consider material deprivation. Crime is reduced to a fairly invariant human nature, and leniency, too many civil rights, tolerance and lack of discipline are not rehabilitative, but the reinforcers of criminal nature. Socialisation at an early age is highly morally influential, and this reminds us of the view of the British Conservative Government and their supporters:

the more society can be policed by the family... and less by the state, the more that such a society will be both orderly and liberal.... The ideal society must rest upon the tripod of a strong family, a voluntary church and a liberal minimum state. The family is the most important.

(Johnson 1982)

and

You don't learn from books... you learn from other people.
(Mrs Thatcher: interview in *Woman*, September 1982)

As Mrs Thatcher told Conservative Women at their 1988 Conference:

> children should be taught moral values, and to understand our religious
> heritage.... We can't leave it to them to discover for themselves what is
> right and wrong.

For Wilson and Herrnstein criminals are both born and made. Nature and
nurture combine to make young men more impulsive, aggressive and less
caring than young females or adults, and these characteristics apparently
show themselves particularly strongly among black people. Reinforcement
or punishment have a very distinct effect on those who experiment with
crime. They carefully avoid attributing constitutional features as the sole
factors producing crime, but they emphasise them, without actually explaining why constitutional features (and hence criminality) emerge at particular
moments in history in specific societies. Poverty and racism are conspicu-
ously absent from their argument.

Wilson and Herrnstein's suggestions for strengthening the family, and
their exhortation of moral leadership in social policy, seem to have no
understanding of the nature of material exploitation in contemporary society.
At the same time they manage to ignore 20 years of critical feminist writing
on domestic social relations. They prefer to romanticise the family, whilst
failing to mention current research on domestic violence and child abuse,
both in Britain and the United States. They cite (Wilson and Herrnstein 1985,
p 301) Rutter's study comparing working-class families in the Isle of Wight
with those in East London, which found that London families suffered more
breakdown than those in the Isle of Wight, unproblematically quoting Rutter
(1978): 'For some reason, the stresses of inner city life impinge particularly
on working class women' adding only their own opinion that this was '... not
simply for reasons of social class'.

The authority of the family, then, is seen as central to the development of
criminality and this theme as we have seen is common in New Right thought.

Wilson has at times taken a distinctly racist stance. As early as the
mid-1970s he commented about Britain:

> If you were to ask a taxi driver, hotel clerk or newsvendor in London, they
> would explain the increase in crime, especially robbery, by the presence
> of West Indians.

> (Wilson 1977, p.69)

Such a statement of ignorance and prejudice is frightening to find in a writer
with claims to scientific detachment. Wilson argues that as the inner city lost
its homogeneity (that is, became racially mixed), it lost its sense of community and also its 'community leaders'. This led to an increase in predatory
crime on the street. The discussion continues with a complete absence of

understanding of the complex, historical, social relations of the British city, and shows a lack of sensitivity to and lack of knowledge of the black British community, in the context of white racism. Wilson tries at times to move away from his linkage of race and crime in the article quoted (Wilson 1977) but he quite plainly reinstates it in *Crime and Human Nature,* his latest and most well-known work (Wilson and Herrnstein 1985).

Whilst there has not been such an open association between race, class, sociobiology and crime in British criminology, the alarming thing about academics such as Wilson, is that they make racism respectable by cloaking it in apparent objectivity. By reducing the causes of crime to moral values and constitutional psychology, and ignoring or denying exploitation and injustice the New Right arrives at a thesis of blaming the victim.

WICKED PEOPLE EXIST: THE INDIVIDUALISATION OF CRIME

> I am convinced that criminals will be criminals just as boys will be boys.
>
> (David Mellor, Secretary of State, Home Office. Panorama Interview, 4 June 1990)

The solution suggested to crime is generally couched in terms of social values, and family responsibility. Individualism, free will and enterprise are contrasted with the cushioning of the Welfare State. We are reminded of the Conservative Party pundits' views on these matters. Schools, because of the principles of progressive education advocated by woolly liberals, no longer teach 'basic skills', and 'good attitudes to work', and it is this, rather than youthful rejection of monotonous poorly paid, routinised labour, which is seen as the reason that young people have difficulty in finding work. In Britain, Patricia Morgan (1978) blames child-centred parents and liberal teachers for encouraging a 'consensus psychology', which is encouraged by social workers and intellectuals alike and which leads adults to:

> short-circuit the cumbersome process of choosing, defending, transmitting and maintaining social rules.
>
> (Morgan 1978, p.51)

This failure leads to a delinquent syndrome, a mixture of behaviour, appearance and attitudes, bringing in:

> a flaunting of contempt for other human beings, a delight in crudity, cruelty and violence, a desire to challenge and to humiliate, and never, but never, to please.
>
> (Morgan 1978, p.13)

There is a retreat from 'the older language of morality and legality to that of morality and welfare'. As Taylor (1987) reminds us, the left are seen as moral abstentionists, uncritical apologists for rebellious black youth and other sections of the delinquent population. As such Morgan refuses to allow that socialist and progressive thought has had anything to say about personal responsibility, writing them off as permissive and amoral.

David Dale (Dale 1984) argues the Conservative case against radical criminology, which for him, is nothing more than Marxism in disguise. Dale accuses British radical criminology of refusing to understand and assess human behaviour in terms of morality, reduced by him to the simple dichotomy of good and evil. To appreciate any act of deviance we must suspend morality and responsibility removing conventional notions of morality. Furthermore, Dale suggests, at a theoretical level Marxism redefines crime out of existence, and by sleight of hand replaces it with sexism, imperialism, poverty and inequality. Marxism is damned for its moral relativism. Racism is written off as 'punk radicalism' or 'ethnic criminology'. For Dale we do not need to understand crime; all that is required is that we see certain acts as wrong and punish them. The objectivity of moral standards must be underlined. This is unproblematic for Dale, since he removes from them any taint of historical or class bias.

The immorality of collectivity is explored by other New Right thinkers, usually in combination with an attack on the Welfare State. In 1983 Rhodes Boyson (then Minister for Social Security) indicated how the Welfare State has undermined independence so that:

> The moral fibre of our people has been weakened. The state which does for its citizens what they can do for themselves is an evil state and a state which removes all choice and responsibility for its people and makes them into broiler hens is a state which will create the irresponsible society. No one bothers, no one cares. Why should they when the state which speaks for all, takes money from the energetic, the successful and the thrifty and gives it to the idle, the failures and the feckless.
>
> (Boyson 1983)

Lack of discipline and the stifling of enterprise has combined with a permissive, educational system and lax social services to excuse immorality and criminality. Liberal and radical intellectuals are responsible for the demoralisation of the inner city. To posit a genetic basis, albeit socially programmed, to criminality allows the State to abdicate all responsibility for rehabilitation or reform, encouraging a lesson of swift and disciplined retribution instead. This is the ideological context of conservative criminology. Taylor (1981) correctly argues that conservative criminology has nostalgically romanticised a cultural history which never existed. Mrs

Thatcher's desire to return the country to 'Victorian values' reflected this. It is an attempt to return to a pre-Beveridge family, a family which did not look to the State to resolve its problems, but had the integrity and guts to deal with issues and discipline itself. As she told the Conservative Women in 1988, self-reliance, personal responsibility, good neighbourliness and generosity to others were both Conservative values and the 'traditional values' of British life. The family becomes the site of moral values:

> It's at home that children first learn right from wrong.
>
> (Mrs Thatcher 1985)

and, as previously noted, the Conservative Party Manifesto of 1987 reminded us:

> The origins of crime lie deep in society, in families where parents do not support or control their children, in schools where discipline is poor; and in the wider world where violence is glamourised and traditional values are under attack.

This overlooks the reality of a divisive and reactionary culture which attempted to impose often harsh and tyrannical legislation upon the poor. It reduces the cruel exploitation of class struggle to a left-wing metaphor, replacing any sense of history with right-wing rhetoric. Taylor reminds us that the appeal of right-wing criminology is its populism which is rooted in the genuine fears and anxieties of the public, and both feeds and allays them by attacking radicalism, and exhorting a punitive morality.

The arguments for a conservative, rather than a liberal or a socialist view of justice have been put by Roger Scruton:

> Human beings as free autonomous agents fall under the rule of justice, which is to say to put it roughly and once again in the abstract terminology of Kant they must be treated as ends not means.
>
> (Scruton 1984, p.29)

A social contract is the clearest case of just relations for Scruton. He suggests that the bond linking the citizen to society 'is not a voluntary but a natural kind of bond'. It is not unlike family ties, and this analogy extends to authority and the State.

> It is clear from the start that a child must be acted upon by its parents power; its very love will accord them that power, and parents no more escape from its exercise by being permissive than does an officer cease to command his troops by leaving them constantly at ease. A child is what

it is by virtue of its parents' will and consequently the parent has an indefensible obligation to form and influence the child's development.

(Scruton 1984, p.32)

Mrs Thatcher extended the role of firm parent further, to that of Prime Minister. She reminded Eastern bloc ministers in 1987 that sometimes one had to be a strict parent with one's citizens, and there have been constant references to the family as the site of responsibility and control in Conservative policy documents. This has frightening consequences for the State.

It is as possible for a conservative as it is for a socialist to be should the need arise, 'totalitarian' although it is not the height of wisdom to declare oneself.... The conservative believes in the power of the state as necessary to the state's authority and will seek to enforce that power in the face of every influence that opposes it.

(Scruton 1984, p.33)

Scruton also takes up another New Right theme of nationalism, which is a respectable front for prejudice against those of different nations or races:

But while it is clear that it is a long standing principle of British law that the fomentation of hatred (and hence racial hatred) is a serious criminal offence, it is not clear that illiberal sentiments have to be forms of hatred, or that they should be treated in the high handed way that is calculated to make them become so. On the contrary they are sentiments which seem to arise inevitably from social consciousness. They involve natural (sic) prejudice and a desire for the company of one's own kind.

(Scruton 1984, p.68)

Sociobiology is then referred to at the basis of racial prejudice. Scruton offers us a prescription which has been followed by the Conservatives; that of strong government:

For the conservative, the value of individual liberty is not absolute, but stands subject to another and higher value, the authority of established government.

(Scruton 1984, p.19)

He points out:

It is unquestionable that if the power of the state is threatened, so too is its authority and with it the structure of civil society. To sacrifice power for the sake of justice is to make the exercise of justice impossible.... the Conservative view of law pays special attention to the constituted artefact known as the 'rule of law'.... the power of state achieves its full dressing of authority only when it is constituted in law.

(Scruton 1984, p.91)

This view is offered in a book which also opposes social justice, equality of status, opportunity, income and achievement and yet which is against attempts to bring major institutions under government control. We see here the defence of government policy, and an academic debate which takes a hard line against 'wet' defences of civil liberties.

Dahrendorf (1986), whilst holding a considerably more liberal and social democratic position than Scruton, also appeals to Kant. We see in this an example of reactive oppositional criticism, part of the new realist response to the ideological battle over law and order, and ultimately over civil liberty. Dahrendorf, for example, looks at the 'terrors of our streets and the riots on our football grounds'. He identifies impunity as the primary feature underlying contemporary concern about the breakdown of law and order:

Impunity or the systematic waiver of sanctions, links crime and the exercise of authority.... The growing incidence of impunity lead us to the core of the modern social problem.

(Dahrendorf 1986)

No connection is made with public concerns over administrative impunity, for example, police accountability. Impunity is seen as leading us to anomie, exemplified by 'no go areas', not prosecuting juveniles, and the failure to control either riots or demonstrations. As with Scruton, the referral to Kant is used to appeal for a strong social contract, which is the 'domestication (sic) of man's unsociability in the interest of progress' (Dahrendorf 1986 p.67). He notes:

the social contract, sanctions and all, is therefore a condition of liberty. We have to rebuild social institutions, we have to bring young citizens into real citizenship, not marginalise them as an underclass. We need a community development with economic and social policies which will create serious institution building.

(Dahrendorf 1986, p.82)

Both writers, like many conservatives and neo-conservatives fear the atavistic creatures of the urban jungle, the rise of the dangerous classes. Whilst in 1968, the fear was of militant fractions of the intellectualised middle-class youth – and in particular students, the dangerous classes are now either organised working-class terrorists, or unemployed youth, especially black youth. The supporters of the status quo are seen as those of the middleground

– respectable employed working class, or the disenchanted lower middle-class adults.

Unlike their American counterparts, the voices of professional criminologists in the United Kingdom, have been somewhat muted in the law and order debate. In one sense this is no more than a reflection of the traditionally marginalised position of social science academics in British political life. Right-wing governments, in particular, have tended to treat them as idealistic intellectuals rather than professional advisors. It also reflects the historical basis of British criminology which has developed within the social science disciplines and has tended to be critical of the political establishment. This critique has ranged from liberal and social democratic to Marxist in content. Its early growth was fostered by Mannheim at the London School of Economics and Radzinowicz at Cambridge, where the influential Institute of Criminology was established in 1959. This same year saw the establishment of what was to become the Home Office Research and Planning Unit, but even this, we would argue, has produced liberal, rather than distinctively conservative criminological research.

Conservative criminology has been a project located on the political level with inputs from criminal justice professionals and especially the police. Mrs Thatcher was able to harness the populist groundswell for strong law and order to her electoral and reforming goals. The intellectual support for tougher law and order policies was provided as we have seen by the work of mainly American criminologists and in particular James Q. Wilson. The British academic criminological community had little impact upon this debate during the 1970s and early 1980s. Wilson's pragmatic approach, denying the efficacy for policy makers of searching for the root causes of crime (although at the same time arguing strongly for a genetic model) and calling for stronger policing and tougher sentences, struck the right polemical chord with the radical right. We shall see how during the 1980s the influence of what Young (1986) has called 'administrative criminology' has grown. This approach, championed by the Home Office Research and Planning Unit, and in particular its former director Ron Clarke, shares with Wilson the rejection of causal theorising as a necessary prerequisite for controlling crime. It differs, however, in concentrating on reducing the opportunity for crime via 'target hardening' and does not have the same immediate reactionary implications as Wilson's calls for tougher deterrence. Indeed some critics have suggested that the situational approach to crime prevention has support across the political spectrum (Reiner 1987). We shall return to this theme again in Chapter Four.

CONSERVATIVE CRIMINOLOGY BECOMES LEGITIMATE

Conservative criminology has become concretised because law and order emerged as one of the key issues in the May 1979 and subsequent elections. The Conservative Election Manifesto of 1979 promised to 'give the right priority to the fight against crime', and to implement in full the Edmund Davies Committee's recommendations on police pay. The assassination of Airey Neave, and the street confrontations which occurred when the National Front held election meetings in black neighbourhoods, highlighted law and order for the public. The police had became more outspoken and openly political during the 1970s. Various individuals, Chief Constables and representatives of the Police Federation, had spoken out on the problems of maintaining order and in particular the dangers posed by 'violent', 'dangerous' or 'delinquent' young men (Taylor 1987, p.312). For the police spokesmen the problem was depravity not deprivation. Indeed in his address to the Police Federation in 1976, the then Chairman, Leslie Male, using words which were to be echoed in following years by Mrs Thatcher, launched an attack on the:

> gross irresponsibility of some teachers and social workers.... These included teachers who are so indoctrinated with their alien political creed that they convince kids that it's all the fault of the system... and social workers who turn a blind eye, sometimes connive at offences by children in their care.
>
> (quoted in Taylor 1987, p.313)

Just before the election, the Police Federation (representing all police officers up to chief inspector), published a full-page law and order statement in almost every daily paper. Its contents were very similar to those in the Tory Election Manifesto. Sir Robert Mark, ex-Commissioner of the Metropolitan Police, declared that trade union support for the Labour Government of 1974–79 was:

> not unlike the way in which the National Socialist German Workers' Party achieved unrestricted control of the German state between 1930 and 1938.

Law and order organisations and personnel were to be exempted by the Conservative Governments, from the public expenditure cuts imposed upon education, health and social services. Prison expenditure was to be increased, although overcrowding in prison is still today an unresolved problem. Some of this was to be put out to private tender. The issues of law and order were to become confirmed during the Conservative Governments of 1979 to the current day, as certain public events, notably the 1981 and 1985 youth 'riots', and the miners' strike of 1984 indicated the deepening of the crisis in Britain.

This has led to the strengthening of the coercive power of the State by the passing of legislation, especially the Police and Criminal Evidence Act 1984, the Public Order Act 1986, the Education Act 1987, the Criminal Justice Acts 1982 and 1986, the Sporting Events (Control of Alcohol) Act 1985, the Employment Acts 1980, 1982, the Prevention of Terrorism Act and Section 28 of the Local Government Act 1988. In addition there has been legislation concerning income maintenance benefits, in the form of loans, and grants from a cash-limited social fund, as well as the Community Charge or Poll Tax, and the Housing Act 1988. Public concern has been voiced over accusations of shoot-to-kill policies against IRA activists, both in Northern Ireland by the RUC, and abroad, notably the Gibraltar shootings, by the SAS. There has been concern over leaks from the RUC to militant protestant organisations, and concerns about censorship of the media in matters of security sensitivity. There has been a large recruitment drive for the police, including campaigns aimed at women, graduates and black people, and the police have become more centralised in their organisation, more militarised in their operations and more efficient in surveillance due to the increased use of computerised technology.

In order to dismantle the Welfare State and encourage economic liberalism, the Conservative Party, paradoxically, has had to maintain and strengthen the State in areas outside the market economy. The basic motifs in the law and order debate have centred upon the maintenance of public order and the control of the rising crime rates. From these, other issues have arisen involving national security and civil liberties, the democratic rights of unpopular groups and the freedom of the press. The rights of civil servants in posts sensitive to national security to join trade unions, or to reveal information when they consider it to be in the public interest, have been curtailed.

One of the themes of this book will be the growth of a control culture in contemporary Britain made possible by the encouragement of a public response drawing on the traditional island mentality of the British, and in particular, the English. Declining as a world power, and threatened by the development of Europe, Britain has become obsessed by insular problems.

There has been an appeal to a simple-minded sense of right and wrong; there are wicked people rather than complex issues. The individualisation of success has allowed the fragments of the class system to be overlaid by individual consumption and style. Strong moral attitudes and more explicit police monitoring has led to the emergence of the 'barrier of steel'. The persons and property of the middle class have to be visibly and symbolically protected. In a market economy, collectivism has to be discredited and democracy expediently replaced by liberty. The law has become a central cipher to protect the market economy and with the law had to come order. We shall see how this led to a control culture in the next chapter.

We believe that the Conservatives' desire to use the forces of law and order in order to defeat opposition to their economic, industrial and social programmes has accelerated and reinforced the trend to paramilitary-style policing. While we would not wish to overemphasise the newness of this move we shall discuss it in more detail in the next chapter. Unfortunately, in our opinion, this 'militarisation' of options to maintain public order and police industrial disputes conflicts fundamentally with strategy required to combat crime and fear of crime. This, we believe, involves the democratisation of the control of the police and a truly community-based force. Chapter Four looks at the development of community-based initiatives and their ideological underpinnings.

3   Private attitudes and public policy

Control culture or the law and
order society

In this chapter we shall enlarge on some of the themes of Chapter Two and consider the development of the 'hard', paramilitary side of policing during the 1980s. We will consider the arguments which have taken place on the left about the nature of these developments: do they represent a fundamental change with earlier decades or are they simply a continuation of already existing trends? This will lead us to a discussion of the major legislation affecting the police introduced by the Thatcher Government, the 1984 Police and Criminal Evidence Act (PACE) and the 1986 Public Order Act. However, legislation is only one part of the story. The police themselves have reacted to various pressures and demands to deal with threatened disruptions of public order, by developing their capacity to respond in a paramilitaristic fashion. We chart key moments in this process and in particular look at how the Irish dimension has informed policing on the mainland both currently and historically.

THE DEVELOPMENT OF A CONTROL CULTURE

There has been much debate amongst social commentators of the left as to whether there has been a shift in the United Kingdom, towards an authoritarian state, particularly with regard to law and order (Kettle 1983; S. Hall 1985), a phenomenon referred to by Hall as authoritarian populism – or whether, in fact, the Thatcher government did not represent a decisive break, but merely continued what had gone before, albeit with a more radical rhetoric (Gilroy and Sim 1985). Those proponents of what Hall (1985) calls 'the great moving right show' argue for an ideological victory for the right. Hall (1985) uses the concept of organic crisis, proposed by Gramsci to develop this argument. For Hall a crisis so deep and long-lasting has emerged, that efforts to defend the status quo cease any longer to be defensive, and become, instead, highly formative.

This leads to:

new political configurations and 'philosophies', a profound restructuring of the state and the ideological discourses which construct the crisis and represent it as it is 'lived' as a practical reality:

(S. Hall 1985, p.23)

It is within this context that the contribution of the anti-collectivism and anti-statism of the radical New Right, with its monetarist, individualist perspective, to a transformation of the dominant ideology may be understood.

According to Friedrich von Hayek, (1982) one of the major architects of New Right thought, and an acknowledged influence on Mrs Thatcher, the State should provide security only against those 'common hazards of life' which are unforeseeable, 'Acts of God' such as earthquakes or floods. All other forms of provision against mishap should be the responsibility of the individual through personal insurance. Market forces should be left free to operate untrammelled by features of the welfare system such as income guarantees. Indeed for Hayek, freedom is the antithesis of the security provided by the state by interference in the market. The state provision of services is to be opposed, he argues, because it eliminates competition which is essential for promoting the efficient, use of resources. In *Law, Legislation and Liberty* (Hayek 1982), his prescription for a free and spontaneous society involves only one area, for which responsibility should be taken centrally by the government: law and order. Other aspects of social life and organisations such as the firm, the factory, the corporation and the farm should remain free of interference. We can see that this has emerged in contemporary Conservative economic policy.

As well as a distinct set of hard-line monetarist policies, there has arisen very particular social values. There has been an attempt to gain hegemonic control, through the promotion of a certain set of cultural values, of which nationhood and respectability are central. These, of course, are not new. Their emergence in popular culture can be traced to the nineteenth century where nation, respectability and empire were central themes, and jingoistic nationalism was of considerable ideological importance, disseminated through such institutions as the music hall. Mrs Thatcher promised a return to Victorian virtues and certainly we have witnessed the resurrection of respectability and nationalism, two distinctly Victorian ideological formations during the reign of her Government. This has helped the implementation of laws and social policies which one jurisprudence expert, Ronald Dworkin (1985) has seen as having been introduced on the grounds, not of justice, but of State convenience and expediency. Laws have been passed which have appealed to 'common sense', and these have attempted to bypass liberal notions such as rehabilitation and social justice. In its attempt to develop a society which is free of the culture of dependency, the Government has moved away from collective responsibility to individual ambition. It has argued that it has created an enterprise culture by giving more rights and responsibilities through the avenue of market choice to its citizens.

The economic doctrine of monetarism needed an ideological counterpart for it to gain electoral support. It developed a discourse which gave priority to common sense, moral imperatives and individualism composed in a populist idiom. In this way, economics becomes justified by moralism; personal responsibility and nationalism are used to vindicate attacks on Welfare State mollycoddling. After all – again following Hayek – a needs-led economy can only produce endless need, endless demand. Hall suggests that this new populism is a combination of organic Toryism such as nation, family, duty and authority combined with an aggressive neo-liberalism, which is both self-interested and individualistic. Social democracy is now confused with market democracy – freedom of the market is made equivalent to freedom of the individual. For law and order (and in public consciousness, this often means public disorder and racial unrest), this has meant substituting a 'realistic' approach in place of rehabilitation. More police, tougher sentences, better discipline in the home, are the way to counteract the rising crime rate seen as an index of social disintegration. All this is set in the wider context of loss of respect for the law, unsafe streets, burglaries and mugging. It touches concretely what people experience or fear, cementing an important hegemonic element – something every reasonable person agrees on – crime and authority. No rational person supports crime or the breakdown of authority. The right was thus able to win important populist support for its policies, because the fears it exploited have a real material base. It is this that many on the left have ignored. Large sections of the population, especially amongst the working classes, are victims of crime. As Hall (1985) suggests, the problems of law and order, and how they are resolved, have become lived practices acted out within popular culture.

THE EMERGENCE OF A LAW AND ORDER SOCIETY

The terrain of this dispute was marked out by Kettle (1983). Law and order may be taken at one level as a policy area covering justice and crime, is administered by the Home Office and involves such agencies and institutions such as the police, courts and prisons. Beyond this, however, it has a broader aspect, involving a belief in the need for discipline in civil society, and the legitimation of the recourse to law and constraint. Furthermore the way in which state agencies such as the police and the judiciary have increased their spheres of influence, and resisted attempts to criticise and control them need to be considered. However, many of the current Conservative law-and-order policies continue and develop trends which had their origins during previous administrations both Tory and Labour.

Gilroy and Sim (1985) argue that the centralisation and militarisation of policing, and the growth of repressive legislation:

> have longer histories than most advocates of the Thatcherism concept would like to admit.
>
> (Gilroy and Sim 1985, p.18)

During the nineteenth century, the police were not accepted in many communities, and the notion of the 'bobby on the beat' – beloved of those who refer to pre-war nostalgia of community consensus policing – is, in fact debatable. Working-class communities have a long history of conflict with the police, which continued into the period between the wars. The 1935 Report of the Commissioner of the Metropolitan Police, defended the publicity given to their stop, search and detain policy, which had led to 1,000 people a week being stopped. Obviously, these were not middle-class sections of the London population. Brogden (1983), has suggested the Liverpool police were historically never under local control and accountability, but made major decisions autonomously from their local authority. For Gilroy and Sim the left has also idealised the post-war period, and they argue for instance that the 1948 Criminal Justice Act introduced by the reforming Labour Government was more repressive than its 1939 predecessor, introducing, for example, detention centres whose regimes were to provide a 'short sharp shock', a term still much in vogue 30 years later. Abolition of capital punishment was abandoned and the minimum age for imprisonment reduced from 16 to 15. Additionally, this Labour administration was to deploy troops to break up strikes by dockers and other workers. This picture, which could be painted in similar shades for other decades of this century, gives a different context in which to contemplate the constant referring back to earlier, more halcyon days of law and order. Crime is often an indicator, a metaphor, as Hall *et al* (1978) suggest for a more general feeling of social anxiety and apprehension, a theme pursued historically by Pearson, who sees preoccupation with disorder by the respectable as serving:

> an ideological function within British public life, as a convenient metaphor for wider social tensions which attend the advance of democratization.
>
> (Pearson 1983, p.230)

Gilroy and Sim (1985) further their argument by reminding us that it was in 1967, under the Labour administration of Harold Wilson that the Special Patrol Group was first deployed in London, and it was the Criminal Justice Act of the same year which introduced provisions for juries to convict by a majority, rather than by an unanimous verdict, and which, following the Mountbatten and Radzinowicz Committees, tightened up conditions for long term prisoners. Again during the 1974–79 Labour Government, the 1974 Prevention of Terrorism Act was introduced. The 1977 Criminal Law Act reduced to three the right of defence lawyers to challenge jurors, and removed the right of jury trial for a number of offences. Under the same Act a coroner no longer needed necessarily to have a jury when investigating sudden or violent death. Planning of intimidatory mass picketing was made illegal. This brief resumé does remind us that Labour has not been necessarily on the side of reform in the law and order debate. For Gilroy and Sim, (1985) in particular, 1979 was not a watershed. Authoritarian policing can be seen as a spin-off from the increased bureaucratisation and professionalisation of policing and the increased politicisation of leading police officers. They trace the long history of policing disorder, from the 1910 Welsh coal strike, the women's suffrage movement, the hunger marches to Grunwicks in 1976. They take issue with E. P. Thompson's attack on those of the left who see the police as enemies and crime as a form of displaced revolutionary activity. Thompson's support for the police, they suggest, is reiterated by many in the Labour Party and underlies the calls for a new realism towards law and order issues. Having denied the existence of a time when policing was for and of the community Gilroy and Sim further oppose the idea that the police force is fundamentally a benevolent organisation sullied only by the occasional 'bad apple'. For them police subculture is central to understanding the rank-and-file police officer – the racist and sexist culture of the 'canteen cowboys', with its contempt for racial minorities, the disreputable poor, gay people and women whose respectability is deemed to be in question, well illustrated in research by the Policy Studies Institute (Smith and Gray 1983), and Holdaway's (1983) participant observation study on police work.

The police, they argue, do not enforce the law impartially, but concentrate on a rootless underclass of the poor, based on a view of class which finds favourable the respectable, working and the suburban middle classes, whilst rejecting ethnic groups and those who make up an impoverished underclass, or are urban deviants, such as gay people, hippies and the lumpenproletariat of the city. What the left has failed to do is to take account of the police's relative independence, its successful resistance of accountability and the influence of police sub-culture. Gilroy and Sim (1985) reject any notion of a conspiracy between the police, the Home Office and the Government. However, they overlook the fact that there is little doubt the police sub-culture could be broken down, by consistent regulatory control of the rank and file from above. Whilst it may be that the police sub-culture is disapproved of by the higher ranks, they certainly collude with it by not engaging it. For Gilroy and Sim, the left has failed to break down the abstract category of 'crime' into the particular experiences, and fears which correspond to city life. Public concern about crime is the outcome of a political process. There is a symbolism about police activity, a feature certainly understood by the Conservatives.

> The sites of police activity often mark significant struggles over social space, or resources and freedom to exist without being subjected to continual surveillance or intimidation.
>
> (Gilroy and Sim 1985, p.47)

They outline the links made between mugging and black youth, then youth in general, as part of the contemporary discourse which conflates street crime with street robberies, street riots and disorders, so that all become, uncritically, part of the same criminal malaise. Social control is thus a major function of the police, and contemporary forms such as multi-agency policing must be discussed in this context.

Central to any analysis of law and order is the view of the State as the site of ideological reproduction of the social relations of capital. With its involvement in such programmes as health, education, welfare, income maintenance, it is not a simple set of coercive instruments working for capitalism. As Gramsci (1978) has argued, the democratic Welfare State, operates to reproduce the conditions for production. The State is therefore a site of struggle concerning ideological reproduction, and law and order is not simply a mechanism of social control, but is in itself an ideological issue. The appearance that law and order is being maintained, is part of a struggle to establish a control culture. Gramsci's (1978) view of hegemony, does not limit it just to struggles over ideological dominance, but gives it a wider educative interpretation. This includes a way of seeing the world, and involves explanations of human nature and social relationships. Clearly Britain has experienced an economic crisis, that is to say a situation where the economy was unable to provide income commensurate with its workers needs, since the mid-1970s. Hall *et al.* (1978) have argued, however, there has also arisen a hegemonic crisis, which arose because of the increasing inability of the State to perform its educative role successfully enough to provide cohesion in civil society. Thatcherism can be read, then, as a form populist anti-statism, as a move towards a control culture, which alongside of its individualism, its privatisation of collectivist welfare provision, from health and education through to water supplies and transport, and its aggressive law and order policies justifies its increased collective surveillance with an appeal to values of self-reliance and individual responsibility.

The rising rate of crime, and the public concern voiced about this has been a major reason cited by the Conservative Government for strengthening the powers of the police. We turn now to a consideration of the major pieces of legislation affecting the Police which have been passed by the Conservatives, the Police and Criminal Evidence Act of 1984 and the Public Order Act 1986.

THE POLICE AND CRIMINAL EVIDENCE ACT 1984

The Home Office presented PACE as a major policy initiative in the field of police powers to combat crime arguing that there was a need to develop legislation with the:

> objective of encouraging effective policing with the consent and cooperation of society at large.

(Home Office 1984, p.15)

There was however, Reiner (1985) argues, a struggle over the implementation of the Act. There had been growing evidence and complaints about police abuse of power since the Fisher Report on the Confait case, which had led to the Royal Commission on Criminal Procedure (RCCP), set up in 1977. Their report was published in January 1981 *(Royal Commission on Criminal Procedure* 1981), and was condemned by civil liberties groups because of the widening of police powers recommended. These, it was felt, were spelt out in great detail whilst any compensating obligations were left vague. The National Council for Civil Liberties (NCCL), the Labour Shadow Home Secretary and the Young Liberals all supported this view. The police reaction was favourable ('Nice one Cyril', said the magazine *Police* in February 1981 – agreeing with Sir Cyril Phillips, the RCCP chairman).

The first version of the PACE published in 1982 strengthened police powers, but omitted or diluted the RCCP recommendations on safeguards for the public. Police opinion was mainly in favour; there was an antagonistic reaction from the left and civil liberties groups. They rightly protested that the notion of balance between suspects' rights and police powers, which had been an important thesis in the RCCP report, was missing. The government was forced to modify some of the clauses (see Zander 1983). A vigorous, if not rough, parliamentary debate ensued, and the Government was obliged to table 170 amendments for the Report stage. Just under a quarter of these had been debated when the Bill fell due to the 1983 General Election.

In 1983 a revised version of the Bill was introduced in the Commons. The police were decidedly less enthusiastic about the new version, but civil libertarians still opposed it. Seen as the result of a long debate about police powers and police accountability, it was felt by the Association of Chief Police Officers to do nothing to aid the fight against crime, and not to achieve the:

delicate balance between the twin needs of law enforcement and the rights of the individual.

(*Police* January 1984, p.4).

Basically, the Act was seen as tidying up legislation, and balancing powers and safeguarding the public. PACE requires people to give their names and addresses on request to the police (who may detain them if they consider it necessary until they are satisfied that these are correct). It extends the powers to stop and search to include searches for 'stolen or prohibited articles'. Basically, the rather disparate provisions of local forces have been replaced by the more extreme powers of the Metropolitan Police. Powers of entry, search and seizure, and arrest with or without warrant, are extended. Anyone under arrest can be questioned for up to 96 hours before being charged (the permission of a magistrate having to be obtained after 36 hours), and fingerprints and body samples can be taken from a person without consent. Draft codes issued by the Home Office on 15 August 1989, which revise those accompanying PACE 1984, suggest that witnesses may make their identification from a video tape of an identity parade. The usual rules involving the conduct of identity parades still remain, but the NCCL has objected that the shooting and editing of the film could influence witnesses.

There are increases in police accountability under PACE, with Codes of Practice, granting specific rights to citizens. A specified custody officer in each police station is given the responsibility for supervising prisoners and for adherence to rules governing interrogation. The Act also requires local consultation between police and community, but in reality the police decide who the community representatives are to be, and set the agenda.

The claims that PACE has meant an increase in police accountability, are dubious. The Government has certainly not encouraged any attempts at local accountability and the police have resisted any influence from the community in terms of operational strategies. Successive Home Secretaries have upheld the autonomy of the 43 chief constables to determine operational matters. The courts have repeatedly supported the independence of chief constables from their local authorities (Uglow 1988a, pp.121–2), and in 1988 the Court of Appeal upheld the right of the Home Secretary to make available plastic bullets and CS gas to the Northumbria police against the wishes of its police authority. The Crown is clearly considered to have the prerogative power to do what it considers necessary to maintain the peace against not only actual, but threatened disturbances. We shall return to this point again below when discussing key moments in the development of police powers.

THE PUBLIC ORDER ACT 1986

The Public Order Act (POA) of 1986 covered new public order offences, processions and assemblies, racial hatred, exclusion orders and other miscellaneous provisions involving trespass, and alcohol at sporting events. In many ways it is a response to trespass, particularly by squatters. As early as 1975 there were the beginnings of a 'moral panic' over squatting:

> Of the many strange and frightening features on contemporary British life, none carries a more obvious and direct threat to society's survival than the growing phenomena of squatting. Innumerable houses up and down the country are now in illegal occupation by organised groups of thugs, drugtakers and revolutionary fanatics... in reality the motive of this squatting is either political – a settled purpose of subverting public order – or simple greed and aggression.
>
> (*Daily Telegraph* 16.7.75)

The result was the Criminal Trespass Act 1975. By the 1980s this fear of squatting and trespass on private property had become amplified in the 'battle of the beanfield', when in 1986 (Jones 1986) a pitched battle was fought during the police eviction of 'hippies' and travellers from the road to Stonehenge for the annual celebration of the summer solstice. In many ways the annual Stonehenge ritual by the police is reminiscent of their response to the Notting Hill carnival, another occasion seen by the guardians of law and order as a symbolic gesture against authority by an 'unrespectable' section of society. At Notting Hill the 'threat' is from the black community; at Stonehenge the unrespectable are white 'hippies', suspected of drug taking and living on welfare.

The present Act is aimed also at pickets, demonstrations, marches and football crowds. Powers of search outside football matches have been increased, and the police have been given power to break up conveys of vehicles, and to eject trespassers. The police can intervene where there is 'serious disruption to the life of a community' a notably vague term which gives the police considerable scope of interpretation.

It would appear that the police have not used either of these Acts against those whom they consider 'respectable', those who are not seen in cop culture as 'criminal types', but have continued to use them against marginalised groups. The use of these Acts against black people, gay people, the young, the militant and quasi-criminal has not made a great deal of difference because the police used informal ways and means before (Levi 1989). This, however, hardly justifies their enshrinement in legal codes.

Having considered the legislative changes affecting police powers, we turn in the next sections to a review of the ways in which the police themselves have responded to the requirements of public order policing.

KEY MOMENTS IN THE DEVELOPMENT OF BRITISH POLICING

An important factor in any consideration of law and order debates, has been the rapid transformation of British policing over the last 20 years (Bowden 1978; Mark 1977; Levi 1989; Scraton, 1985). Increasingly, there has been a tension between the 'militarisation' of policing, organised around the imperatives of social surveillance and quick reactions to public incident reports, or requests for assistance, and the traditional view of neighbourhood-based policing, the legendary bobby on the beat. We shall have more to say about the 'softer' side of policing, particularly multi-agency strategies and the emphasis on community involvement in crime prevention through schemes such as neighbourhood watch, in the next chapter. Here we will focus upon the hard end of policing, which may be seen in the creation and expansion of specialised quasi-military police units such as the Metropolitan Special Patrol Groups (SPG), established in 1965 originally as a mobile reserve to target areas of high crime, and the Police Support Units (PSU), established by all forces since 1974, capable of rapid mobilisation in public order situations, ranging from fights outside public houses, soccer hooliganism, demonstrations, strikes and the prevention of trespass. Most provincial forces now have groups similar to the SPG with various names such as the Tactical Patrol Group, Task Force or Tactical Aid Group, but the SPG itself was disbanded in 1987 after an internal inquiry by the Metropolitan Police. They were replaced by eight Territorial Support Groups based on the area commands (Uglow 1988a, p.46) but are still formed around a nucleus of SPG officers and have similar roles to the SPG as well as supporting more traditional police work.

An analysis of this transformation in policing reveals several key moments which have been significant. The conflict in Northern Ireland, public order situations influenced by events of 1968, concerns over street crime, the inner city 'riots' of 1981 and 1985, and industrial disputes, the most famous being the miners' strike of 1984, have all had an impact on police and public attitudes.

In this chapter we look at changes in the policing of Britain, *vis-à-vis* certain of these key moments, and discuss other significant developments such as the Police Act of 1964 which reduced the number of provincial police forces in Britain and accelerated the use of sophisticated technology. The Act also changed the accountability of police forces to the local police authorities – the Watch Committees in the boroughs and the Standing Joint Committees in the counties. However, it should be remembered that these discontinued bodies, which had, in any case, a dubious democratic base, being dominated by local landed and business elites (Uglow 1988a, p.123), always had a relationship with their chief constables which was at best ambiguous. Chief constables insisted on their autonomy to do whatever they considered necessary to maintain the law, whilst, on occasion, the committees expected their chief police officers to follow their instructions. True, the Watch committees and Standing Joint Committees had more powers over the police than the present police authorities, but the law was sufficiently equivocal in terms of their powers over their chief constables that, in practice, during the twentieth century there has been a significant decline in local control. According to Bunyan (1977) this decline was related to the increasing enfranchisement of the working class and the desire to counter socialist influence in the local authorities. As Uglow puts it:

> Treating the police as independent avoided the inevitable local opposition that would arise from creating a 'national' force yet ensured that Home Office influence would be a central factor, given the background of senior police officers.
>
> (Uglow 1988a, p.123)

A series of controversial incidents in the late 1950s concerning the actions and misdemeanors of individual police officers, which would now seem relatively minor, led to the setting up of a Royal Commission in 1960. It considered the case for a national police force, the roles of chief constables, police authorities and the Home Secretary, police public relations, police remuneration and the complaints system. Its recommendations, presented to Parliament in 1962 (Royal Commission 1962), which proposed rationalizations somewhat short of a national force, were implemented in the 1964 Police Act. The Act provided for chief constables to be able to send officers to assist other forces, a provision which was to have significance particularly during the 1984 miners' strike as we shall see below. It also created new local police authorities (LPAs), consisting of magistrates and councillors and usually a sub-committee of the full local council, and was intended to provide institutional controls over chief police officers while not impeding the efficiency of their forces, but its measures on accountability and complaints were, in the words of Reiner (1985, p.63), 'widely seen as vague, confused and contradictory'. Furthermore, he continued, 'the net effect of the act was clearly to strengthen the hands of the Home Office and of chief constables at the expense of local police authorities'. The Metropolitan Force is exceptional as there is no LPA for London and it remains directly under the control of the Home Secretary.

The Act also granted the Home Secretary considerable influence over the provincial police forces, and in practice little direct public accountability was required of them, the LPAs, under Section 4 of the Act, having responsibility for seeing that an adequate and efficient force was maintained but operational decisions, the direction and control of the force, were left to the Chief Constable, who was removable only with great difficulty. Whilst the role of the LPA was essentially to keep an eye on the budget, they can decide on the overall establishment of the force, decide on the provision of vehicles and other equipment. The LPA is responsible for the appointment to senior ranks, chief constable and deputy and assistant chief constables, but only if the Home Secretary confirms the choice, which must, in any event, be made from a shortlist approved by the Home Office.

As we shall see the 1964 Act was the last affecting the police to receive a smooth passage through Parliament. By weakening further local control, despite the efforts of some LPAs to become more active (see Uglow 1988a, pp.125–6), the Act set the scene for the changes in policing discussed below.

One of the first key moments in the post-war transformation of policing was the response to the large anti-war demonstrations which arose concerning the complicity of the Labour Government in the US/Vietnam war in 1967–68. These took place in the context of considerable public and official anxiety over the hedonism and permissiveness among the young middle class, and a concern about 'student power' at a time when Paris had erupted, and a determined civil rights movement had developed in Northern Ireland. A demonstration in March 1968, outside the American Embassy in Grosvenor Square, nearly led to an international incident when the police line almost gave way. Mounted police charged the crowds in a violent, little publicised, police attack. These demonstrations, organised by the Vietnam Solidarity Campaign had a fundamental effect upon the British police's orientation to public order events. The poor image, on national television, of a police force clubbing down students, and poor pre-demonstration planning, led to more sophisticated preparation by the police. There was an increase in the gathering of intelligence, of surveillance and special training was given so that officers could organise flying-wedge attacks on crowds, and operate snatch squads to seize those seen as ringleaders.

Hall (1979), Kettle (1980) and Taylor (1981) have all suggested that the years of 1967–68 are crucial for any informed discussion of changes in policing. They contextualise this against the emergence of the conflict in Northern Ireland and the Vietnam War demonstrations. Until then, they argue, policing had been organised around the assumption of a fundamental social and political consensus, which had allowed the local constabulary to fulfil its mandate with considerable public support. Certainly, working-class districts had a long history of police surveillance and brutality, but this had always been responded to in the context of crime prevention. However, the police have always been used to survey problem working-class families and have always been involved in industrial disputes. This became apparent as clear political rifts in British post-war democracy thrust the police into increasingly transparent, partisan positions, and necessitated the development of more coercive policing.

The second moment in transforming police practice was the 1980–1 inner city riots, but the ground had been well prepared by the moral panic over mugging which developed during the 1970s (Hall *et al.* 1978; Gordon 1983). This brought to a head the already poor relations between the police and the black community. There had been a series of serious confrontations leading to an erosion of confidence in the police by the black community since the 1950s. Racially motivated arson, physical attacks and even murders were felt not to have been pursued seriously. Black British youth felt itself stereotyped as drug dealers, criminals or illegal immigrants.

The image of the mugger as young, black and male developed during the years prior to the 1979 election. Hall *et al.* (1978) systematically attempted to unpick the moral panic over mugging. They examined the pattern of offences, and the official and societal reactions to them, in the context of the crisis of hegemony affecting the British State during that period. They show how mugging became symbolic of lawlessness and a breakdown of social order. The white population conflated its fears of young people and immigrants into a new folk devil – the mugger. Anxieties about the general economic and political decline of Britain became projected onto black youth, the image of the unBritish black 'immigrant' became combined with that of threatening male youth. In contrast to the moral entrepreneurs of the time, who saw the rising crime rate of the late 1970s as a product of the 'permissive society' combined with too lenient an approach to the apprehension and punishment of wrongdoers, for Hall *et al.* street crime, especially amongst black youth, was connected with fundamental contradictions in the British political economy which had resulted in yet another bout of recession. What was a crisis of legitimation for the State became rewritten as a crisis of authority. Crime became a symbolic source of unity in an increasingly divided and embittered class society. Where the traditional armoury of consensus is exhausted, a state facing a threat to its hegemony will have to manage consensus and in Britain the war against crime became a focus for this re-legitimation. We see here the historical antecedents of the ideological uses of law and order during the 1980s. Hall and his co-workers shape street crime, moral panics and folk devils into a broader project 'the politics of mugging'. Political crises, ideological struggles and racial tension are to be understood in the broader parameters of Britain's economic decline. Hall *et al.* trace in this beginnings of an 'exceptional State', the emergence of a culture of control. The British State's main task at this time was to explain away the crisis, or to move it from the context of class relations. The crisis becomes one of legitimate authority, which is prevented from carrying out its responsibilities by the permissive mores peddled by the left, and evil groups – strikers, criminals, scroungers. Crises in class relations became rewritten as crises in authority relations. Policing the crisis becomes a matter of policing the blacks, the poor and the unemployed. The Tory Party, in opposition during this period, was as we have seen, able to exploit these themes and present them as the fault of the Labour Government, held captive by the trade unions and free thinkers of the left. We can see the development of the foundations of the control culture of the 1980s.

A perennial problem in the relations between the institutions of State control and fractions of British society has been the breakdown in relations between the police and black communities. A particular site of struggle has been the confrontation between police and black youth in the inner cities. The black community has been seen by the police as intruders from another culture and has felt itself policed rather than protected from racist attacks. During the 1979 Election the police were perceived as offering that very protection denied to blacks to right-wing racist organisations such as the National Front. Relations between the police and black communities were strained by several notorious cases – starting with the killing by the Special Patrol Group of two Asian youths who, in February 1973, armed with toy pistols, tried to take hostage staff at the Indian High Commission. In 1974, Kevin Gately was killed during an anti-racist demonstration, after an SPG charge. In April 1979, during the General Election campaign 5,000 police were mobilised to protect a National Front march in Leicester. Two days later, police cordoned off the centre of Southall because of a National Front election meeting, and during the subsequent disturbance there occurred the killing of Blair Peach, allegedly by the SPG. This was always strenuously denied by the police, although in 1988 they were to offer compensation to Peach's parents. Racist attacks were ignored or played down by the police. This all fuelled white racism, and led to the sense of isolation by black communities.

This sort of societal reaction is the background to the uprisings of 1980–81 and 1985. There is a history of police raids on cafes, youth clubs and social centres in black areas. Local police tended to regard them as places where drugs and stolen property are sold. However, they are often the meeting places of young black people, which also function as legal advice centres. As such, they are seen by the police as sites of political organisation. The community regards attacks on them as attacks on organised black resistance. The disturbances in the St Paul's district of Bristol in 1980 started with an attempt at an arrest at a black social centre and café. Local youths reacted by attacking the police vehicles, with the result that the area became unpoliceable for several hours whilst rioting occurred. Avon's Chief Constable withdrew his force because it took 6 hours for support from other West of England forces to arrive. This action was severely criticised in Parliament, being perceived as the setting up of a 'no go' area. The agenda was set by the mass media with such headlines as 'Race Mob Runs Riot'. A high-level consultation between the Government and the police led to arrangements for the 'handling of spontaneous public order'. This was an important development which reviewed mutual-aid arrangements, and recommended that all police officers should be trained in crowd control, involving riot shields (see *Review* for arrangement for handling spontaneous public disorder, Home Secretary memo, 1980).

During 1981, several similar incidents followed the St Paul's disorders. However, these youth uprisings should not be seen as race riots but as clashes between young people, black and white, and the police. Brixton, South London – an area subject to a long history of heavy police surveillance – also erupted, partly as the result of 'Operation Swamp 81' – an exercise in saturation policing made without any consultation with the community leaders or indeed the home-beat officers. The Scarman Report (Scarman 1981) details the use of arbitrary roadblocks, the stopping and searching of pedestrians and mass detention – 943 stops, 118 arrests and 75 charges, only one of which was for robbery. Other areas to explode included Moss Side (Manchester), Handsworth (Birmingham) and parts of Liverpool. In the last location the situation was contained only when the police used CS gas for the first time on the British mainland, and only after a young disabled man had been killed in a charge by police vans. The Prime Minister indicated where her concern lay, 'Oh those poor shopkeepers,' (quoted in Young and Sioman 1981).

There were major riots in over forty cities. The (then) Chief Constable of the Merseyside Police, Sir Kenneth Oxford, argued:

> This is not a racial issue as such. It is exclusively a crowd of black hooligans intent on making life unbearable.
>
> (*Guardian*, 6.7.81)

Mrs Thatcher intoned that the very high levels of unemployment amongst Merseyside and Manchester youth 'were no excuse'. Perhaps not, but it may be an explanation, a possibility we shall explore in Chapter Five. The Commission of Enquiry which investigated the Brixton disorders, offered a carefully diffuse explanation:

> the police must carry some responsibility for the disorders.... The

community and community leaders must take their share of the blame for... distrust and mutual suspicion between the community and the police.

(Scarman 1981)

Scarman identified the problems of policing areas with a high crime rate (such as Brixton), whilst retaining the confidence of the community – especially the black community. As Hall (1982) wryly noted, Scarman was not liked by the police lobby; he made a dent in the 'powerfully constructed popular/populist groundswell'. Scarman indicated that the root of the Brixton 'disorder' was the deprivation, severely exacerbated by a recession, in which its inhabitants lived. He understood that the 'combination of long-term conditions and short-term contingents combine to make the unpredictable occur'. Critical of saturation policing, he nevertheless avoided confronting the structural and institutionalised racism which is at the core of police/black community policing. Scarman suggested, however, increased consultation between local community leaders and the police, the permitting of 'lay visits' to local police stations at any time, and more independent investigations of serious complaints.

Shortly after the Scarman report was published, there was a reaction against its findings in the tabloid press which supported the police in their 'war' against street crime. On 9 March 1981, the *Daily Express* ran a two-page feature on 'Britain's most brutal streets' with a report on Railton Road, Brixton, headed 'The Front Line ... a line of hatred dividing black from white'. On 25 February 1982 the *Daily Mail* reported on rank-and-file discontent over the instructions not to raid community centres without high-level consultation. On 11 March 1982, the Metropolitan Police published, for the first time, the race of offenders and victims in its crime statistics. These annual crime figures focused on the crimes, robbery and violent theft, which comprised a mere 3 per cent of the total recorded offences and emphasises the racial composition of the statistics – notably absent in all the other figures: 55.4 per cent of all robbery and violent theft was perpetrated by blacks, most victims were white and a quarter were over 50 years of age. The media reaction to these figures fed the popular belief in the relation between ethnicity and crime, reinforcing white racism.

There were further similar violent disturbances in 1985 in Brixton again, and at the Broadwater Farm Estate in North London. Both arose out of incidents involving families of suspects wanted by the police. There had been an increased concern about police use of firearms, when 5 year-old Barry Chamberlain, son of a white suspect, was shot and killed in his bed in a police raid in Birmingham in August 1985. This concern intensified when, in September 1985 in Brixton, the home of Mrs Cherry Groce was violently broken into by the police searching for her son, who no longer lived there.

During this raid, Mrs Groce was shot in the back, suffering permanent injuries. On Broadwater Farm Estate in Tottenham, in November of the same year, Mrs Cynthia Jarrett died of a heart attack when police entered her home in search of her son, Floyd. In all three cases these were innocent people who died or were injured, due to police activity in searching for suspects.

Broadwater Farm and Brixton erupted in protest at the police actions and the conflict culminated with the killing of a policeman, P C Keith Blakelock, in a struggle at Broadwater Farm between police and youths. Local residents tend to see close police surveillance as an attack on a community seen by the police as being well organised. In a survey carried out on Broadwater Farm, half the estate thought the police acted unfairly in surveillance. This view was held regardless of age and ethnicity (Gifford 1986). The breakdown in relations between the community and police in London was so severe, that Metropolitan Commissioner Newman declared that he was putting 'all people of London on notice' regarding the possible use of CS gas and plastic bullets (*London Standard* 7.10.85).

There seems to have been little change in the situation. Toxteth in Liverpool was still complaining of heavy-handed policing 8 years later. Although the private investigation into law enforcement in the area, by Lord Gifford, published in July 1989, found the police in Toxteth insensitive and racist in their behaviour, the then Home Secretary, Douglas Hurd, refused a call for a public enquiry. The Merseyside police refused to participate in the inquiry. Their current chief, James Sharples, described the report as 'very negative and unconstructive'. He rejected allegations of racist policing made by a former Toxteth community policeman, David Scott, and rejected claims that the police started street incidents to increase their overtime.

The third moment which is important to our discussion spanned the miners' strikes of 1972 and 1984. Again, there is a history of tension between organised trade unions and the police, with perhaps the most notorious post-war case being the picketing of Grunwick in 1976–77. The non-union plant, founded and owned by a leading member of the right-wing free-enterprise pressure group, the National Association of Freedom, employed exclusively Asian immigrant women at rates far below those negotiated by trade unions elsewhere. When the workers struck for union recognition they received massive support from the Trades Union Movement.

A big police action was mounted for what became almost a daily confrontation with pickets, and the strikers felt particularly angry about:

> the special relationship which appeared to exist between Grunwick and the police on duty at the picket.
>
> (Gilroy and Sim 1985).

The police have appeared more willing during the last decade to accept an increasingly coercive and partisan role in the industrial relations of a divided society in crisis. This involvement in policing industrial disputes is not, in itself new, as Gilroy and Sim (1985) remind us, but the openness with which the police appear willing to take on this task is. The police were also active in the harassment of women peace demonstrators at Greenham Common, the first European site of American cruise missiles, and were highly involved in the miners' strikes of 1972 and 1984. Essentially a civil matter, the confrontation between the National Coal Board and the National Union of Mineworkers (NUM), was seen by the second Thatcher Government as an opportunity to take on and defeat an old rival.

For criminology there were two relevant issues in the defeat of the miners; firstly, the legislation and the legal strategies involved and secondly, the role of the police. A law and order response, emphasising the use of criminal law, was made by the Government to deal with, what were in essence, social problems arising from their economic policies. The Government seemed reluctant to test the legislation which had arisen in the Employment Acts between 1980 to 1984, but instead encouraged the use of the criminal law to avoid becoming directly involved in the dispute whilst orchestrating public sympathy by appeals to union democracy, and condemning the violence of the pickets against the police.

This involved the attempt to encourage working miners to take legal action against the striking NUM, and the issues of picketing ballots and the closed shop. Under the 1984 Trades Union Act (passed 26 July 1984), unions were required to ballot their members before taking strike action – albeit rule 43 of the NUM requires a ballot for a national strike. The issues of union democracy were used to counteract the NUM's attempt to preserve their jobs and their communities.

The Employment Act of 1980 had arisen out of the Government's determination to end secondary picketing (so highly successful during the 1972 miners' strike). This act narrowed the definition of a trade dispute to that between an employer and his direct work force, distinguishing between official and unofficial disputes and primary and secondary picketing. It restricted the 'permission' of a worker to picket at or near his place of work. Such picketing is not a right in law; there is merely a recognition in the Act that such action is not necessarily unlawful. Anyone breaking the Act may be subject to charges ranging from civil action to conspiracy. The Department of Employment Code of Practice under the 1980 Act, suggests that no more than six pickets should be present in one place. The legislation to curtail the power of pickets also increased under Section 15 and 16 of the 1982 Employment Act which made the pickets' unions responsible for illegalities where it had authorised industrial action. Furthermore, under the 1980 Act (Section 4) and the 1982 Act (Section 3), an employee could sue if a closed shop operated and if he or she were expelled from the union for a form of wrongful dismissal. But this battery of legislation was largely ignored during the miners' strike.

By September 1984 some 7,000 miners had been arrested. 52 per cent of those arrested were charged with offences under section 5 of the Public Order Act 1936, basically for conduct which might lead to a breach of the peace, 25 per cent with obstructing a police officer, 11 per cent for obstructing the highway, 10 per cent with criminal damage and 6 per cent with assault on the police (*Policing London*, September 1984). This focus on the use of criminal law, for relatively minor offences, with the publicity over the daily struggle between the pickets and the police, moved the struggle onto a ground, that of the courts, preferred by the Government. By so doing, the actual political issues of the struggle were defused, and the main issues replaced by appeals to legality and democracy. The miners' strike was seen as a major test for government committal to law and order:

> As the strike has worn on, the police on the picket lines have become more and more convinced that an NUM victory in terms of substantial concessions on pit closures would be seen as a triumph for mass defiance of the law.

> (Tony Judge, Editorial *Police* July 1984)

The handling of the struggles of 1984 showed that the Conservatives had learnt the lessons of 1972. The 1972 miners' strike can be seen as a victory for the flying pickets system by the Yorkshire NUM. The successful mass picket of Saltley Coke Depot in Birmingham (believed by many observers to have laid the ground for the defeat of the Heath Conservative Government) was used to justify a centralisation of police organisation:

> The picketing of Saltley traumatised the police by exposing a basic strategic weakness in their organisation; while the trade union movement was organised nationally and could sweep pickets across the country to converge on one target, the 43 police forces in England and Wales were trapped by the tradition of local policing into a fragmented reply.

> (Coulter *et al.* (1985)

The National Recording Centre (NCR) was created as a result of the 1972 strike, and in particular as a response to the confrontation at Saltley Gap. It is managed by the president of the Association of Chief Police Officers (ACPO) and was used both in the 1981 riots and the 1984 miners' strike. It helps organise, and has indeed pushed to the foreground the deployment of the Police Support Units. As we have noted the PSUs are available for special operations within or outside their own police force area. They remain ordinary officers on normal duties but have received special training for their

PSU role. They are distinct from new forms of militarised police units such as the Special Patrol Groups or Territorial Support Groups, who are a permanent reserve with specialist duties.

The existence of the NRC means a national mutual aid operation is now possible using the PSUs. The effectiveness of this was seen most graphically during the miners' strike, when at Orgreave in Yorkshire, for example, on 29 May 1984, there were 1700 officers from thirteen different forces confronting 1,500 miners. The police had their revenge for Saltley! The NRC reports to the Home Office, but although the Home Office does not directly instruct it, it is naive to suppose that it is not highly influential in terms of advice on operational decisions. The PSUs act as a collective force, and they were used to support the Government's political position during the 1984 strike. They were used to police the drift back to work, and some units after confrontations with the pickets had used a violence which caused George Moore (South Yorkshire Police Committee Chair) speaking of the police violence at Grimethorpe colliery (17.10.84) that:

> They come into the force as decent chaps, and we send them to training centres and they come back like Nazi storm troopers.'

While the assertion of central control during the miners' strike has always been vehemently denied, the evidence seems strongly to support it (see, for example, Loveday 1986). Indeed, in innovative research into the work of chief constables, Reiner concludes that an

> accountability debate has tended to under-emphasise the growing control of police by central government.
>
> (Reiner 1989)

Reiner's research suggests that contrary to the accepted view that ACPO influences the Home Office, the reverse is in fact the more significant factor in the relationship. Given the upwardly mobile class background of chief constables and the fact that they rely on the Home Office for career advancement, this is hardly a matter for surprise.

The 1984–85 miners' strike underlined the relatively powerless position of the LPAs. The mutual-aid provisions of the 1964 Police Act were directed at chief constables with the Home Secretary having the power to order such cooperation if they refused requests. The Chief Constables were instructed to do precisely this, and furthermore the Home Secretary told them not to allow financial constraints, supposedly under the control of the LPAs, to interfere with the 'operational discharge of your duties' (Uglow 1988a, p.126). Some LPAs found their forces were suddenly greatly undermanned as the officers went to assist forces in the coalfields, while the LPAs in the striking areas were suddenly faced with large bills to pay for assistance they often did not want. The LPAs in practice had little control over their forces even in areas, such as finance, which were theirs under the 1964 Act.

Another notable change in the police is the increased political astuteness and publicity awareness of many chief constables. Some have moved from their traditional role of maintaining political neutrality in their public statements, reporting only, without comment, on serious crimes. James Anderton, Chief Constable of Greater Manchester, remarked in 1982 that:

> A quiet revolution is taking place around us, and the prize is political power to be wielded against the most cherished elements of the establishment, including the monarchy. It is the duty of the police to guard against this as much as it is to guard against crime.

Anderton, in his address to the Institute of Housing at Harrogate in June 1984, said that:

> Holding the breaking pieces is a crucial role for the police. In some respects society now resembles an ice cap crumbling dangerously as the temperature rises. Small wonder, therefore, that people fermenting disorder for political ends have turned the heat on the British police.

The same speech contained the following comment on industrial disputes:

> Mass picketing – if I can use that popular misnomer – and violent street demonstrations, are acts of terrorism without the bullet and the bomb.... There must be few countries in the world prepared to watch so patiently a politically motivated mafia at work causing friction between police and the people.... There are serious attempts now being made to undermine the independence, impartiality and the authority of the British police service. I honestly believe we are now witnessing the domination of the police service as a necessary prerequisite of the creation in this country of a society based on Marxist Communist principles.

Anderton was in conflict with his police committee, which was not surprising as he had already made his position clear:

> I recommend that police committees should be totally abolished and replaced by non-political police boards.
>
> (*Guardian*, 17.8.82)

It has been argued that Anderton, because of his extremeness, is an exception. Especially after his public statements of his 'born again' Christian views and his belief that he received instructions from God, he might be seen as merely eccentric. However, it should be remembered that he was elected president of ACPO in 1986. Less 'extreme' CPOs have also commented on the political scene. Sir Robert Mark, for example, when discussing the 1973 trade disputes involving the Shrewsbury pickets wrote that they:

> had committed the worse of all crimes, worse even than murder, the attempt to achieve an industrial or political objective by criminal violence, the very conduct, which in fact helped to bring the National Socialists Workers party to power in 1933.
>
> (Mark 1978)

Mark had made a similar remark about the Nazi party and the British 'left' in the month of the 1979 General Election, when he argued that trade-union support for the Labour government of 1974–79 was:

> not unlike the way in which the National Socialist German Workers Party achieved unrestricted control of the German state between 1930 and 1939.
>
> (Mark 1979)

Charles MacLachlan, President of ACPO during the Miners' Strike said on television:

> Supporting the freedom of people who want to prevent people going to work is not supporting freedom but supporting anarchy, violence, riot and damage and everything else.
>
> (Interview, Channel 4, 'Diverse Reports', 13.10.84)

and when criticised by Nottinghamshire Police Authority, responded that he served:

> the people who got the living daylights beaten out of them, not those who beat them.
>
> (*Guardian*, 23.6.84)

Certainly it was during the miners' strike that the CPOs made their most public statements. It is not extraordinary that senior police officers hold conservative views, but it is a new development to find them expressed deliberately to the media so as to gain maximum coverage. These views are supported by the rank and file as may be seen from the comments of Tony Judge, editor of the *Journal of the Police Federation*, quoted on p.53.

After the long reign of a strong Conservative Government, senior police officers, and representatives of the lower ranks obviously feel free to comment, not only on matters of crime and public order, but also on the activities of organised trade unions. What is alarming is that they have obviously received tacit, if not open, support in this.

A Labour Research survey conducted in 1985 (Labour Research 1987a) indicated that of legal injunctions granted to employers since 1979, one-third originated in one industrial sector – printing and publishing. In the period up to 1985 the National Graphical Association (NGA), for example, had been fined £125,000, £175,000 and £73,000. The printers' unions represented workers in a craft industry, and had considerable power operated through an effective closed shop. They resisted the introduction of new technology which threatened employment, and so were a natural target for the Government. The News International (NI) dispute at Wapping was to become the focus for this resistance and to produce yet more bitter violent clashes between police and strikers.

The strike was provoked when 6,000 printworkers at NI received dismissal notices from management the day before the plant was due to move to new premises in Wapping (London Strategic Policy Unit 1988). NI were attempting to move to Wapping without reaching agreement with the printing unions, and were recruiting members of the electricians union, the EEPTU, rather than printworkers, to run the new plant. The dispute was to last over a year.

The lessons of the miners' strike had been learned by the police. During the 7 months' strike, 1,139 arrests from a work-force of 6,000, and solicitors' records suggested that the majority were members of SOGAT 82 or NGA 82. On average, 5,350 police were deployed on picket lines in the miners' strike, but at Wapping there were 1,014 police on duty each week – or one for every six dismissed printers – as opposed to one for every 22 miners. The SPG were used regularly. For example, on 15 February 1986, eight SPG units were used. The policing cost was in the region of 5.3 million.

We have noted that in the miners' strike, most defendants were charged with public order and obstruction offences. Again, solicitors' records suggest that at Wapping about 86 per cent of defendants were charged with public order and obstruction. In this strike charges relating to unlawful assembly, conspiracy and riot were not used because of the difficulty the police had in obtaining convictions during the miners' strike. All 137 riot charges were dismissed in the miners' cases (*Labour Research* October 1986). The police tended to pursue the policy of binding over, because their tactics essentially amounted to random arrest. Binding over excludes trade-union members from being involved further with the dispute in public demonstrations. Where this was challenged – a policy adopted, for example, by the SOGAT 82 London Machines Branch – the cases tended to be dismissed for lack of evidence.

One development of irritation to local residents was the setting up of roadblocks to prevent pedestrian and vehicular traffic around Wapping. The instructions forbidding this, under the Metropolitan Police Act 1939, were issued the day before the unions and NI talks broke down, and presumably the police had notice of Rupert Murdoch's intentions to dismiss the strikers. Again, the police complained about the use of violence against them: a total of 572 injuries, but only 52 officers took sick leave. This needs to be considered against the violence meted out to the pickets. On 3 March 1986 alone, pickets reported 44 injured supporters, with 24 head injuries, two leg injuries, a heart attack and two cases of severe shock. Head injuries consistent with truncheon blows were common. One notable feature was the number of police attacks on photographers, including television news teams, which was sufficiently large to prompt Assistant Commissioner Sutton to send a letter to London police stations, warning of the detrimental effects these were having on press and public relations.

Away from the picket lines police attitudes were less insensitive, although police behaviour could be unpredictable even after meetings between the police and the unions to try to avert trouble. On 3 May 1986 for example, after a smoke bomb went off, the police charged a crowd of 10,000 demonstrators marching from the Glasgow NI plant. On 24 January 1987, at the first-anniversary protest rally, the police, including mounted officers, charged the crowd repeatedly with shields and truncheons. The Haldane Society organised legal reporters who, after this event, produced their interim report arguing that the police had broken the 'Tactical Options Manual' by dispersing and incapacitating people rather than arresting them when violence was involved. There was not room for people to disperse, and many demonstrators were struck deliberately on the head. Many officers had no identification numbers, and police used unmarked vehicles. Red dyes were used to mark demonstrators. However, the police obviously learned valuable lessons at Wapping, as on 23 August, 1986, they announced that they used the same crowd-control methods and surveillance techniques for the Notting Hill Carnival.

NORTHERN IRELAND – ITS EFFECTS UPON BRITISH CRIMINOLOGY: PUBLIC DISORDER AND CRIMINALISATION IN ULSTER

The normalisation of special powers

The troubles in Northern Ireland and the response to them of the British State, remain constantly in the background of contemporary law and order issues. Whilst this is too large a subject to cover in any detail here, it is nevertheless essential to consider some of the main issues. Hillyard (1987) argues that the form of repressive strategy developed in Ulster since 1985:

> far from being exceptional and a product of the unique circumstances of the political violence in Northern Ireland is, on the contrary the form which many modern capitalist states are evolving.
>
> (Hillyard 1987, p.279)

This 'normalisation of special powers' as he calls it is reflected in the history of British rule in Ireland. Essentially the problem of Northern Ireland is a material one, the solution of which requires massive infra structural invest ment in order to develop an economy which will be attractive to both the Protestant and Catholic working class. Instead the British State has preferred to maintain the divided society in the province by the use of a sectarian armed police force, rather than attempting unification through economic development. Northern Ireland is treated as an underdeveloped colony whose political eruptions are controlled by the security forces. One consequence of this has been that much of what have become accepted forms of policing, surveillance and social control on the mainland, were legitimated and rehearsed in Northern Ireland. In the absence of a political solution, the State has defined the problems in Northern Ireland as law and order issues, and the police and army have worked together to maintain them.

The effects of Northern Ireland on policing on the British mainland may be seen in both its form and content. Sophisticated forms of surveillance, detection, interrogation, the use of plastic bullets and water cannon, and the suspension of trial by jury have become commonplace in Northern Ireland. Many of these have been transferred unevenly to the mainland, as for example, the training of the SPG (under Sir Robert Mark in 1972) in the methods of snatch squads, flying wedges, random stop-and-search and road blocks – tactics used by the Royal Ulster Constabulary (RUC). Other spin-offs have been press censorship, under the Terrorist Broadcast Ban 1989 and the changes in rules concerning detection and detention in the Police and Criminal Evidence Act of 1984. There has been anxiety over the allegations of a shoot-to-kill policy by the security forces in Northern Ireland which has spilt over into Europe.

The British use of Ireland, and especially Northern Ireland first as an experiment in militant policing and special powers, then as a normalisation of extraordinary law and order policies has a long history. British criminologists ignore legal developments in Ireland, reinforcing its 'invisibility' by a disclaimer that it is a special case. However, Ireland, and Northern Ireland in particular are important when considering British official attitudes to law and order (for further details see Jennings 1989).

The development of special powers

Between 1920 and 1969 Britain used special powers to deal with the particularly difficult problems of policing the six counties. (The following discussion on Britain and Ireland owe much to the work of Hillyard 1987.) As well as the IRA it had to cope in 1920 with sectarian attacks carried out on Catholics. It used the Royal Irish Constabulary (RIC), and units of the

British army. Because of pressure to send British troops to the south of Ireland, the Ulster Volunteer Force, a totally Protestant paramilitary unit was set up in 1920, as was the Ulster Special Constabulary (USC), which included the B specials, part-timers willing to serve in their own locality. We had therefore the creation of a sectarian paramilitary force, to control the six counties, including the two which had a Catholic majority, and which had no wish to be included in Northern Ireland. The Specials were seen from their inception as an undisciplined, partisan sectarian group (see Farrell 1983). These forces were the basis of the RUC which was founded in May 1922. In that same year Civil Authorities (Special Powers) Act allowed the Minister for Home Affairs powers to take such steps 'as may be necessary for preserving peace and maintaining order'. The forces of law could arrest and detain who they liked. In this sense Northern Ireland was set up as Hillyard puts it 'a state with extraordinary powers'. The Special Powers Act was regularly renewed until made permanent in 1933.

The Catholic communities were so closely surveyed and controlled that political opposition in Northern Ireland became ineffective. Under the Special Powers Act, anyone who was acting, had acted or was about to act, in a manner prejudicial to the preservation of the peace and the maintenance of order could be arrested and interned. The same minister who made the internment order was responsible for signing release papers, and whilst there was an advisory committee to review these cases, the minister could ignore its recommendations. The courts were notably associated with the Unionist Party, and particularly in the appointments to the judiciary.

The re-emergence of the 'Troubles' 1969–71

The failure to pay attention to the material development of Northern Ireland was coupled with a sectarian, centralised, repressive law-and-order policy supporting the Unionist Party and serving the exclusive interest of the majority Protestant community. The systematic discrimination against and exclusion from power of the Catholic minority eventually led to a civil rights campaign in 1969. British troops were deployed in Northern Ireland in August that year, initially to protect the Catholic community. At the same time the British Government attempted to initiate reforms for the treatment and freedom from discrimination for Catholics. The Hunt Committee, an advisory body on the police in Northern Ireland, reported in 1969, and its recommendations, which included making the police force less sectarian and partisan, were implemented. The B Specials were disbanded and as a first step towards the goal of an unarmed, civilian police force the Ulster Defence Regiment was established under British army control. The RUC was disarmed briefly but the continuing violence led to a rapid reversal of this decision. As the army took a stronger line against riots, the relations between them and the Catholic community deteriorated. Whilst the Government attempted to correct discrimination it did little or nothing to monitor the effective implementation of the reforms and the continued pressure from the Protestant community meant that a more coercive strategy once more developed to deal with the violence.

The introduction of internment and military supremacy: 1971–75

Internment was introduced in 1971 and within 6 months of its introduction 2,357 arrests had been made. Of these, 1,600 were released in the same period (for further details see McGuffin 1973). This example shows yet again that whilst there may be a serious law and order problem in Northern Ireland, the responses to it were always used as a means of suppressing political opposition. Violence increased after internment and a rate and rent strike began. After 'Bloody Sunday' in 1972, when 13 Catholics were killed by the Army, the Catholic communities became even more alienated from a British State which had singularly failed to protect them. Their bitterness increased when the official enquiry into the massacre exonerated the soldiers responsible for the deaths.

The situation in Northern Ireland was now one where, because of alleged intimidation of juries and witnesses, the British State used internment for suspects, but in order to maintain the facade of the rule of law, wished to deal with as many cases as possible through the judicial system, even if this meant suspending the ordinary rules of criminal procedure. The Diplock Commission, which was to influence this strategy from 1975 onwards, reported in 1972. It never actually went to Northern Ireland, and so the bulk of the evidence it considered came from those responsible for the administration of surveillance and justice in the province. Because it was a policy document, it focused upon the maintenance of public order, and ignored the broader, complex, political context. Long-established common-law principles were reconstituted as mere technical rules. The Diplock provisions for court procedures have been central to the Irish situation, and its recommendations were implemented in the Northern Ireland (Emergency Provisions) Act (EPA) 1973. Basically, the commission suggested trial without jury and legalised prolonged interrogation. The EPA allowed the army and the police to stop and detain anyone suspected of being a terrorist for up to 72 hours. Extensive powers of search were created, juries and many rules of evidence abolished, so that civil rights and the rule of law were seriously abrogated.

Interrogation centres became the subject of controversy, particularly after 1977 when torture and ill-treatment were alleged, both by the Association of Forensic Medical Officers and Amnesty International (Amnesty International 1977). Earlier allegations of torture against Republican detainees in 1971, had been rejected by the Compton Committee (1971), which concluded that only ill-treatment had occurred. However, the treatment of detainees led in 1976 to the Republic of Ireland filing an application to the European Commission of Human Rights. This held that, whilst the techniques used during interrogation were inhuman and degrading, they were not torture, but nevertheless the British Government had to pay £188,250 in damages to the persons involved. The high degree of confession (e.g. 86 per cent between January and April 1979 and Walsh's (1983) more recent figures) suggests that the courtroom had taken a back seat to the interrogation centre as regards prosecution and proof.

The normalisation of special measures is indicated by the fact that 40 per cent of all cases coming to the Diplock Courts had nothing to do with the Troubles (Taylor 1980). The acquittal rate declined after the suspension of jury trials, suggesting judges became cynical and case-hardened. The majority of suspects were interrogated for long periods after confession, which suggests that interrogation was used to gather information (Walsh 1983).

In 1974, in response to public panic after the Birmingham pub bombings, the Prevention of Terrorism Act (PTA) was rushed through parliament in 42 hours. It extended powers of arrest and detention, based on the concept of an emergency situation in Northern Ireland to the rest of the United Kingdom. Arrest was possible with 'reasonable suspicion', and could be prolonged by a further 5 days by the Secretary of State. This has clearly influenced the implementation of the PACE Act 1984 which extends to 96 hours the period for detention without charge.

Ulsterisation, supergrasses and 'shoot to kill'

The first indication of 'Ulsterisation' of the situation in Northern Ireland came in 1974 after the Labour Party election victory when it became clear that an attempt was to be made to reconstitute the economic and political problems of Northern Ireland into a law and order issue. The Government Ulsterised the situation by restoring the responsibility for law and order in the province to the RUC, while at the same time attempting to portray the problem in terms of criminality, by, in 1975, stopping the use of internment, relying more upon the court process and withdrawing the special-status category from prisoners. This had been granted since 1972 to people who had been convicted in court but who claimed that their offences had been politically motivated. The withdrawal of special status led to 'on the blanket' protests in the Maze prison in 1976 and 1978, and by women prisoners at Armagh in 1980. The protests were so called because special category prisoners had not been required to wear prison uniform and when this status was withdrawn they refused to put on prison issue and so had only blankets for clothes. These demonstrations escalated and led, in 1980 and 1981, to hunger strikes which resulted in the death of Bobby Sands. Nine others were to die before the strike ended and the Government made some concessions. Despite appeals to, and criticisms by, the European Human Rights Commission, the Government's intransigence during the four and half years of protests over special status, was a stark signal of the lengths to which they were prepared to go to maintain the criminalisation policy.

Ulsterisation, restoring the full responsibility of law and order to the police, meant the replacement of British security personnel by the predominantly Protestant RUC, which with increased re-arming became once more a quasi-military organization rather than the civil force recommended by the Hunt Committee. Hillyard (1987) sees as particularly important its increased intelligence capacity via the growth in the number of confidential telephones and the use of informers and surveillance techniques. The police had as we saw earlier extensive special powers under the EPA and PTA as well as ordinary powers under criminal law. Hillyard (1987) points out that the most frequently used power is section 11 of the EPA which allows the police to arrest anyone they suspect of being a terrorist. The extensive questioning under arrest further suggest that the powers are being used to gather information rather than to charge and prosecute. In Hillyard's words:

> The almost exclusive use of Section 11 rather than ordinary powers of arrest illustrates very clearly the way in which emergency powers become the norm. More importantly, the effect of mainly using this particular power has been to shift the basis of arrest from suspicion of a particular act to suspicion of the status of the individual.
>
> (Hillyard 1987, p.289)

From the end of 1981, the authorities, because of the lack of other independent witnesses, and public protests about methods used in interrogation systems, were forced to increase the use of the so-called 'supergrass' system to obtain convictions, and as an alternative form of gathering information. In that year, for example, the evidence of Christopher Black was used against 38 people, 35 of whom were found guilty; in total, between 1983 and 1985, 120 people were convicted in this way, half of them on the uncorroborated evidence of a supergrass alone (Hillyard 1987).

Asmal (1985), in a report into the Security Forces' use of firearms calculates that between 1969 and the publication of his findings, 270 individuals – at least 155 of them civilians – had been killed by the security forces. Of the 21 members of the security forces prosecuted for some of these deaths 19 were acquitted. More recent evidence on the use of firearms and plastic bullets may be found in Jennings (1989). The Gibraltar shooting of three IRA members suggested that a shoot-to-kill policy may have been extended abroad. The use of firepower is common against civilians: 16,656 plastic bullets were used in one month alone in 1981 during protests around the hunger strikes, and 17 people, 11 of whom were children, were killed between 1972 and 1986 by rubber/plastic bullets (Jennings 1989). Aggressive tactics have become a familiar part of the strategy used, for example, by the RUC's Special Branch unit, E4A, a deep-surveillance squad trained by the army's Special Air Services team, and the RUC's Headquarter Mobile Support Units. These units have been involved in several disputed killings, and those which took place during a 5-week period in 1982 were the subject of the Stalker enquiry. The enquiry, initially led by John Stalker, then Deputy Chief Constable of Manchester, but subsequently taken over, under controversial circumstances, by John Stephenson, began in 1985. Stalker submitted a critical report to RUC headquarters in September of that year, concluding, amongst other things, that there were grounds for the charging of a number of police officers with offences ranging from conspiracy to pervert the course of justice to murder.

Prior to presenting his findings, Stalker was himself accused of fraternising with known criminals, suspended from duty, reinstated by his police committee and then resigned from the police. In his own book (Stalker 1988) he confirmed that his brief did not include an investigation of a shoot-to-kill policy as such. He was given the impression by the Northern Ireland Chief Constable, Sir John Hermon, that he was simply to read a few documents, and when he tried to go further he was met with hostility and suspicion. He felt his investigation was hampered by the RUC. He states:

> The circumstances of those shootings (of 6 men suspected of terrorism) pointed to a police inclination, if not policy, to shoot suspects dead without warning rather than to arrest them.
>
> (Stalker 1988 p.253)

There is, at the very least, a strong suspicion that an attempt was made to delegitimate a report by exposing the private life of its investigator. One is reminded of the fate of Dr Robert Irwin, who in 1979 reported the results of his examinations of 160 people injured while in police custody. His allegations were written off, the RUC describing him as a 'drunk' who was 'sour and bitter'. Furthermore, they portrayed him as having a grudge against the RUC because they failed to find the rapist who attacked his wife (Taylor 1980). Stalker was removed from the investigation, and publicly disgraced, and his advice to his successor was to contemplate suicide. In January 1988, the Attorney General, Sir Patrick Mayhew, announced that the eight RUC officers accused of obstructing the Stalker enquiry would not be prosecuted, for reasons of national security. In August 1989 evidence came to light that there had been security leaks to the Protestant paramilitary groups about IRA suspects, culminating in murder in some cases.

The 1985 Anglo-Irish agreement was set up in an attempt to improve border security, and to respond to fears in the Republic about the threat to stability in Ireland posed by Sinn Fein and the Provisional IRA. Security co-operation between the two countries has increased, and extradition from the Republic of those claiming political motives for their alleged offences is now allowed. The situation within Northern Ireland remains the same. A garrison State exists, despite the evidence that Catholics are not necessarily in support of a united Ireland, and that desire for equal rights is favoured over unification (Jennings 1989). Certainly 40 per cent of Catholics vote Sinn Fein in areas where there are candidates, but this is part of a democratic process which cannot be ignored. In Northern Ireland civil liberties have been eroded and emergency powers have become normalised. All discussions of legal reform presume that the special powers are permanent, because they are too convenient to the State to remove. Policies are being developed in conjunction with the higher levels of the police and the army. What is required is a political solution including legal reforms, for a State whose legal process has become based on discrimination. The difficulty is finding a solution to a historically unjust society, the roots of whose injustice go back to Ireland being treated as a colony and founding of Ulster.

Policing in Northern Ireland and Britain

the methods and strategies for dealing with the high level of political violence in Northern Ireland are increasingly being introduced into policing and the administration of justice in the rest of the United Kingdom.

(Hillyard 1987, p.304)

Hillyard argues, that while not identical, developments in policing in the two areas have many similarities. In particular he suggests there have been parallels both in the form and organisation of policing. This is not, to paraphrase his words, because the province has been used as some social laboratory for experimenting with different methods, but because there has been a common core of people involved. There has been a constant interchange of personnel in all sections of the Civil Service in Britain and Northern Ireland (and especially between the Northern Ireland Office, the Home Office and the Ministry of Defence). Furthermore, the police forces in the United Kingdom, despite being decentralised, have close working-, and especially training-relationships. Senior police officers visit the province to study police tactics and officers from the RUC attend courses in England with their colleagues from mainland forces. Prior to becoming Commissioner of the Metropolitan Police, Sir Kenneth Newman spent over 8 years as Deputy Chief and then Chief Constable. With such close relationships similarities are to be expected. Northam (1988), in his discussion of changes in public order policing in Britain in the 1980s, traces a longer history of the use made of Ireland for the development of paramilitary-style tactics. In his account, in the nineteenth and early twentieth centuries, the Royal Irish Constabulary (RIC) founded in 1836, was the prototype for the military-style colonial police forces, used throughout the Empire to keep down rebellious natives, while the Metropolitan Police served as a model for the law-enforcing, peace keeping role of the mainland police. Indeed much of the training of the colonial forces took place in Dublin:

> So for a hundred years, Ireland became the base for an enormous training operation controlled from London. Officers of the RIC were sent abroad to recruit and give basic training to police forces all over the world, and on return trips officers who needed advanced training for promotion returned to Dublin.... After partition, the force, renamed the Royal Ulster Constabulary, simply carried on the same business of training colonial police officers from its new address in Belfast. Training on a large scale was transferred to mainland Britain only after the Second World War.
>
> (Northam 1988, p.128)

For Northam the move towards a more 'rugged' approach to public order policing can be traced to the increasing use of colonial, and especially Hong Kong, methods in Northern Ireland and Britain. Since these colonial forces developed in the style of the RIC the circle was complete.

The convergence in form, in increased militarisation, of policing between Northern Ireland was seen most spectacularly in the 1984–5 miners' strike which in Hillyard's words:

> provided the majority of police forces in Britain with the opportunity to develop military methods of policing.... Police tactics ranging from the extensive use of road blocks to the specific methods of crowd control owed much to the experience of policing in Northern Ireland.
>
> (Hillyard 1987, p.305)

Another change in the form of policing has been the increased policing of people rather than crimes, the targeting of black people, trade unionists and travellers. In Britain, as in Northern Ireland, large sections of the community are seen as posing a threat to the status quo and are placed under regular and systematic surveillance. Even those aspects of police work in which they like to present their socially concerned face, such as multi-agency policing, have their antecedents in North Irish initiatives.

There has also been a convergence between Northern Ireland and Britain in how the police are organised and in particular the increased centralisation. The tradition of local autonomy for the forces in Britain has, as we discussed earlier, been put increasingly under strain. Another area in which developments in the province have foreshadowed those in the rest of the country is in the form of the criminal justice system. In Northern Ireland changes in the early 1970s involved:

> the vast expansion of the police powers of arrest, search and detention; fundamental changes in the rules of evidence particularly in the admissibility rule; the abolition of trial by jury; and the introduction of the public prosecutor system.
>
> (Hillyard 1987, p.306)

In England and Wales PACE 1984 allows detention for up to 4 days (as compared to 3 under the Northern Ireland emergency legislation). PACE also weakened the provisions that prevented the admission of non-voluntary admissions thus weakening court control over police interrogation methods. The right to silence has also been weakened, in that now judges may draw attention to it in ways detrimental to defendants. While trial by jury has not yet been abolished there have been restrictions on the number of cases which may go for trial. Furthermore, the number of challenges which the defence may make to a jury has been reduced and there is evidence of jury vetting by the authorities (Harman and Griffiths, 1979). The Crown Prosecution service was introduced in 1986.

The dubious situation which exists in Northern Ireland was underlined by the revelation in August 1989 that MI5 documents about military operations against them in West Germany, had been leaked to the IRA. These files seem to have come from the offices of BSSO, a joint MI5/Ministry of Defence organization (Campbell 1989). This is in addition to leaking within Northern Ireland of persons suspected of being members of Republican organisations to Loyalist paramilitary groups.

The worrying thing about academic discussion about criminology and law, is that the colonial attitude to Northern Ireland has continued in this debate. Northern Ireland is seen as something too complex, or too exceptional to be considered as part of the normal discussion about civil rights and legal reform. Hillyard asks us whether police accountability would work for the RUC, and the Protestant and Catholic communities. Would the belief in a Labour Government reform of law hold for Northern Ireland, given their record on Ulsterisation? Would the same conclusions have been reached as regards the contemporary analyses of British policing in the large literature that has been produced recently? Britain's liberal academics and lawyers unwittingly support the colony attitude towards Northern Ireland by continuing to treat it as an exceptional case.

CONCLUSIONS

The bifurcatory nature of British policing became more marked after 1979. Whether one sees the increasing militarisation of public order policing as nothing more than a continuation of earlier practice (e.g. Gilroy and Sim 1985), or as a more fundamental shift, introducing techniques previously reserved for controlling the unruly colonies (Northam 1988), there is little doubt that it has placed great strains upon 'normal policing'. In this chapter we have traced the development of this paramilitary style via a discussion of certain key moments. This style proved extremely effective in underpinning the Conservatives' claims to be the party of strong law and order in its early years in office. Inner city eruptions by the dangerous classes protesting at the impact of the Government's economic and social policies during a period of deep recession were dealt with by force masquerading as firmness. Nor should the role of the police in defeating organised union resistance to the Government's economic and social problems be minimised. The miners' strike in particular showed how they had developed into an extremely effective arm of the Government's strategy to break union power and reconstruct British industrial relations on terms more favourable to the employers. As we have seen, during this period the police, in common with other parts of the criminal justice system, were cocooned from the cold winds of monetarism, protected from the repeated rounds of public expenditure cuts and indeed received additional resources. Yet crime of the type which made the headlines in the tabloids continued to rise. Since hard-line approaches seemed to provide no solution, the answer was increasingly sought in more softly-softly strategies which placed great emphasis on community involvement. It is this softer approach which is the focus of the next chapter.

4 The police as social workers

Community and multi-agency policing

If in the 1980s paramilitary tactics had become the order of the day for a police in the front line of defence against the 'enemy within', they had had little impact either on crime prevention or detection. There had been a growing sense, backed by Home Office research (Clarke and Hough 1980, 1984; Morris and Heal 1981) that increasing police numbers and resources has little impact upon crime. This led to a rethinking on strategies for controlling crime. As we shall see in this chapter this dovetailed neatly with the Conservatives' ideological propensity to keep public expenditure as low as possible and with their commitment to transfer as much as possible of the State's responsibility onto the shoulders of the private citizen. In this chapter we examine the development of this community-based approach to crime control. According to Hope and Shaw (1988) this was brought about by two main considerations. Firstly, there was the increased awareness of the social problems created by fear of crime, independently of crime itself, and in particular the damage such fear can wreak on community life. Secondly, the growing belief, referred to above, that there are:

> limitations of what the criminal justice system can do: that the burden of crime prevention cannot be carried solely by the police, the courts and the penal system. As well as citizens themselves, those responsible for housing, for schools, for employment and leisure provision also have a more crucial role in crime prevention than has been acknowledged previously.
> (Hope and Shaw 1988, p.11)

These considerations led to two interrelated approaches to the problem; multi-agency policing and citizen involvement in crime prevention. The main part of this chapter will concentrate on examining these developments.

We begin by looking at the changes in policy towards young people and crime since it is in this area that many of the policy innovations were first introduced. The introduction of multi-agency policing and the implications of such a move are then considered prior to a brief diversion to consider the civil libertarian aspects of Conservative policies. We conclude the chapter with an examination of the Conservatives' new answer to the rising crimes rates: the active citizen.

YOUTH AND LAW AND ORDER

The Children and Young Persons Act (CYPA) of 1969 can be seen as the culmination of social welfare influence which emphasised the caring rather than the controlling aspect of juvenile work. Its tone was rehabilitative, non-punitive and treatment oriented. It is debatable, however, whether its principles ever had any impact in practice. If we examine the juvenile sentencing figures for 1971 to 1981 (see Smith 1984), we find that in practice the relative use of measures such as probation, supervision and care orders declined whilst correspondingly there has been an increase in punitive measures, especially custody. Smith argues that the Criminal Justice Act (CJA) 1982 reflects these attitudes, shifting legislative emphasis from treatment to control. The Act finally disposed of any lingering rehabilitative aspect of the Children and Young Persons Act, 1969. What we see here is the 'short sharp shock' illustrated by the introduction of very short detention-centre sentences, in as disciplinarian a regime as can be managed. The CJA 1982 not only restored to the judiciary the power to commit young persons to prison, a power the earlier Act had severely restricted – at least in principle – but it has also extended the age limit downwards from 17 to 15 years. However, some care must be taken with these figures, especially when if we extend Smith's argument into the 1980s. Smith's analysis refers only to percentages of those sentenced. If we consider 14–16-year-old males we find that between 1981 and 1988 of those sentenced between 11 and 12 per cent received custodial sentences of one sort or another. However, this ignores the impact of police cautioning. In the same period the numbers of 14–16-year-old males appearing before the courts declined from 62,000 to 29,600. If we look at the combined numbers cautioned and sentenced then between 1983 and 1988 the total numbers have declined from 91,800 to 72,600. The percentage cautioned has increased from 41 to 59 per cent, whilst the percentage receiving a custodial sentence has declined from 7 to 4 per cent. The diversion of 14–16-year-olds from the courts has been a major feature of the 1980s.

Pitts (1988) argues that the 1982 CJA had two major objectives: to strengthen the law relating to juveniles and young offenders aged 15–21, but also to limit the use of imprisonment for this group. The CJA wanted to limit imprisonment, which was becoming grossly overcrowded, but also to maintain the idea of the 'short sharp shock'. The State needed to reduce the borstal population (15–21-year-olds) which showed a reconviction rate of 70 per cent, whilst the 14–15-year-old age group had a reconviction rate of 79 per cent. The 1982 CJA allowed courts to imprison young offenders in the mainstream of the prison system. Borstal was reabsorbed into the main prison system. This was a real turning back of the clock, as from May 1983, courts could sentence anyone aged over 15 to prison, and this meant that juvenile courts could impose custodial sentences without remitting to crown court for sentence. Once again rehabilitation is abandoned for punishment. Pitts points out that Britain could have followed Holland and set a limit to prison places which the courts could sentence to (Junger-Tass and Blok 1984), but this would have been seen as weakening responses to adolescents, and against the ideology of the law and order Party. By the end of the first year of CJA 1982, there was an increase of 65 per cent in the borstal/youth custody population. This led to a massive increase in the log jam in the prison system, partially because the old borstal training was flexible in terms of time spent inside a borstal, a factor which no longer held. This is why the Government had to promise the shock should be short, but definitely sharp. This explains the tougher regimes in detention centres, which unfortunately did not work, as there was no discernible change in the reconviction rate. The juvenile bench firmly favoured custody, and it is the custom of the juvenile bench to impose stricter sentences on lesser offences, when given an increase of powers, rather than reduce sentences on more serious offences. Stricter punishment is moved down-tariff.

The CJA 1982 also had introduced a stronger form of intermediate treatment (IT), under a supervised activity order. The magistracy now had more control over IT, and it was hoped that IT would establish a network of alternatives to custody. On the one hand, more alternatives to custody were being created, in the same legislation which allowed more custodial sentences. Juvenile crime rates had, however, remained static, and the adolescent population was on the wane. The youth custody population grew by 65 per cent by May 1984, and the detention-centre population declined. Less problematic offenders were being locked up for longer. IT, the rehabilitative wing of juvenile justice, now had to deal with the group who needed an alternative to custody. Community Service Orders under the CJA 1982 made it possible to create a prison in the community regime. 'Night restrictions' forced parents to supervise children in their own homes, as well as being responsible for their fines. Unfortunately, community service orders were imposed on those who would have received a less serious non-custodial sentence, not those who would otherwise be imprisoned.

In any discussion of juvenile crime a central agency is the probation service. The courts' loss of confidence in the probation service as an effective measure in crime reduction had led to 50 per cent fewer men being placed on probation between 1969 and 1979. This was due to new alternatives in sentencing, such as suspended and deferred sentences, and community service. One result of this decline has been the 'coercive tilt' (Walker and Beaumont 1981) with suggestions for introducing a more controlling form of probation supervision, which it was felt would be more attractive to the courts, coming from within the service itself. The Younger Report in 1974 (again under Labour), had suggested probation officers should be given power to detain offenders in custody for 72 hours. Despite the outrage which followed this proposal, in 1980 a Probation Control Unit opened for 17 to 24-year-olds in Kent. Its strict regime led to it being closed in 1985. The detention centres gained a bad reputation, because Glenochil Young Offenders complex in Scotland, which was the prototype of the short-sharp-shock regimes, by 1983 had 171 young men on strict suicide observation, and by 1984 had its fifth suicide since its inception in 1981. The short-sharp-shock in detention centres, whilst pandering to the more controlling elements of the law and order supporters in Parliament and on the bench, was found to have little effect on inmates, but a bad effect on uniformed staff morale (HMSO 1984). There was also:

> evidence that the trainees actually enjoyed the para-military trappings of the new regimes.
>
> (Shaw 1987)

The then Home Secretary, Leon Brittan, however, responded by extending the regime to all detention centres.

The 1982 Criminal Justice Act in fact gave magistrates powers to order the removal from home of young people by social services, to sentence young people to Prison Department institutions, and introduced care orders with residential conditions. Despite suggestions that custodial sentencing should be reduced, the magistracy followed its usual inclination to use any new powers to increase imprisonment. What usually happens is that if non-custodial measures are introduced into the sentencing tariff, the magistracy tend to use these instead of fines, discharges or supervision orders, whilst maintaining and even increasing custodial sentences. The Appeal Court eventually laid down guidelines for custodial sentencing under the CJA (Whitehead and MacMillan 1985; Cavadino 1985). Under the act, curfews were made possible as a condition of probation or social service supervision, but the professional social work unions refused to implement these. The probation service's view of itself traditionally has been that of befriending prisoners, and negotiating with the court on their behalf, has come under increasing pressure from the current Government. A probation order is an alternative to a custodial sentence, but the 1982 Criminal Justice Act had a provision for offenders to be required to attend a specified place for up to 60 days. The 1972 Criminal Justice Act reduced by the use of bail hostels, probation hostels and probation homes, those who would have been incarcerated because there was nowhere else to send them, usually they were homeless. With probation day centres and community service orders these can be seen, then, as alternatives to prison, as long as they take the higher-risk offenders. Where this does not happen, sentencing is merely being extended to low-tariff offenders. Detention centres orders were finally phased out in 1988 when they were merged with youth custody orders into a single sentence of 'detention in a young offender institution'.

At a probation conference on 2.7.89 (*Guardian* 3.7.89) a senior Home Office civil servant suggested that changes were to be brought about which would transform the probation service into one which administered punishment in the community rather than one which befriended offenders. The probation service seemed to be catching much of the backlash felt by the social work profession. Ministers, it was reported, believe that probation officers should no longer see themselves as the 'nice guys' of the criminal justice system. It was suggested that reforms would include the introduction of cash limits, and hiving off a range of functions such as hostel schemes and day centres into the private or voluntary systems, implemented in the Criminal Justice Bill 1990–1. A proposal to develop a central agency, rather than a locally based service was held back, but it was felt by probation unions that this would be used ultimately as a technique for imposing a new service ethos if persuasion fails. This attack on the view that probation is a soft option is not new, but the idea of attaching dusk-to-dawn curfews and bans on going to pubs to probation orders was seen as a distinct move away from the soft-option image. The problem of actually enforcing these, however, is the difficulty.

In many ways tagging, curfews and bans are preferable to prison, and the use of these for non-violent offenders is likely to increase. Electronic tagging is likely to be introduced in the 1990 CJB, to supplement an experiment about to be carried out for those on bail. However, the National Association of Probation Officers argues that these conditions can become counterproductive. Offenders refuse to comply, and end up back in court. An experiment using tagging as an alternative to custodial sentencing following the Green Paper of 1988 was introduced in Tower Hamlets to run alongside those trials already operating in Tyneside and Nottingham. This area seems to have been selected because of the fears that large numbers of black youths were destined to become the target of tagging. This could escalate into resistance along the lines of racial solidarity, and this the government wants to avoid. Preliminary results (*Guardian* 4.4.90) seemed to indicate the three experiments had been failures but nevertheless the Government seemed determined to press ahead. The statutory aspect of probation has prevented privatisation, but the Home Office seems to be moving towards the involvement of more voluntary and private agencies becoming involved. The 1990 Bill intends to introduce cash limits for the funding of the 56 probation committees, funded 80 per cent by central Government, and 20 per cent by local authorities. The private agencies to be involved would be accommodation schemes, employment services, drugs and alcohol groups, day centres and community services. This could place probation officers in the position of referring offenders and assembling packages of services rather than delivering them. This would move a social-work function to a referral function. In this situation multi-agency work for the Government seems to mean the privatisation of agencies.

Forms of closer surveillance and tighter structures are popular in the United States for young people, and have been introduced in this country. Tracking (Brockington and Shaw 1986) a community-based sentence, used as an alternative to custodial sentences was organised in the United States by Key, a private agency. Key tried to provide alternative care and support for offenders released from training schools whose harsh conditions had brought them into public criticism. Fundamentally, the programme was based on the tracker knowing where a youth was at all times, ensuring a highly structured daily routine, constructing a system of structures which, drawing on school or work, could be maintained after supervision and providing intense activity, counselling support and close monitoring. Most trackers, unsurprisingly, burnt out after 18–24 months. Modified versions of these schemes were introduced into this country in the late 1970s. Again they met resistance from professional social workers who disliked the punitive element it might introduce into their work. It has been patchily developed by social service and probation departments, usually developed as part of an intermediate treatment requirement (and usually) as part of a supervision order. Some schemes use a residential component, others use tracking within a 28-day bail order, some projects provide training, others expect the offender to continue at work or school (see Ely *et al.* 1987). Professional responses have varied from seeing it as dependency-creating and too demanding for staff (Ross 1984) or inflexible, routinised and overt control (Ely 1985). Pratt (1985) sees it as yet another instance of a current intensification of the regulation of the lives of the young. The scheme which was taken up in the Medway, Leeds and Coventry areas among others provides little hard evidence as to its superiority over other forms of intervention. Whilst it can provide an alternative to custody, it has raised disquiet about the role of social work supervision and surveillance (Brockington and Shaw 1986).

What we see in this development of policy is a swing away from rehabilitation as a principle, to a more viable, and often privatised form of social control. This leads to a challenge to probation officers in particular, moving their role towards a more controlling than caring one. We see the gradual removal of the principles of the CYPA 1969, to an approach more acceptable to the political views of the law and order lobby.

A particular strategy developed mainly, but not exclusively for youth, is the multi-agency approach to community policing. This term and structure was developed by Sir Kenneth Newman after he became Commissioner of the Metropolitan Police in 1982, prompted at least in part by the Scarman Report on the Brixton disorders, but also as a response to the more general problems faced by the police. The Newman strategy, as outlined in the Metropolitan Commissioners' Annual Reports for 1982 and 1983, was clearly conceived as being a sweeping reorientation of policing policy and organisation. Apart from the impetus of Scarman, Reiner (1985) argues that it stemmed from three basic problems facing the police: (i) a crisis in legitimacy and public confidence, (ii) the failure, already noted, to clear up or prevent crime and (iii) the message enshrined in Home Office Circular 114/83 that further resources would not be available for forces who did not demonstrate efficiency. This third factor, part of the Government's Financial Management Initiative to curtail public expenditure and to achieve the three E's – Effectiveness, Efficiency and Economy – in the public sector, has, as we have noted, been slower to bite in the police than other public service areas. However, the continued interest of the National Audit Office, which has published several studies critical of police efficiency, and the increasing emphasis being placed upon the use of performance indicators by the Inspectorate of Constabulary, suggest that the police will need to become more accountable, at least in a financial sense. Newman's approach was centred around the idea that any successful crime control must clearly involve the public. Neighbourhood watch schemes, to be reviewed in more detail later in this chapter are one consequence of this attitude. To encourage public involvement Newman extended the idea of policing by consent to include a 'notional social contract' between police and public. This was to be done through greater public involvement in consultative committees and crime prevention panels and by the multi-agency approach to policing. In return the police as their part of the contract would be more responsive to the types of policing required by the public. Basically, it involves other agencies, e.g. social workers, teachers, besides the police becoming responsible for a surveillance and intelligence role over young people, and working closer with the police. According to Hope and Shaw:

> The basic premise underlying the approach has been that, inasmuch as crime within local communities is likely to be sustained by a broad range of factors – in housing, education, recreation, etc. – the agencies and organizations who are in some way responsible for, or capable of, affect-

ing those factors ought to join in common cause so that they are not working at cross purposes or sustaining crime inadvertently.

(Hope and Shaw 1988, p.13)

The leading role which the police saw for themselves may be gauged from the following:

officers should be seen to be the front-runners in social change, whether it is urging architectural change to help in the 'designing out' of crime, advocating alternative housing policies or actively persuading commercial enterprises to build greater safety or crime prevention factors into house or vehicle design.

(Metropolitan Police Commissioner 1984)

In addition to the police initiatives as part of their move towards community-based policing, Hope and Shaw note a second trend towards multi-agency work has been, as we noted earlier, in youth work where:

there have been moves, usually at a local level, towards developing co-ordinated approaches to juvenile justice, involving increased collaboration between police, social work agencies and schools

(Hope and Shaw 1988, p.13)

The co-operation between police and other agencies involved with juveniles has, of course, a history which predates Newman. As early as 1952 a Juvenile Liaison Department had been created by the police, and its importance increased in the 1960s, with the move in the juvenile justice system towards a social work model, emphasising care rather than control of juveniles. Police work with juveniles led to their involvement in social services departments and schools. In 1968 the Metropolitan Police set up a Juvenile Bureau to collect information about juveniles from schools and social work departments. By 1978 there was a joint circular from the Home Office, DHSS and DES emphasising the need to develop joint activities concerning juveniles, and in 1980 the Home Office issued its own circular urging such co-operation.

The school became to be seen as the centre of pro-active programmes, and police work with schools has been developed considerably since the mid–1970s. Police have held education classes on their role and spoken not only on traffic dangers, but also vandalism and drugs. Some police forces have used the schemes as an opportunity to ask children to pass on information about vandalism and theft. This clearly has dangers for the role of teachers and has been resisted by some local branches of the National Union of Teachers, who have opposed police presence in schools. In particular, in 1987 teachers in the Inner London Teachers Association banned any further co-operation with the police, including using their video material warning of the dangers of sex attacks, because:

> The police motives are anti-black and anti-working class. They want to get into our classrooms to clock the likely lads so that they can pass their names to the juvenile bureau and the collators at their local stations.
>
> (*London Evening Standard*, 15.2.87, quoted in Uglow 1988a)

The Government, with this view in mind, has seen fit to write into the 1987 Education Act a requirement which makes it incumbent on school heads, when discharging their duties to the curriculum, to have regard to representations made by the chief officer of police.

Section 30 of the same Act instructs the school governing body to include in its annual report steps taken to develop links with the police. Menter (1988) argues that important developments have taken place in the police/schools debate since 1980, and this involves attempts to develop better relations between the police and the local black youth. The stated intention of the programmes are to foster better relations, but this has been challenged by some teachers. They are concerned about police expertise in presenting programmes, and about their perceived hidden motivation – information gathering. The multi-agency approach placed teachers in the difficult situation of being seen as extensions of the police surveillance system, and some teachers have argued that the racism left out of the programmes is police racism (Kolenzo 1984). Policing by consent is partially achieved by policing through ideology, and the school is in the front line.

The school in fact plays a large part in Conservative ideology, being seen as important in developing the right work attitudes and habits. Part of the Conservative education policy is to wrest schooling from the vested and ideological interests of teachers, to create a curriculum in the national interest.

Gordon (1984) suggests that community policing has a dubious side, gathering information about members of a local neighbourhood. The police community-beat officers have access to local populations which would normally would be closed to them. Multi-agency policing allows the police entry into new areas of civilian life, for example, as in Glasgow where by being members of local authority committees, the police had become an essential ingredient of local authority corporate policy. This is, of course, rather different from democratic accountability by the police. Gordon also sees such schemes as neighbourhood watch, not just as a crime prevention programmes, but aimed at mobilising support for the police amongst the middle and respectable working classes. Community policing in this view is seen in the context of increased surveillance and discipline by the strong

State, which takes the form of trade-union legislation, immigration control, criminalisation of sections of the community and the use of the family to control children and keep women in the home. Community policing is used to 'break down community resistance, to engineer consent and support for the police and to reinforce social discipline'. It is part of what Hall (1979) has called policing the 'social crisis of the cities'.

Community policing has been implemented in a top-down style. To be truly effective it needs to confront its own rhetoric and tackle the question of why there is a reluctance of agencies other than the police to become involved. At present there is a feeling that the police involvement is simply a public relations exercise.

COMMUNITY CRIME PREVENTION AND THE ACTIVE CITIZEN

> At the very centre of our ideas on how to control crime should be the energy and initiative of the active citizen.
>
> (John Patten, Minister of State, Home Office
> (Foreword in Hope and Shaw 1988))

The particular use of the law and order card by the Conservatives in the 1979 election campaign meant that in the years immediately following, a liberal-minded Home Secretary, such as Willie Whitelaw, was always likely to be given a torrid time by the Conservative Annual Conference and so it proved. While he may have had the twin aim of persuading the courts to send fewer people to prison, and reducing the sentences of those who were sent, the constituency activists, egged on by the tough-sounding clichés of the election campaign, and with the (mostly) passive support of the Prime Minister, clearly had other ideas. For example, the resolution chosen for debate at the 1980 conference insisted that 'the penalties inflicted upon convicted criminals be made severe so as to present a formidable deterrent to those people who would break our laws'. The majority of the resolutions in that year called, in the words of the *Guardian* (8.10.80), for simplistic solutions, military service deportation, ending remission, abandoning parole, reintroducing corporal and capital punishment and lowering the age of criminal responsibility without any recognition of the complexity of controlling crime. Standing his ground, while at the 1981 Conference the Prime Minister publicly applauded the sentiments of his rank-and-file critics, Mr Whitelaw was nevertheless unable to proceed with the reforms he might otherwise have wished. His successor, Leon Brittan, made no attempt to oppose the Party's right wing. At the first conference after the 1983 Conservative Election victory he made what one commentator referred to as 'one of the most unpleasant speeches heard in years.' (Peter Jenkins, *Guardian* 12.10.83), in which he announced a package of punitive measures for dealing with violent crime and a further expansion of the prison-building programme. He further pledged that while the Government had given top priority to bringing down inflation in the 1979–83 Parliament now its most crucial job was the fight against crime. To this end he also emphasised his commitment to a wider strategy for crime prevention and in particular to the encouragement of neighbourhood watch schemes. But the tone of his speech may perhaps best be captured by the following extract:

> Our party alone challenges the indiscipline in our schools which has led to disorder in our streets. We alone robustly proclaim the overriding need to defend life and property. Whatever the threat and whatever the consequences. Our mission is to defend the rule of law and the values of freedom wherever they are in peril.
>
> (*The Times* 12.10.83)

Between 1983 and 1987 the total number of offences recorded by the police increased by just under 20 per cent and far from being an electoral asset their law and order policies were, if anything, the area of their biggest failures. Clearly a cost-conscious Government could not continue just repeating the same old tune when faced with such a stark picture of ineffectiveness. A different emphasis was clearly required, and the answer lay in crime prevention. But as Jock Young, writing in the *Independent* newspaper, commented, the political ideas had always been present waiting to be mobilised. 'They represented the application of Thatcherite ideals to the hitherto sacrosanct area of law and order.' The Conservatives were not alone in championing crime prevention. It was endorsed by all major parties in the 1987 election. But while for the Labour Party the approach was to be a collective one through the local authorities, the Conservatives, in line with their general policy of privatising services wherever possible, stressed the responsibility of individual householders and voluntary neighbourhood schemes. Mrs Thatcher herself got into the act, when in her key-note speech at the 1987 Party Conference, after her third election victory, she emphasised that once more the Government's greatest concern was to 'reverse the tide of crime which disfigures our lives' and that to do this there was scope for self-help through neighbourhood-watch schemes, business watch, crime prevention and co-operation with the police. As we shall see below, the Conservatives were to use crime prevention as a way of promoting their familiar theme, that individuals should become more responsible for their own conditions.

In their third term in office, then, the emphasis in Conservative statements on the crime problem shifted even more from what Walklate (1989) calls the 'blaming the offender' approach – reducing crime by increasing the resources of the police, and by increasing the certainty and severity of punishment – to 'blaming the victim' – changing individual behaviour or making property or the environment a 'harder target' to reduce the risk of victimisation – and 'blaming the community' – encouraging increased local involvement in the fight against crime. The approach of 'victim blaming', while it contains much sensible advice, also runs the risk of heightening fear of crime by placing responsibility on the shoulders of the individual and creating no-go areas especially after dark. The 'Reclaim the Night' demonstrations of the Women's Movement highlight graphically the problems of this strategy.

We concentrate for now upon the community-based-crime-prevention strategies. While the idea that community failure in some sense results in crime has precedents which stretch back at least to the work of Shaw and McKay (1942), it has taken on a greater significance during the last 10 years and has become especially associated with the work of researchers within the Home Office Research and Planning Unit. Hope and Shaw (1988) suggest that this is due, in part, to the growing recognition of the problem of fear of crime, and its detrimental impact upon the life of the community, but also because of the increased awareness that most of us have direct or indirect experiences of crime. These two factors have according to Hope and Shaw combined and elicited two policy responses. The first, and the one to concern us here is the focus on greater community participation and involvement of the individual, the active citizen, in crime prevention. The second, one example of which, multi-agency policing, we discussed earlier, has encouraged greater collaboration and co-ordination between public and private agencies operating within the community.

The Home Office, as we noted earlier, had been interested in crime prevention for some time (see *inter alia* Laycock and Heal 1989). The Home Office Standing Conference on Crime Prevention was established on the recommendation of a committee set up by the Home Secretary in 1960. This committee was also responsible for establishing the post of Police Crime Prevention officer, central crime prevention training and the Crime prevention Panel (Laycock and Heal 1989, p.315). However, as Heal and Laycock observe:

these attempts to foster prevention were largely overtaken by other contemporary changes within policing which led to a massive expansion in vehicular patrolling, a development which reduced contact between the police and public, and the growth of information technology which, in the first instance, was deployed to reduce police response time – the bench-mark of reactive policing.

(Heal and Laycock 1989, p.316)

Crime prevention, then, remained relatively undeveloped until the mid-1980s when, as we have seen, the obvious failure of the traditional Conservative tough approach to law and order once more gave it a place on the political agenda. In 1983 the Standing Committee on Crime Prevention was resurrected with a Home Office Minister in the chair. In the same year the Crime Prevention Unit was set up in the Home Office to promote crime prevention. But perhaps the most telling sign of the importance given to this initiative was the setting up in 1986 of a Ministerial Group on Crime Prevention and the holding of two seminars on crime prevention at 10 Downing Street, the first chaired by Mrs Thatcher and the second by the Home Secretary.

Consequently, other government departments as well as the Home Office became more involved, most notably the Department of the Environment via its Priority Estates Project (PEP) which was aimed at improving physical and social conditions on problem housing estates, particularly through the increased participation of tenants. Perhaps ironically, given the debate over the relationship between unemployment and crime, the Department of Employment, or to be precise the Manpower Services Commission (MSC), through its Community Crime Prevention Initiative, also played a major role. By 1987 the Community Programme, a temporary employment scheme which claimed as its aim to bring together long-term unemployed with work which needs to be done 'for the practical benefit of the community' (Laycock and Heal 1989, p.326) had 8,000 job places allocated to crime prevention work. The Home Office itself, drawing upon the MSC experience, set up the Five Towns Demonstration Projects which operated during 1986–87. Following on from this came the 'Safer Cities Programme' which was launched by the Prime Minister in March 1988 as part of the Action for Cities Initiative. By September 1989 sixteen projects had been launched and four more were in the pipeline. (Home Office 1989c).

The cornerstone of the Conservative variant of the community crime prevention programme, has been the 'active citizen' and his or her involvement particularly in neighbourhood watch (NW) schemes. In Britain the first of these was set up in 1982 in Mollington, Cheshire but the real impetus came in September 1983, in London when the then Commissioner of the Metropolitan Police, Sir Kenneth Newman, announced the launch of NW throughout the area under his command. The London initiative was based upon the Turner-Barker Report (Turner and Barker 1983) which recommended an extensive strategy based upon four main components: (i) NW (a network of members of the community who watch out and report suspicious incidents to the police); (ii) Property identification (the identification of valuable property with a personalised mark); (iii) home security surveys (free home surveys conducted by the police to provide advice on minimum levels of protection); and (iv) community crime prevention and environmental awareness (the promotion of crime prevention and community campaigns to address particular local problems) (Bennett 1989a, p.139).

NW was to be 'a working partnership between police and the community to reduce crime and the fear of crime' (Metropolitan Police 1983). For the police the primary aim of NW was to reduce crime, especially household burglary and that which is 'opportunist' (Bennett 1989, p.141). This was to be achieved in two ways. First, the greater willingness of the public in NW areas, to look out for, and report suspicious incidents to the police, would become known to potential offenders and deter them from operating in those areas, and second, this increased reporting might improve arrest and conviction rates and hence deplete the pool of offenders operating in the NW area. A secondary aim of NW, by encouraging a growth in 'community spirit', was to reduce fear of crime. There is some evidence (see *inter alia* Box *et al.* 1988), that fear of crime is related to neighbourhood decline, signs of incivilities (litter, graffiti, noisy parties, etc.) and lack of community cohesion. By involving individuals in group activity, such as NW, it was hoped to counteract this decline.

Certainly the growth in the number of schemes was rapid. In April 1987 there were over 29,000 registered schemes (Hope 1988, p.146), and by November, John Patten, in a parliamentary reply, quoted a figure of over 35,000 schemes in operation outside Greater London. According to the Conservative Party this had increased to 42,000 by February 1988, covering an estimated 3.5 million households, (*Politics Today* 1988, p.35), although this figure is a million more than that estimated by the 1988 British Crime Survey (BCS) (Mayhew *et al.* 1989). They found that 14 per cent of households questioned were members of NW schemes and that membership rates were highest in the North-West and South-East, and lowest in East Anglia and Wales. When David Waddington addressed the national NW conference in March 1990, there were reported to be 81,302 schemes covering 10 per cent of the population (*Guardian* 2.3.1990).

According to the 1988 BCS, the typical NW member would be better-off, owner-occupiers with a rather older head of family. Conversely, those who might be expected to benefit most from the schemes, those living on poorer council estates and racially mixed inner city areas were least likely to join (Mayhew *et al.* 1989, p.60). These findings suggest in the words of Walklate that NW 'tends to be popular in areas where the worry of crime is high but the actual risk of residential crime is relatively low.' (Walklate 1989, p.165).

She suggests that NW may be unpopular in areas where the crime rate is high, because people who live there believe the offenders are local, and hence see the threat as being internal to the community, rather than an external one against which they must defend themselves. Under these circumstances she suggests NW is not necessarily the mechanism on which trust can be built or fear reduced.

What evidence is there that the NW has been successful in reducing crime and fear of crime? The answer has to be very little. Indeed, in his paper on the North American experience presented at a 1986 Home Office conference on Communities and Crime Reduction, Denis Rosenbaum, Professor of Criminal Justice at the University of Illinois at Chicago, concluded that the schemes have been oversold:

> Specifically there is some North American evidence to suggest that: (a) if given the opportunity to participate, the residents in the majority of high-crime neighbourhoods would not participate; and (b) when citizens do participate, the social interaction which occurs at meetings may lead to increases (rather than decreases) in fear of crime and other crime-related perceptions or feelings.
>
> (Rosenbaum 1988, p.141)

Indeed, Rosenbaum goes even further, suggesting that there is no clear evidence that NW increases residents' involvement in surveillance, social interaction, bystander intervention, and specific crime prevention activities. As to whether or not crime levels are reduced he quotes two thorough evaluations one of which shows a reduction and the second of which showed no consistent effect.

The most careful research so far into the impact of NW in the UK is that carried out for the Home Office by Cambridge criminologist Trevor Bennett (Bennett 1987, 1988, 1989a, 1989b). He found no evidence that there was a NW effect upon crime rates (Bennett 1988, p.251) but there was evidence of a reduction in fear levels in one of the schemes.

Mayhew *et al.* (1989) attempted to use the 1988 BCS data to examine the impact of NW, even though, as they themselves acknowledged, cross-section data at one point in time is not really appropriate to this task. They found that the proportion of members and non-members who suffered a burglary loss in 1987 was the same, 3 per cent, but that during the period 1982–86 NW members suffered a significantly higher risk (12 per cent) than non-members (8 per cent). This they suggested may be taken as evidence that joining the NW has made members less vulnerable than previously (Mayhew *et al.* p.58). They also found that belonging to NW increases sensitivity to risk, in that members are generally more fearful than non-members. Furthermore, according to Hirst (1988) the Association of Chief Police Officers was warned in early 1987 about the schemes' poor results at a confidential seminar at Bramshill police college.

The second Islington Crime Survey (Crawford *et al*. 1990) also found no evidence that NW schemes stopped burglaries though they could have a role in tackling offences such as illegal dumping of rubbish. The report's authors were highly critical of crime prevention initiatives in general, arguing that there had been no independent monitoring of the effectiveness and cost of such projects.

Leaving aside for the moment the efficacy of such schemes in reducing crime or fear, we should consider whether there are not more fundamental problems with NW and indeed with the whole community-based approach to crime under the Conservatives. We agree with Kinsey and co-workers that:

> community based initiatives in crime prevention are in themselves, an important innovation.
>
> (Kinsey *et al*. 1986)

but recognise that the notion of community is itself not unproblematic. We draw here upon a perceptive article by Michael King (1989) to look at the ways in which NW schemes are viewed by the Government. As King points out, it is clear from ministerial speeches and the government's crime prevention literature that NW schemes 'are also seen as a means of promoting neighbourliness and social cohesion'.

> (King 1989, p.300).

In the Home Office (1989b) publication *Practical Ways to Crack Crime* there are extracts of long interviews with NW scheme co-ordinators which stress this feature in a way which in King's words:

> is all rather reminiscent of the 'community spirit' which is supposed to have flourished during the war years and, as such, represents a nostalgic, idealised view of 'the community' and 'the neighbourhood', where, in the faces of threats from an external, invisible enemy, everyone, regardless of class, colour, creed and political affiliations, gets together to repulse the enemy and help and support one another through difficult times.
>
> (King 1989, p.301)

As King comments, this idealised notion is similar to that promoted by the French Socialist Government (see also King 1987) with the crucial distinction that while the French acknowledge that certain groups are marginalised by society and traditional social institutions the Home Office sees 'a seamless web of like minded people' (King op. cit.). For us, however, the most crucial point is that the Government's way of promoting NW bypasses local authorities, and seeks the direct involvement of 'the people'. Here we see a further example where, along with the opting-out schemes in education and housing, a Government, supposedly committed to the democratisation and devolution of power, actually has, because of its dislike of Labour controlled local authorities, increased the role of non-elected bodies, in this case the police, in the local community. In *Practical Ways to Crack Crime* as King again notes:

All those social organizations involved in crime prevention whether planners, police, courts and probation service, crime prevention panels, the M. S. C. Community Programme or the voluntary sector are seen as revolving around and depending upon the police crime prevention officer.'

(King 1989, p.302)

Indeed, when discussing the various crime prevention activities at the local level Heal and Laycock, members of the Home Office Research and Planning Unit, use the headings 'Local police activity', 'Local voluntary activity' and 'Central government at local level' but have no separate section for local authorities.

It is here that we can distinguish ourselves from the Conservative position without abandoning the commitment to community involvement. To us the determining factor is that organisations which are involved in the local community should be subject to local democratic control. As long as the police and not elected representatives from local government are the primary instigators of NW schemes they cannot be the basis for true democratic involvement in the local community. 'Situational' crime prevention programmes, 'measures designed to reduce the opportunities which are available for offending' (Hope and Shaw 1988) are the way forward for socialists only in so far as they are located within plans for wider strategies to combat unemployment, poverty and deprivation. Only such developments will counteract the marginalisation of the dispossessed, so that they become less involved in criminal acts of theft, violence and vandalism. Nor can these programmes ignore the physical side to community regeneration. This requires improving whole neighbourhoods and includes safer transport services, better lighting and more sympathetic architecture so that areas become less vulnerable to street crime.

RECLAIMING LAW AND ORDER

Taylor (1987) argues that the Tories' law and order position owes little to the free market vision of Hayek and much more to the old-fashioned values, and sense of morality, of its supporters in the non-commercial middle classes: the teachers, the magistrates, the police and those who supported the campaigns of Mrs Whitehouse's National Viewers and Listeners Association. The use of the law in pushing through their ideas of the free market was however important, as we argue in Chapter Seven, in enabling them to break the power of the trade-union movement.

The Tories' attempts to push their new line on law and order: that they were not really to blame, continued after their 1987 Election victory. The first shots were fired at the Conservative Party Annual conference in 1987 when the law and order motion chosen to be debated, 'This Conference recognises that there is no instant solution to the problems of lawlessness and disorder but calls upon Her Majesty's Government to maintain the fight against crime by further strengthening the police, the courts and the penal system.', which, while still clinging ritualistically to the rhetoric of earlier conferences: more police, tougher courts and more incarceration, implicitly adopted a defeatist tone. Mr Hurd, in his reply to the debate, agreed that it was not within the power of the Government, police, or courts alone to reduce crime levels and ended his speech by arguing that:

> The active citizen is the key to success of our Conservative third term. The active citizen is now responding to the lead which we have given against crime.
>
> (Reported in the *Independent* 8.10.87)

Mrs Thatcher, in her closing address, reiterated this theme, pointing out the scope for self help through neighbourhood-watch schemes, business watch, crime prevention and co-operation with the police. She reminded the party faithful that:

> Civilised society doesn't just happen. It has to be sustained by standards widely accepted and upheld. We must draw on the moral energy of society. we must draw upon the values of family life.
>
> (Reported in the *Independent* 10.10.87)

And lest it be thought she or her Government were responsible for any moral decline since 1987 she reminded the conference that:

> When left-wing councils and left-wing teachers criticise the police they give moral sanction to the criminally inclined. When broadcasters flout their own standards on violent television programmes, they risk a brutalising effect on the morally unstable.
>
> (ibid)

The campaign to locate the responsibility for crime prevention with the individual reached a crescendo during 1988 with a series of speeches from Mrs Thatcher and Mr Hurd outlining the responsibilities of the active citizen, and the need for the family, the schools and the church to maintain moral discipline. This, coupled with the reported upsurge in rural violence, apparently by white employed youth, was to provide interesting confirmation of the Conservative's views on the aetiology of crime. In a speech at a meeting to celebrate the bicentennial of the birth of Sir Robert Peel, Mr Hurd contrasted the deprived inner cities, where crime was (at least at that time) edging down with the traditionally better-off shire towns, where it was increasing. There was, he said:

> no question here of deprived, unemployed victims of discrimination or of something called Thatcherism. In dozens of cities and market towns up and down the shires we have seen disturbances caused largely by youths who were white, unemployed, affluent and drunk.
>
> (*Daily Telegraph* 6.2.88)

According to *The Times* report of the same speech it was designed to rebut criticism that Thatcherism had been exclusively concerned with achieving economic recovery and efficiency at the expense of social progress. Mr Hurd pointed out the failure of parents, teachers and church leaders to exert their influence. He asked where were the teachers and the churches who should have moulded a sense of 'responsibility, obligation and discipline' in young people:

> too many parents seem to have opted out. Giving youngsters their head is all well and good but only when they have been equipped with fixed points, a sense of responsibility and values, by which to steer a course.
>
> (ibid)

Mr Hurd repeated his demand that the church should take a firm moral line when in an address to the General Synod of the Church of England he argued that:

> We have to influence the behaviour of those who may be tempted into crime. What society most desperately needs from the churches today is a clear, definite, and repeated statement of personal morality. It often strikes me that many of those who commit violent crime seem genuinely to have no sense whatsoever of the consequences of their actions.
>
> (*Independent* 11.2.88)

Mrs Thatcher entered the fray in the following month. When addressing the Conservative Central Council she spoke of the need to:

> restore a clear ethic of personal responsibility – we need to establish that the main person to blame for each crime is the criminal.... But if anyone else is to blame, it is the professional progressives amongst broadcasters,

social workers and politicians who have created a fog of excuses in which the mugger and burglar operate.

(Independent 21.3.88)

This produced a 'culture of excuses' which enabled criminals to 'evade their own conscience and the bad opinion of others'.

When Mr Hurd addressed the Devizes Conservative Association he did so secure in the knowledge that the latest statistics showed the slowing down of the crime rate. He confidently asserted that this:

suggests that our strategy for tackling crime may be beginning to work.

(Guardian 26.3.87)

As the *Guardian* pointed out in its leader, a Government which had spent so much time reminding the public that the fight against crime is the responsibility of 'all of us' clearly must be chary in claiming too much credit. And, while accepting that the crime prevention programme would have affected the burglary and car theft rates, the leader writer wondered whether the drop in numbers of those out of work and the increase in training programmes for unemployed youth might not also be a factor. The *Guardian* stressed the importance of the Government's general social strategy by urging Mr Hurd to:

recognise the dangers posed by some of the new policies in the pipe line: the cuts to social security, the reduction in housing benefits and a new social fund which will require welfare claimants to finance emergency needs (like holes in the roof or cots for new babies) from loans rather grants. Claimants from the most depressed regions could conclude crime is the only way they can pay back such debts.

(Guardian 26.3.88)

As might have been expected these words fell on deaf ears.

Meanwhile, Mr Hurd continued his travels around Britain. In May 1988 he delivered a speech to the Police Federation Conference in Scarborough where he again stressed that rural unrest, which continued to make the headlines, was occurring in areas where not much poverty or social deprivation was to be found. Of course as a politician he was careful to tailor his remarks to his audience, and announcing approval for requests for additional manpower, told the Federation that the:

police are already at record strength, because they need to be. Now they will be stronger still.

(Daily Telegraph 19.5.88)

He was, he said, 'a willing listener' to demands for more police resources.

Mrs Thatcher went to Scotland in May 1988 to address the General Assembly of the Church of Scotland and in a widely reported and analysed speech set out the spiritual beliefs which underpinned her political philos ophy. She told the assembly:

> any set of social and economic arrangements which is not founded on the acceptance of individual responsibility will do nothing but harm. We are all responsible for our own actions. We cannot blame society if we disobey the law. We simply cannot delegate the exercise of mercy and generosity to others.

> (*Observer* 22.5.88)

The role of politicians, she argued, 'was to bring out the good in people and to fight down the bad: but they can't create the one or abolish the other'. And at the heart of our society are the 'basic ties of the family... (which) are the very nursery of civic virtue'. It is on the family, she argued, that those in government should build their policies for welfare, education and care. While Government involvement in these areas was essential in a complex modern society, she continued, it must 'never become so great that it effectively removes personal responsibility'. The main thrust of her speech was that 'it is not the creation of wealth that is wrong but love of money for its own sake. The spiritual dimension comes into deciding what one does with wealth.'

Speaking the following week at the Conservative Women's Conference, she repeated her moral justification for the emphasis on 'self reliance' in society, this time appealing to Methodism, using the words of its founder John Wesley: 'Gain all you can, save all you can, give all you can.' However, she went further in her depiction of the dangers of a breakdown of the family:

> We must strengthen the family. Unless we do so we will be faced with heart-rendering social problems which no government could possibly cure – or perhaps even cope with. The family is the building block of society. It is a nursery, a school, a hospital, a leisure centre, a place of refuge and a place of rest.... Yet today in some of our inner cities, as many as one in three children are being brought up without the security of two parents. Family breakdown on this scale leads to poor results in school and to worse. It is serious not only for these children but also for the health of society.

> (*Independent* 25.5.88)

Warming to her theme of the traditional conservative virtues of self-reliance, personal responsibility, good neighbourliness and generosity to others (prescriptions for individuals but not apparently for Government?) she placed the neighbourhood-watch schemes in the centre of the fight against crime.

In a speech to the Conservative's Women's Conference she compared leaving crime control to the police to leaving health to the medical profession (see p.10). Crime is seen a random event which strikes like some virus. We must keep ourselves safe and healthy, that is our personal duty. However, she did not abandon the hard line completely, continuing that:

> In dealing with crime we have to make life as tough as possible for the criminal. We must never allow the rule of law to be replaced by the rule of fear.
>
> (*Independent* 25.5.88)

But the shift to individual responsibility, the tacit acceptance that crime was beyond the control of the Government, especially as it was nothing whatsoever to do with their social and economic policies was clear. The active citizen was to be the way forward.

We are of course not alone in wondering at the ignorance of the impact of the Government's own social and economic policies:

> Does the plight of the youth service, always in the front line for local authority spending cuts, influence the behaviour of the young? Will changes in social security regulations, reducing benefits for the under-25's, tempt more young people into crime? Do changes in the availability of grants for offenders leaving prison increase the likelihood of recidivism? Do plans to allow child benefit to wither away, and to reduce other forms of family support, threaten more family breakdown and thus undermine an institution that can effectively restrain delinquency? Are ministers undermining the authority of schools and the churches by their constant attacks on them?
>
> (*Independent* 14.3.88)

RESPONSES TO THE LAW AND ORDER DEBATE

The left's response to the developments outlined above has been fragmented, and in many ways reflects broader division within left-wing politics. In most areas, the consistent attack on welfare, health provision, organised labour, civil and welfare rights, the expectation of employment and the public sector, has managed to prevent any united opposition.

Jock Young (1979) and his co-workers at the Middlesex Polytechnic's Centre for Criminology – and elsewhere – have developed what they have called a realist, or left realist, criminology. Young has argued that a central element in any analysis of the left of the question of crime, is that of its impact upon working-class people. He poses this as a feature of left idealism. This he argues:

plays down the impact of working class crime against the working class, it maximises the anti working class effects of ruling class crime.

(Young 1979)

Left realism intends to engage in the problem of crime, with the intention of helping to reduce substantially the crime rate. The problem of this, however, is that race has arisen as an issue in crime. As we have noted earlier, the ethnic origins of both assailants and victims in street crime has been publicised by the police. Lea and Young (1984) posed the question that if there was a black presence in official criminal statistics, then this had to be taken note of by socialist academics. Such a contentious issue is bound to give rise to criticism and angry reaction, and perhaps what is notable about Lea and Young's work at this point, is their naivety at not consulting with, or explaining their intentions to, either black academics or the black community. Insufficient attention was paid in their analysis to the institutionalised racism of the immigration legislation, and the criminal justice system.

As Sim, Scraton and Gordon (1987) – who oppose Young's realistic/idealist dichotomy – point out, unemployment has developed as a persistent condition of advanced capitalism, and produced a relative surplus population:

The inevitable consequence of the economic, political and ideological location of black communities is that they are over-represented in this surplus population.

(Sim *et al.* 1987, p.44)

Black people are consequently on the wrong end of the rough/respectable, non-deserving continuum of the working class. They are identified as the new 'dangerous classes'. A false link has been made in the mind of the public, between crime and ethnicity. This clearly has its roots in the tradition of white, mainland British xenophobia. The effects of this is felt by the black population, and is often left out of crime surveys. The Haringay Research Centre's study (1987) for the London Borough of Newham found that a quarter of Newham's black residents had experienced racial harassment in the previous year, but only 5 per cent of this group had reported this to the police. Of this group, 80 per cent were dissatisfied with police responses.

The most notable presence of black people in criminal statistics is within the group receiving custodial sentences. However, as Pitts (1986) argues, what this illustrates is that young blacks in particular, receive custodial sentences for other reasons – such as unemployment and homelessness. They are moved too far up the tariff in criminal justice terms, and should be the subject of supervision orders to the probation service.

The left realist perspective has also attempted to take issue with the police, their role in the State and police accountability. They rightly take issue with the lack of accountability and the consequent crisis in confidence in the police. This, as with other aspects of left realism, ties itself to the Labour Party's policy for policing and crime.

While it is plain that something has to be done about policing and accountability, historically the police have never been a force which supported working people, but rather a force involved in surveillance of the working class, and maintenance of public order amongst them. Crime prevention is secondary to this, and there are certain crimes, such as racist attacks, sexual assault and domestic violence, where the police have traditionally been notoriously reluctant to prosecute. The same is true at present for petty theft. Any strengthening of legislation, or increase in the efficiency of crime control must have serious implications for civil liberties. This is at the heart of the police struggle against accountability to civilians, investigations against the police by non-police bodies, and a powerful defence against any accountability in operational matters.

The ideological core of this is an historical nostalgia by both police and left-realist criminologists, about a past where people had a more deferential attitude to authority, and where permissiveness was absent. Perhaps the weakest aspect of the new realism is its belief that the Labour Party, despite historical evidence to the contrary, is the organ of change as regards policing and the State. The truth of the matter is that the police will resist vigorously any attempt, especially by a Labour Party, to bring them to accountability. There is no reason to believe that any future Labour Government, in its present form, and with its present policies, will want to take on this thorny issue, any more than past governments. It may well try to redirect police priorities away from public order towards crime prevention and control, but it clearly has no intention of confronting the issue of police power within the State.

This does not mean it has to accept the same law and order agenda, with the same anxieties about the rise of crime, as the Conservative Party. The release of rising crime statistics becomes a response to the escalation in crime, rather than responding with a cautionary analysis. In fact the commonest crime in Britain is motor vehicle theft (just under 30 per cent), whilst violence is approximately 5.2 per cent of crime – although sexual and racial attacks are under-represented. Rather than unpicking the criminal statistics, oppositional parties gleefully use them to show how the Conservative crime policy has failed. The moral panic remains unchallenged. The political differences within the working class has been exploited by such issues. They are deep divisions, the consequences of colonialism, nationalism and patriarchy, and are to do with racism, gender, order, discipline and respectability. The parties of opposition including, sadly, the Labour Party, instead of challenging this have accepted the main terrain of the law and order debate.

5 The failure of Conservative criminology under Thatcher

In this chapter we will consider the impact of the Conservative's law and order policies on the crime rates themselves. We begin with a brief look at the official figures, since, whatever the shortcomings of these statistics, and no matter how distorted a picture of 'real' crime they portray, they do nevertheless have real effects, since they are used, for example, in political debate and inform, at least partially, the public's perception of the crime problem. The 1980s has seen the victimisation, or crime, survey become a major growth industry in the UK. The spotlight they have cast on 'real' levels of crime and its impact are important new factors in the criminological debate. Our discussion of such surveys both at the national and local level lead us on to examine the impact of crime on women and ethnic minorities, and to a broader consideration of how these groups are treated by the criminal justice system. Finally, noting the prominence of assertions to the contrary, by Conservative speakers, we will conclude this chapter by looking at the relationship between crime and unemployment.

MORE POLICE AND MORE CRIME

We have noted changes in procedural legislation, as well as changes in the actual nature of policing in previous chapters. The increase in police powers and the subsequent curtailment in civil liberties, rest on the Conservative Party's alarm over the increase in crime. But have these expanded powers and the concomitant increase in punitiveness had the desired effect upon crime?

Between May 1979 and March 1988 the number of police officers increased 11 per cent (from 111,493 to 124,080). The number of serving police officers per 1,000 population had increased by 20 per cent during the 1970s (Burrows and Tarling 1987, p.230) and the increase continued during the Thatcher decade. By 1988–89 there were 3.89 officers per 1,000 population in the Metropolitan Police District, while the average outside London was 2.18 (CIPFA 1990). Civilian workers employed by the police went up by 12 per cent between 1979 and 1988 (34,630 to 41,800). Police salaries adjusted for inflation went up from £983 million in 1979 when the Conservatives came to power, to £2,378 million by 1987, a rise of some 47 per cent in real terms. By 1988–89 they had reached £3,825 million, with police manpower increased by 16,000 officers. Total police expenditure (operational expenditure including salary costs, buildings, equipment, increased 64 per cent in real terms by 1987, (£1,178 million to £3,163 million). Add to the enlarged programme of prison building, the feeding and housing of more and more convicted prisoners, the costs of the exploding remand population, and expenditure on the justice system presents a stark contrast with the swingeing cutbacks of other areas in the public sector.

It is the highly publicised rise in crime, and the Government's exploitation of the fear that it produces, which has justified increased expenditure since 1979 on the police, at a time of cutbacks on other sections of the public sector, such as health, income maintenance schemes, education and housing. Has this increase in manpower and resources been effective? Has the Conservatives' emphasis on strong policing and punishment succeeded where the supposedly soft approach of the Labour Party had failed? Not according to Downes and Young (1987), who found that in the post-war period, the rate of increase of crime under the Conservatives was, on average, twice that under Labour. As we have seen, the Conservative Party made much, prior to the '79 General Election, of the increase in crime during time in office of the 1974–79 Labour Government. While we shall comment further below on the use of such officially constructed statistics, which may reflect, *inter alia*, changing public attitudes to reporting crime, police practice in recording crime or changing priorities concerning crime seriousness, as well as changes in underlying crime levels, we may be excused some ironic enjoyment in examining the patterns in these figures during the Thatcher decade. Between 1979 and 1988 the total number of indictable offences known to the police (ignoring offences of criminal damage of value £20 or less) increased by just under 50 per cent (the 1988 total was in fact 4.5 per cent down on the previous year). According to Criminal Statistics for England and Wales 1988, during these 9 years of Conservative law and order, violent offences increased by 66.5 per cent, robbery by 151.2 per cent, burglary by 50.3 per cent, theft by 37.3 per cent and fraud and forgery by 13.4 per cent. Increases in the 1990 crime rate were to be even worse. The figures for the first quarter of 1990 showed an increase of 15 per cent on the corresponding period of 1989, the largest rise in crime since records began in 1857. But the statistics for the second quarter, announced just before the October Conference of the Conservative Party, were even more damaging to the Government showing a rise of 17 per cent on 1989. Indeed these figures made even sorrier reading for the Conservatives when one realised that demographic shifts were working in the Government's favour. Historically, the major group of offenders are 14-to 20-year-old males and these peaked as a proportion of the population in 1982 at 6.77 per cent (of the total population over the age of 10) before declining to 5.99 per cent in 1988. Taylor (1987) points out that in the United States during the 1980s, the Reagan Administration, pursuing similar policies to those of the Conservatives, presided over a decline in crime and asks why the United Kingdom was different. He sees part of the answer in the massive recession suffered by the British economy at that time, a point to which we shall return below. Steffensmeier and Harer (1987) have argued that at least part of this decline in the US may be attributed to demographic factors i.e. to a declining number of young males. Clearly the same did not occur in the UK; the increased propensity to offend more than counterbalanced the decline in the high-offender groups in the population (Liddelow 1990).

While it is difficult to draw any definite conclusions from such bald statistics on recorded crime, they clearly posed a major embarrassment for a Government pledged to reduce the crime rate. What is clear, as we shall see below from both victimisation studies and official statistics, is that the crime rate had not decreased under the Conservatives and Home Office projections for the 1990s suggested that the increase was likely to continue. The forecasts were for a 28 per cent increase between 1983 and 1993 (although the demographic shifts noted above may reduce this), and indeed by 1989 the increase was already 19 per cent. These figures provide political ammunition to chief police officers arguing for more resources, although this is clearly a double-edged sword since the figures could be interpreted as showing the police being unable to do much about crime levels.

One problem with statistics of recorded crime is that they are functions both of police administrative practices and of the public's propensity to report offences. Changes in either or both will produce changes in recorded crime trends. For example, since 1972 the General Household Survey (GHS) has, at irregular intervals carried questions on household burglaries. Over the period 1972–87 Mayhew *et al.* (1989), combining GHS and British Crime Survey (BCS) figures, suggest that household burglary rose by 17 per cent while police figures showed an increase nearly 8 times more – 127 per cent. This discrepancy in trends was greater for the earlier years of this period – between 1983 and 1987 'there is no statistically sound evidence that the trends diverge' (Mayhew *et al.* 1989, p.20). Mayhew *et al.* follow Lewis and Mo (1986) in arguing that the discrepancy may be due to a greater rise in the serious burglaries which involve insurance claims, and hence are more likely to be reported, especially given the increase in the number of personal telephones and the higher levels of home ownership. Alternatively, the public may simply have become more sensitised to crime, through media and press reports or the Government's crime prevention publicity, and so believing crime to be on the increase they are more likely to report offences leading to a rise in recorded crime which will lead to further media attention and so on in a 'deviancy amplification spiral'. Other changes in reporting may be due to shifts in public perceptions of police attitudes towards specific crimes. Sexual offences and particularly rape may fall into this category.

We will look at other methods of assessing the level and effects of crime in a moment, but we note here that both survey-based estimates and police statistics show increasing levels of crime, the differences are of degree not direction. A second question to ask when considering the effectiveness of the increased powers and resources commanded by the police since 1979 is have they become more successful at clearing up crime. Again from Criminal Statistics (1988) we see that there has been an increase in the number of offences cleared up by the police, between 1979 and 1988 of 27.3 per cent (from 980,700 to 1,248,900). However, if we look at clear-up rates, those cleared up as a percentage of the total number of recorded offences we find that a 15 per cent decline from 41 per cent in 1979 to 35 per cent in 1988. Moreover, looking at total clear-up rates flatters the police, since it includes crimes which, by their very nature, are usually cleared up as soon as they are reported. For example, fraud and forgery usually only come to light when an organisation discovers the offender. Similarly shops will often only report shoplifting when they have apprehended the culprit. As Burrows and Tarling (1987) note, the major offence categories of burglary, robbery and criminal damage all have relatively low clear-up rates (29 per cent, 23 per cent and 24 per cent, respectively in 1988).

However, there are more fundamental problems with clear-up rates. A crime may be recorded as cleared by the police for a variety of reasons: where an individual has been charged or summonsed for the offence (whether or not they are found guilty!); where an individual admits an offence and receives a formal caution from a senior police officer; where an individual convicted of an offence asks, before sentence for other offences to be 'taken into consideration' (TICs); where forces officially take 'no further action' and the offence is written off. This may occur for various reasons; the suspect may have died or be below the age of criminal responsibility, the victim may not wish to press charges or a witness may be unwilling, or unable, to give evidence or a person already in detention after conviction admits to further offences.

Following revelations in the *Observer*, (Nick Davies' 'Crime, the great cop out', 13.7.86, p.1) and 'More policemen confirm crime figures scandal' (*Observer* 20.7.86, p.6), which suggested that the clear-up rate, in Kent and elsewhere was inaccurate and sometimes fabricated, Gill (1987) challenged the use of the clear-up rate as an assessment of police effectiveness. He looked at the crime figures reported by the Merseyside police, where the increase in clear-up rates could be shown to be related to the number of prison visits by police officers. These visits were extremely fruitful sources of confessions to hitherto unsolved crimes which subsequently were classified NFA, and hence cleared up. They were drastically reduced in 1985–86 because of overtime cuts forced upon the police by the local police authority as one of the ways of responding to the budgetary impact of rate capping. The consequent decrease in clear-up rates was almost entirely due to a drop in NFA numbers.

A second interesting example of how police practice affects crime figures is given by Farrington, and Dowds (1985). In a study of Nottinghamshire, Leicestershire and Staffordshire police, they found that 25 per cent of all crimes discovered in Notts came from admission by those in custody, while in Leicestershire and Staffordshire the figures were 4 per cent and 8 per cent respectively. The apparent higher crime rate in Notts was almost entirely due to this factor and the Notts police's greater tendency to record trivial offences. A further quirk in the Notts approach to gathering statistics is that until 1982 they counted as TIC those offences offered to the court but denied by the offenders!

If changes in detected crime levels need to be monitored with some scepticism, the real rate of crime is also problematic because of unrecorded crime. As well as distortions to the official figures produced by police recording practice, there are a variety of reasons why victims of crime often do not report offences. They may consider them too trivial or feel that the police would be able to offer little assistance. The offences may occur within the family or between acquaintances and to report them may be socially disruptive. Alternatively, and this applies particularly to domestic offences, the victim may feel that the police are unwilling to take the matter seriously. Certain groups of individuals – ethnic minorities, homosexuals, young people – may also be suspicious of the attitudes of the police towards them. For all these, and other reasons, official crime figures will underestimate the true figure. In attempts to obtain alternative estimates of crime levels but also to gain information on various topics such as fear of crime, attitudes to the police, public views on punishment and impact of crime, the last decade has seen the proliferation of the crime survey in Britain. The major impetus for this work have been the national surveys carried out by the Home Office, the British Crime Surveys of 1982, 1984 and 1988. These have been followed by a number of local area surveys usually commissioned by Labour-controlled councils and usually focusing on inner city areas. The most quoted are the two Islington surveys carried out in 1985 and 1988 and the Merseyside survey of 1984. Crime surveys attempt to bypass the problems of police statistics noted above, by asking a sample of respondents about their experiences of crime, both reported and unreported, to obtain a more accurate picture of crime levels. They are not without their own problems of course. Young (1988) has, for example, noted that for local and national crime surveys, the response rate (the proportion of individuals chosen for inclusion in a survey who actually complete a questionnaire) has never been above 80 per cent. Young points out that this means the victimisation of over 20 per cent of respondents is still unknown and that such a large proportion could easily skew findings from the surveys. He argues that this number:

> probably includes a disproportionate number of transients, of lower working class people hostile to officials with clipboards attempting to ask them about their lives, and those most frightened to answer.
>
> (Young 1988)

The 1988 BCS estimates of crime levels show that in 1987 the amount of under-reporting of crime varied substantially between types of crime. For example, only 10 per cent of vandalism and 12 per cent of theft from the person were estimated to be reported, while for burglary, the estimated percentage was 41 per cent and for motor vehicle theft 86 per cent (Mayhew *et al*. 1989, p.10). Overall the survey suggested 37 per cent of offences were reported. The problem of the 'dark' figure of crime, the 'real' crime level, which is so much greater than the official statistics for recorded crime, seems to indicate a far more serious problem than previously acknowledged. However, the picture which Home Office researchers have used the successive surveys to portray is one where the majority of unreported crime is of a trivial nature. They have attempted to use the survey figures to counteract fear of crime. They have argued that most crime is petty and that the increase in recorded crime is more to do with the public's decreased tolerance than anything else:

> The real message of the BCS is that it calls into question assumptions about crime upon which people's concern is founded. It emphasises the petty nature of most law breaking – a point which also emerges from Criminal Statistics but is often overlooked.... Of the offences uncovered by the BCS only a tiny proportion were crimes of serious violence, and very few were serious property offences such as burglary or car theft. The vast majority were, for example, petty thefts, acts of vandalism, and minor assaults. A corollary of this is that the risks which people face of being victims of serious crime are remarkably small.
>
> (Hough and Mayhew 1983, p.33)

The British Crime Surveys (BCS) were set up at least partly because of official scepticism over police statistics, and in an attempt to counteract the portrayal in parts of the media of crime rates soaring out of control. It is a liberal questioning of criminal statistics collected and collated by the police themselves. As we noted above, the latest 1988 BCS indicates, that indeed, crime is not rising as steeply as police statistics imply. The BCS suggested that in fact the prospect of suffering from sexual assault, robbery or burglary was unlikely when considering the country as a whole. For example, the 1982 survey reported that:

> a 'statistically average' person aged 16 or over can expect: a robbery once every five centuries (not attempts), an assault resulting in injury (even if slight) once every century, the family car to be taken by joyriders once every 60 years, a burglary in the home once every 40 years.
>
> (Hough and Mayhew 1983, p.15)

Furthermore, the BCS distinguished between the fear of crime, i.e. people's fear of being victimised, and concern with crime, people's more general anxiety about crime which did not have to do with personal risk. Basically, fear of crime, it is argued, is out of proportion with the actual probability of being a victim. Maxfield (1987) in looking at the fear of crime, found that this profoundly affected a minority of people's lives. We obtain a national picture of crime and people's attitudes towards it from the three BCS, but for their critics these surveys have emphasised this national picture at the expense of the inner cities, which suffered more than their fair share of crime. Furthermore, while quotes like those above have an immediate impact they ignore the variations in the patterns of victimisation due to age, race and gender. These considerations led to the awareness of the need for local crime surveys which focused on the crime problems of smaller geographical areas and their impact upon specific sub-groups of the population. For example, Kinsey (1985) states that:

> It appears that on Merseyside personal crimes are only marginally more common than in England and Wales generally. In relation to offences involving personal violence there would appear to be little evidence from the survey to substantiate claims that Merseyside is an exceptionally violent area. In relation to household crimes, however, the rate in Merseyside is substantially higher and in the case of burglary three times higher than the national average.
>
> (Kinsey 1985, p.5)

Perhaps more importantly the Merseyside Crime Survey (MCS) showed clearly that the impact of crime fell disproportionately on the elderly and the poor:

> While men and women under 30 are most often the victims of crime, the impact is greatest upon those over 50. However personal and household

crime in Merseyside appears from the survey to be most pervasive in the poorest areas of the count: there is more of it and the effect is most severe. There can be no doubt that both in terms of the quantity and impact of the crimes examined the poor suffer more than the wealthy. The problems appear critical for the 20 per cent of the Merseyside population living in the poorest council housing and especially in the District of Knowsley where 48 per cent of the population (six times the national average) live in such areas.

(Kinsey 1985, p.16)

and again:

Throughout the whole of Merseyside crime is seen as a major social problem but, as has been seen, it is in the poor areas where the victimisation rates are highest, the impact of crime is greatest and the anxiety most intense. Merseysiders in general worry a lot about crime but those under the greatest social and economic pressure also suffer most from crime: they worry more, perhaps too much, but they do have the most to worry about.

(Kinsey 1985, p.24)

This focus upon the real impact of crime upon the poor, women and ethnic minorities is also an important part of the left realist approach to criminology. The realists have undertaken several crime surveys for London councils and have placed great emphasis on the need to look at the pattern of victimisation of the oppressed, claiming that:

If you add to the concern for blacks as victims a concern for the working class, for the poor, for the vulnerable and for women, you have an understanding of the realist approach today.

(Jones *et al.* 1986, p.1)

The Islington Crime Survey (ICS) of 1985 was the first study to focus solely on an inner city area. According to the Department of the Environment Islington is the seventh most deprived area of England and the fifth worst area where housing is concerned. In order to ensure reasonable numbers of respondents from ethnic minority groups the survey oversampled from them using an 'ethnic minority booster sample', a device which the 1988 BCS also adopted. They found that even within Islington there were wide differences in offence rates. For burglary, for example, the area with the highest risk of this crime, Mildmay, the rate is eight and one half times as high as that for the area with the lowest risk. Young people, black people and men were more at risk from burglary, particularly if they lived in the Mildmay area. For theft from the person, women are in general more at risk than men, blacks are more likely to be victimised than whites and the risk of victimisation decreases with age. The ICS gives a detailed picture of the incidence of assault in the area. During the period covered by the survey there were an estimated 11,878 incidents which respondents considered to be assault. Figure 2.8 in Jones *et al.* (1986) shows that only an estimated 6 per cent of such offences were reported to the police. An estimated 22 per cent of all assaults were domestic, 7 per cent were racist and 3.5 per cent police assaults. The authors note:

> Younger people are on average thirteen times as likely to be assaulted as people in the over 45 years of age category. Black people on average are almost twice as likely as other people to be victims of assault and women are almost twice as likely again as men to be assaulted.
>
> (Jones *et al.* 1986, p.65)

The differences between the ICS, an the one hand, and the BCS and official statistics on the other, in the treatment of domestic violence and sexual assault will be returned to later.

The second ICS was carried out during 1989. It found that in the 3 years since the first survey, crime had moved from third place to the top of people's list of problems affecting their neighbourhood. Furthermore, the respondent's confidence in the ability of the police to deal with problem had declined. It reinforced the image of women under siege. Taking all age groups it estimated that 74 per cent of women stayed in very or fairly often. Kinsey (1985) found a similar story in Merseyside:

> The picture which has emerged is one of people of the inner city – especially the women – living under curfew. While, as has been seen, the actual chances of victimisation are less than many people believe, none-theless, in Granby, for example, three quarters of those interviewed believe there are real risks for women who go out at night and half said they often or always avoid going out after dark.
>
> (Kinsey 1985, p.23)

We turn in the next section to consider in more detail the effect of crime upon women.

OFFENCES AGAINST WOMEN

We argued earlier that the crime surveys commissioned by Labour Local Authorities in areas such as Islington, Merseyside, and Hammersmith and Fulham attempted to put the findings of the BCS into an inner city context. One aspect of this was to focus on the experiences of particular groups: the poor, women and ethnic minorities. In the words of Kinsey *et al.* (1986) 'It needs emphasizing that crime and fear of crime hit working class women more than any other major section of society.' In particular, these local surveys suggested that the fear that young women had concerning sexual assault was quite justified. Jones, *et al.* (1986) found that in Islington during the period covered there were about 1200 cases of sexual assault. Of these only 21 per cent were reported to the police and only an estimated 9 per cent were recorded in the criminal statistics. Young females are 18 times more likely to be sexually assaulted than those over 45. Class shows itself in the fact that women who are council tenants are three times more likely to be sexually assaulted, than those who are owner-occupiers. The 1982 and 1984 BCS between them only uncovered two cases of attempted rape and 17 and 18 sexual assaults respectively (Jones *et al.* 1986, p.69). R. Hall (1985) suggested this under-reporting is perhaps partly because the BCS used some male interviewers. This was not supported by the results of the ICS, whose authors claim that their male interviewers actually uncovered more cases of sexual assault than did female interviewers. What was undoubtedly import-ant, however, was that the ICS briefed and trained its interviewers to deal with the part of the questionnaire which dealt with sexual offences, and indeed when a case was uncovered by a male interviewer he always offered a follow-up interview conducted by a woman. These were usually declined (Jones *et al.* 1985, p.71).

A survey by *Living Magazine* (14.8.89) which questioned 1,000 women, found that one-third had received obscene phone calls in the last year, 20 per cent of this group more than once, yet only 26 per cent had told the police, 13 per cent had been interfered with and 87 per cent of these kept silent; 9 per cent had suffered indecent exposure and 92 per cent failed to report this. Of the sample 49 per cent felt that being pestered by men was inevitable.

The rise in recorded sexual offences (Criminal Statistics 1988) is usually explained as an artefact of more sensitive and sophisticated police recording procedures and improved victim treatment, rather than a real underlying change, but hard evidence to support this is not clear. A major problem is still undoubtedly womens' negative attitudes towards the police stemming from their historically well-founded fears that the police do little in cases of domestic violence, and are unsympathetic to sexual offences.

The local surveys have also emphasised the impact of domestic violence on women. As Walklate points out:

incorporating an understanding of domestic violence, in particular, begins to alter somewhat the influence of gender as variable in the patterning of victimization as compared with BCS findings.

(Walklate 1989, p.37)

Domestic violence against women probably has the greatest number of unreported offences. In the United States the FBI believes it is probably ten times more underreported than rape (quoted in Smith 1989). The 1982 BCS found that 10 per cent of assault victims were women who has been attacked by present or previous husbands or boyfriends (Hough and Mayhew 1983). The 1984 survey estimated just over 200,000 incidents of domestic assault in England and Wales in 1983. It found in 12.5 per cent of assaults and crimes of violence the respondent reported the involvement of family, lover or ex-lovers. Hough and Mayhew (1985) regard these figures as underestimates and Worrall and Pease's (1986) re-analysis of the BCS data which looked at all crimes, and attempted crimes, involving contact and where the victim could identify whether or not they knew the offender, found that women were much more likely to say that they knew the offender well and that the offender was a spouse in nearly 40 per cent of cases.

The ICS showed, that while, as we have seen, domestic violence was a considerable problem, comprising an estimated 22 per cent of all assaults in the borough, it was one usually not taken very seriously by the police. The London Strategy Policy Unit (1986) suggests that this estimate would mean an annual figure of over three quarters of a million for London as a whole. The Metropolitan Police as a whole receive over 1,000 calls concerned with domestic violence from women each week (Cowell, *et al.* 1986).

As well as being victims of crime women also suffer from the effects of fear of crime. We noted above the MCS findings of self-imposed curfew by many women in Merseyside. The ICS paints a similar picture:

> 'women generally, and particularly older and black women, feel it is necessary to restrict their behaviour and avoid certain situations as a precaution against crime. *In this sense, the Islington Crime Survey helps to illustrate that a 'curfew on women' appears to be implicitly operative.*
> (Jones *et al.*, 1986, p.169; italics in original)

RACE AND CRIME

One of the hidden agendas in the crime statistics issues has already been raised in our examination of the phenomenon of mugging. We have seen how the issue of race was first raised in the 1982 Metropolitan Police statistics which recorded the race of both victim and assailant in London. The emphasis in 'black crime' has focused on youth, and consequently it is black youth that have been portrayed as folk devils who make the streets unsafe.

Tuck and Southgate (1981) had found that 50 per cent of offenders reported by black victims were black, which reflects American data on intra-racial violent crime. Matthews (1987) using American Bureau of Justice figures for 1987, found that in America there is considerable variability in class and racial distribution of offender victim relations for different types of crime, compounded by age and gender and geographical location (see also O'Brien 1987). However for crime in general:

> 'approximately ¾ of whites are victimised by whites, while on the whole over 80 per cent of blacks are victimised by blacks. However robbery, rape and assault are predominantly intra-racial for white offenders in America, but significantly inter-racial for black offenders.
>
> (Matthews 1987, p.389)

The British picture is different; rapes, robbery and assault are predominantly intra-racial as far as can be analysed, except for racial attacks on blacks. Young and Lea note that:

> a young black male (aged between twelve and fifteen) is twenty-two times more likely to have a violent crime committed against him than an elderly white woman (over 65) and seven times more likely to have something stolen from him.
>
> (Young and Lea 1984, p.26)

The 1988 BCS argues that Asians and Afro-Caribbeans were more likely to become the victims of crime but that this is:

> largely explained by social and demographic factors, particularly the areas in which they live.
>
> (Mayhew *et al.* 1989, p.50)

However, even discounting geographical reasons, 'ethnic minority risks still tend to be higher' with Asians more vulnerable to mugging and vandalism. Of the ethnic minority population, 10.8 per cent had been the victims of assault as opposed to 5.5 per cent of whites. Furthermore, Asians were more likely to be victimised by strangers, 27 per cent of the incidents involving groups of four or more offenders unknown to them. Perhaps not surprisingly given this, they believed that crime against them was racially motivated. Afro-Caribbeans were more likely to know the offender well and were more likely than Asians or whites to be victimised by other Afro-Asians. The 1988 BCS also found that 70 per cent of personal property thefts happened at work, and that those in risk of assault were in entertainment, catering, nursing, welfare and security personnel.

Locality, class, race and gender are central in serious crime happening to a person. We have seen that Asians and Afro-Caribbeans are likely to be assaulted more than whites (Asians twice as much as whites), and whilst we have statistics where white victims are 'mugged' by black assailants (a small part of robbery figures), we have no figures for street robbery, rape or racial assaults on black people by whites. We know about black people as victims, but not about white people as perpetrators of crimes against black people.

We do have evidence that the first generation of Afro-Caribbean immigrants was exceptionally law abiding. We have indications that black people have, over the past 30 years, become more present in the criminal statistics than the previous generation, reaching a level with, and in some categories, exceeding the indigenous population. They certainly receive more custodial sentences than would normally be predicted from their presence in the population. In the matter of stop-and-search powers and cautioning decisions there is evidence suggesting that a disproportionate amount of black young males are stopped by the police. Black juveniles are more likely to be prosecuted and less likely to be cautioned than white juveniles. Stephens and Willis (1979) noted that the chances of black youths being arrested for 'other violent theft' or 'being a suspected person' were 14 and 15 times higher, respectively, than those of young white persons. They argued that the apparent over-representation of black youth in the criminal statistics may be that youth is such a large part of the black population. In 1971 the Runnymede Trust noted that 90 per cent of black Britons were under 15 years of age. It is normal, then, to expect a high representation of black youth in youthful crime statistics. The impoverished areas that black Britons settle in means that young people are far more at risk both in terms of levels of offending, and in terms of police surveillance.

Pitts (1986) notes that there is massive over-representation (up to 60 per cent of the inmate population) of black youth in remand and assessment centres (see also Fludger 1981). He quotes Kettle (1982) who argued that according to the Home Office, 50 per cent of the population of Ashford remand centre were black, and for Brixton and Aylesbury prisons, remand prisoners were between 25 per cent and 35 per cent black. This was true for Rochester, Dover and Hewell Grange Borstal and Balantyre House detention centre. The implication is:

> that as we move down the age range, so the proportion of young black inmates confined in custodial or child care institutions increases.
>
> (Kettle 1982)

This has to be seen in the context that the fastest growing section of the penal population is the 15–25-year-old age group, and indeed the Young Offenders White Paper 1980, and the CJA 1982 are responses to this. Indeed, nowhere is the problem of overcrowding in prison more acute than in this age group. Several factors are involved in the process of black youth through the criminal justice system. Taylor (1982) showed that in the Crown Court, black defendants are two or three times more likely to receive a custodial sentence. The sentence is not related to the offence so much as whether the defendant is homeless, jobless, or has been the subject of a care order, and this is more likely to have happened to black youth. Consequently, sentences for black youth tend to move up tariff (receive too severe a sentence for the offence) in the criminal justice system too early on. Where supervision orders to the probation service would normally have been made for the offence, we find that because of homelessness and unemployment, black youths tend to be remanded in custody, or given custodial sentences. Pitts (1986) found that few black juveniles find their way to the IT schemes, or to day centres. Instead, there has been a pressure for community homes for education for young black people who have been made the subject of care orders because of their offending. Many of these institutions will keep their black intake down to 20 per cent. There are consequently a large number of young black people in remand, observation and assessment centres. Given that the CJA 1982 gave magistrates the powers of Youth Custody sentences of up to a year, and that these sentences increased by 67 per cent in the first year of its operation, it is hardly surprising that Taylor (1982) found that 43 per cent of black youth defendants opted for crown court trials.

It is further worth noting that the lack of confidence in the police by black people is now reaching other parts of the criminal justice system, notably the courts. The Court of Appeal on 9 August 1989 found that a trial judge has no power to empanel a multiracial jury, even if he believes to do so would be right in the particular circumstances of the case. A jury is believed to be selected randomly from the population, but for example, in a study of 326 juries in Birmingham from 1975–77, only 0.7 per cent of jurors were black, whilst the census suggested one should expect between 10 and 15 times that number. A defence cannot challenge the composition of the whole panel on the ground of an inadequate number of the relevant racial group. This must extend Taylor's (1982) findings of the suspicion by black defendants of magistrates courts, being extended now to crown courts. Black defendants are three times more likely to receive a custodial sentence than whites. This sentence Taylor found, does not reflect the seriousness of the offence, but correlates with homelessness, joblessness, and whether the defendant was subject of a care order. Structural inequality affects the process of criminal justice, because black defendants lack material and structural support systems which would normally keep them out of prison.

Pitts (1986) quotes Midland Probation Service figures which indicate that the second highest category of offence resulting in arrest for young blacks are those arising from confrontation with the police, offences he notes, which occur after the police arrive. Landau (1981) suggested that (before its repeal) 'sus' (arrest for being a suspected person) was the biggest difference in arrest rates between races, and that the police thought black youth more antagonistic to them, and they were 50 per cent more likely to be referred to the juvenile bureau. Hence black youth is subject to closer surveillance and control by the police, a form of policing more likely to generate further offences and more likely to be diverted to the juvenile bureau. Willis (1983) found that black males aged between 16 and 24 were stopped ten times more than average (although prosecuted in the same proportion as white juveniles). Landau and Nathan (1983) found that in the juvenile bureau of six London boroughs white juveniles were significantly more cautioned than black, including juveniles with previous convictions. Pratt (1980) showed for Lambeth that young black men between 10 and 18 are the most likely perpetrators, but also the most likely victims of street crime. The Policy Studies Institute (PSI) (Smith and Gray 1983) study of police and people in London found that the proportion stopped by the Metropolitan Police were 63 per cent of Afro-Caribbeans, 44 per cent for whites and 18 per cent for Asians, and that of those arrested 17 per cent were Afro-Caribbean.

The first figures published by the Home Office (Home Office 1986) indicated that of prisoners, 8 per cent of men and 12 per cent of women were Afro-Caribbean, yet these groups make up only 1 per cent and 2 per cent of the population in general (see also Walker 1987). In 1983, the Metropolitan Police had claimed that 13 per cent of defendants were black (Home Office 1984). Relatively, more black people were held in secure prisons. Walker (1988), in a study which looked at the race of young males disposed of by the courts in London in 1983, found that of those prosecuted, more blacks had their case dismissed without trial due to insufficient evidence, suggesting according to Walker, that either '... the police more readily prosecute black people', or that 'the court requires more convincing evidence for black defendents' (Walker 1988, p.459). Furthermore a higher proportion of blacks were acquitted after trial, which again suggests insufficient evidence. Additionally, a slightly higher proportion of blacks were sentenced in adult rather than juvenile magistrates courts and of these a higher proportion of blacks were tried in the crown courts. Of those sentenced in the crown courts proportionately more black defendants received a custodial sentence.

The situation does not appear to have altered dramatically since then. The Home Office Statistical Bulletin 6/89 (Home Office 1989c) found black defendants were more likely to be remanded in custody than white defendants, yet a higher proportion were subsequently acquitted. Compared to their numbers in the general population, black men are 8 times, and black women 6 times over-represented in the prison population.

An examination of magistrates courts revealed that for the under–21 population, black youth on average received 12 months imprisonment, whilst white youth only 9 months for similar offences. The NACRO Briefing (1989a) which provides a useful review of research into racism in the criminal justice system found that there:

is strong evidence that black people are unfairly treated by the criminal justice system.

(NACRO 1989a, p.14)

Commenting on the numbers from ethnic minorities in prison, Vivien Stern, the director of NACRO went straight to the point when she suggested:

these figures do not show that black people are more prone crime, but they do suggest that black people who offend are more likely to go to prison.

(*Daily Telegraph* 13.6.88)

Of the 48,609 people in prison in September 1989, 9173 (18.9 per cent) were from ethnic minorities, rising from 6000 in 1985 (Lord Errars in a written answer to House of Lords question 3 March 1990, quoted in NACRO *News Digest* May 1990). Of the 36,496 sentenced male prisoners on the same date, 3,629 (9.9 per cent) were Afro-Caribbean, 1,059 (2.9 per cent) were Indian, Pakistani or Bangledeshi and 667 (1.8 per cent) of Chinese, Arab or mixed origins (ibid). For all types of custody the proportion of all ethnic minorities in the prison population was higher than in the general population. Black prisoners had fewer previous convictions than white prisoners sentenced for the same type of offence and were less likely to be granted bail. Black youth were more likely to be prosecuted and less likely to be cautioned than white youth. A study of juvenile sentencing in Hackney between 1984–86 (Tipler 1986) found that blacks were twice as likely to receive custodial sentences as whites for similar offences. An analysis of custodial sentences passed on juveniles in North London in 1985–86 (Green *et al.* 1987) found that black youth received longer sentences and that the black Afro-Caribbean youths given custodial sentences had fewer previous convictions than their white counterparts. A Home Office study (HO 1/89) which looked at probationers in 1984 found that of some 110,000 people on probation, only 4 per cent were black, 2 per cent were Asian and 1 per cent were 'other'.

Gilroy (1987) has taken issue with the common reading of criminal statistics and black people. He points out that most ignore the astonishing number of racist attacks which are part of the everyday life of black people in many of the inner city areas, and that the police in such areas are notoriously selective in their surveillance of black people. The police, in common with other members of the white population, he argues, see black British life as characterised by pathological family relations and generational conflict. Black crime is presented as biological culturalism in Conservative thought, and as a cultural problem in by the left, who speak of deprivation and restricted opportunity. This, Gilroy argues, overlooks the multiracial character of what occurred in the 1981 and 1985 youth riots, and relegates British urban street crime to an Afro-Caribbean deviation. Gilroy points out that rising street crime has been used as a justification for increased police militarisation, and blames this rise on the deviant activities of a minority of black youth. An annual symbol of this relationship is the policing of the Notting Hill Carnival. However, it is the continued surveillance, the feeling of lack of police protection from organised and spontaneous racist attacks upon black persons and property that have led to the breakdown in police/black community relations. It is not that police statistics are misleading on recorded crime, but they need to be considered in the context of the BCS and the local crime surveys. They need to be compared to the evidence of such documents such as the Institute of Race Relations 'Policing against Black People' with its accounts of police harassment, assault and deaths in custody, and the Anti-Fascist journal *Searchlight's* files on racial assaults on black people by the civilian population.

Gilroy reminds us that black political protest in the streets and urban crime have very successfully become fused in the public eye. The black population has been under police surveillance for a long time. Sivanandan (1982) noted that in 1975, for example, the Metropolitan Special Patrol Group stopped and interrogated 14,000 people on the streets.

Lea (1986), in a discussion of police racism, suggests that a common theory of apologists for the police force is the 'bad apple' approach which views the problem as one of individual officers being bigoted. This can tie into the occupational or 'canteen culture' explanation of police racism, which in the words of the Policy Studies Institute (Smith and Gray 1983) suggests that racialist talk:

> helps to reinforce the security and solidarity of the group against a clearly perceived external threat.
>
> (Smith and Gray 1983, p.127)

This view puts the dynamic of police racism in the norms and values through which the police define their roles and legitimate their activities. However, Lea points out that for writers like Gilroy racism is embodied in the conscious policies and practices of the police as an institution and that it is difficult to argue that the police are de-politicising black struggles, and criminalising them, when some of them, such as the Spaghetti House siege, used crime to obtain political funds, and hence the police responded to the event as crime. However, what this assumes is that the police never make decisions to de-politicise crime, which they plainly do in their endeavour to argue that many assaults by whites upon black are not racist in their intent, merely matters of public order.

By positing the issue of black crime as a central feature of law and order, the black community becomes viewed as a potentially violent and lawless group. The large proportion of law-abiding black people, for example, black health and social services workers, becomes subsumed under an association of black people and deviance. Certain crimes become symbols of the ethnicity of those who carry them out. Black communities become sites of struggle, defended on the one hand by black youth, and attacked on the other by the police, determined to prevent 'no-go' areas as in Northern Ireland. What can be seen is that the attempt to correlate black youth and crime is a latent but definite element in the law and order debate. Its complexity makes it the rock upon which the left realist argument has foundered. Left realism is not intentionally racist, but it has been responded to as such, because of the complex element of police racism. What has been left out of the argument is that racism is tragically too common to black people. For example, in some districts in Central London, black children have to be escorted to school to defend them from assault; white estates have deliberately driven out black tenants. Racism like this is not faced by whites, and is only too everyday for black people in a highly xenophobic society, and this has terrible effects on their everyday lives.

UNEMPLOYMENT AND CRIME: A DIGRESSION

> We believe unemployment to be among the causes of ill-health, mortality, crime and civil disorder.
>
> (House of Lords Select Committee on Unemployment,
> May 1982)

In a sense we do not really need to ask the question 'Does unemployment cause crime?' or 'Do the under-privileged offend more than privileged.' The debate about whether unemployment, poverty and deprivation are causally related to crime is perhaps less interesting than the observation which we discussed more fully elsewhere that crime, and in particular, street crime, becomes highlighted during times of economic crisis. While agreeing with, if not the language, the sentiments of Taylor that:

> Crime in general is not, therefore, a product of worklessness but a product of the way in which a capitalist mode of production sets man against man and 'systematically' prioritizes individual self interest as rational social practice. But especially in conditions of capitalist crisis, it is only the street crime of the poor which is identified as a danger to the social order.
>
> (Taylor 1982, p.10)

Nevertheless, with the prominence given again and again to assertions that unemployment and crime are unrelated we must, at least briefly, review the arguments.

The orthodox sociological position, which may be derived from various different theoretical perspectives, is that rising unemployment leads to more crime. This proposition has been the subject of much empirical debate, but at present there seems no overwhelming consensus as to its veracity. Reviews of the existing work may be found in Box and Hale (1986) and, at more length, in Box (1987, Chapter Five).

More recent studies using British data do, however, support the argument. In work which addresses the impact of the Womens' Liberation Movement on female crime rates, Box and Hale (1984) found that increases in the rate of female unemployment were significantly related to increases in the rate of conviction for violent crime (assault and wounding), theft, handling stolen goods and fraud.

Farrington *et al.*, (1986), from the Cambridge Study in Delinquent Development, showed that members of the cohort of London youth being studied were more likely to commit offences when out of work than when employed.

Sampson and Wooldredge (1987), made elegant use of the data from the 1982 British Crime Survey and found that the probability of burglary victimisation and household theft victimisation increased with the rate of local unemployment. When personal thefts and larcenies were considered, unemployment was statistically insignificant. However, when the personal thefts were restricted to those which occurred within 15 minutes' walk of the victim's home, unemployment was again a statistically significant factor. This study goes at least some way towards overcoming the problems of other work discussed by Box and Hale (1986, pp. 74–5), in that it relies on self-reported victimisation rather than police figures on recorded crime, and it controls for other socio-demographic variables.

In work using cross-section data for England and Wales, Pyle (1987, 1989) argues that the deterrence effect of the Conservative's policy of increased expenditure on the police and tougher sentences for convicted criminals has been swamped by the massive increases in unemployment during their period of government. Pyle (1982) examined age-specific groups, unemployment and recorded property offences for the year 1975. The results, he believed, 'support the view that increases in unemployment are likely to significantly increase recorded property crime rates (most notably robberies)' (p.15).

Carr-Hill and Stern (1979) are usually quoted as providing clear evidence that unemployment and crime are not related. Their work, which combines census data with other cross-section information for the 3 years 1961, 1966 and 1971, uses econometric techniques to estimate an interdependent model of crime rates and police activity. However, Hakim (1982) re-analysed the data and found that 'the results... confirm the association between crime and unemployment, and suggest it has been increasing over time' (p.453). The reason for the conflicting conclusions is, Hakim suggests, because:

> a careful reading of this study (Carr-Hill and Stern) shows that the authors never carried out the test in question... but instead test the contribution of unemployment to explaining the number of police per capita in each area. In effect the authors reject the hypothesis about unemployment contributing to crime on theoretical (or subjective) grounds, but they imply that they tested it fully. However, they are unable to sidestep the results that show that areas with a high proportion of young men aged 15–24 years and a high proportion of the working class have significantly higher crime rates – and both these groups have the highest levels of unemployment experiences.
>
> (Hakim 1982: 452)

Lord Scarman (1981), in providing the social background to the Brixton disorders of 10–12 April 1981, was at pains to point out that deprivations do not justify attacks on the police or excuse such disorders. But at no stage did he deny that these conditions are part of the explanation. Indeed, amongst the deprivations he lists, unemployment figures prominently. It stood at 13 per cent in Brixton in early 1981 and 'for black people, the percentage is estimated to be higher (around 25 per cent)'. Furthermore, young blacks were even more affected, for 'unemployment among black males under 19 has been estimated at 55 per cent'. (Scarman 1981: p.27).

Indeed, the view that unemployment and crime are related has not always been anathema to the Tories. In 1976 in the *Conservative Monthly News* Lord Whitelaw was clearly of the opinion that 'Undoubtedly, economic mismanagement... where it leads to high levels of unemployment, especially amongst young people, also contributes considerably to increasing the number of those tempted into a criminal life.' Less convincingly, perhaps, he continued: 'The only real remedy for this situation is a vigorous pursuit of Conservative economic and social policies.'

Nor does the view represent the position of some police spokespersons. For example, at the Police Federation's Annual Conference in 1987 the leader of the constables' section told delegates that:

> Decrepit housing, poorly designed estates and unemployment make our job that much more difficult, in that people become more despondent.
>
> (*Independent* 20.5. 1987)

Earlier, in 1984, Metropolitan Police Commissioner Cree had linked youth unemployment with the increase in crime and drug addiction in the London Borough of Southwark. In a letter to Harriet Harman MP, reported in the *Guardian*, he wrote:

I do not think there is any doubt that high unemployment is related to high crime rates in certain parts of the borough. What is even more disturbing is the proven connection between unemployment, crime and the purchase and sale of illegal drugs, both the hard and soft varieties.

(*Guardian* 24.3.84)

We would not wish the preceding argument to be read as suggesting that unemployment is the only independent variable which affects crime. Such a view would clearly be banal. Indeed, work published by the Home Office (Field 1990) suggests that other indicators may capture the effect of economic conditions better than unemployment. In a sophisticated analysis of the variation of crime rates, Field found that, for property crimes in particular, personal consumption was an important correlate. When spending power goes up relatively quickly the long-term growth in property crime slows down. When personal consumption becomes static or declines, property crime rates take off:

In England and Wales the relationship has held throughout the 20th century, and has been particularly strong in the last twenty years.... A similar association between property crime and consumption may be demonstrated for the United States, Japan and France.

(Field 1990, p.5)

For crimes of sex and violence, but not domestic violence, he found the opposite effect. Violence was the only crime for which he found any link with unemployment. Domestic violence like property offences tended to increase when times were hard. The importance of this work is that it puts economic factors firmly back on the agenda as explanations of crime. Clearly it flies against the conventional wisdom of the Conservative Government who, as we have already seen, prefer to blame slack parental control or moral fibre. Indeed, at the Home Office Press Conference held to discuss the catastrophic crime figures for April to June 1990, John Patten attempted to distance himself from the research by asking if Field was the member of his staff 'who wore an earring' (*Guardian* 27.10.90) before stating that the work was exploratory and could not be regarded as definitive.

We conclude by noting that Young (1987), in a paper which attacks the one-sided partiality of much criminological theory, is rightly critical of what he calls the adversarial positivism which characterises the debate over unemployment and crime. He argues that crime is likely to increase when one or more of the following conditions predominate:

When State deterrence is less effective.
Where informal social control is reduced.
Where State and/or public definitions of crime become less tolerant.

When the number of those motivated to offend increases.
When the number of victims and targets increases.

We would suggest that in times of economic crisis and recession several of these conditions are indeed likely to predominate and that in fact they did during the 1980s in the UK. This is not the same as arguing that unemployment will always, inevitably and inexorably, produce more crime. In a society which took seriously its responsibility for the economic and social welfare of all its members this might not happen. But in a society where the official rate of unemployment doubled between 1979 and 1981, from 5.3 per cent to 10.4 per cent and reached over 3.5 million or nearly 15 per cent during 1986, where the Government, in the name of the market, is committed to weakening the ability of workers to defend their jobs, where the Government, in its desire to break what it sees as the 'dependency culture', has systematically set about dismantling the welfare provisions which protected the poorest and weakest in society, where the Government, as part of its programme to establish a new thrusting entrepreneurial society, has encouraged a widening of differentials in income and wealth, we would expect the societal tensions produced to be expressed in, among other things, rising levels of crime.

6 Fraud

White collars and grey areas

As the Sundance Kid said to Butch Cassidy, as they were being hotly pursued by a posse of Pinkerton detectives 'If they paid me to stop raiding banks, what they paid them to stop me robbing banks, I'd stop robbing banks.'

(Box 1987, p.201)

Conservative criminology concentrates on crimes committed by those it considers members of the dangerous classes, those who are seen as part, either of the criminal underworld, or of the *lumpenproletariat*. Thus offences such as the traditional petty or grand crimes, welfare swindles, theft by young males, burglary and street crime (in itself a rather vague term) dominate both popular and academic conservative discourses on criminality. A complaint made by radical criminology against its conservative counterpart is that it has ignored upper-world crime: fraud, corporate crime and white-collar crime. Care must be taken not to confuse corporate crime, crime committed by or on behalf of businesses, with white-collar crime, which refers to the occupational status of the perpetrators and may often be directed against businesses. Whilst the issue of 'crimes of the powerful', to use Pearce's (1976) evocative phrase, is now often portrayed as a left-wing cliché, this does not make it any the less a problem. An ideology of greed and selfishness, passed off as self-sufficiency, and of untrammelled individual aspirations passed off as ambition, cannot fail to have an effect upon upper-world crime. Several notorious cases, involving either fraud or neglect of health and safety legislation have, however, forced a usually reluctant conservative criminology to face the issues of corporate crime. These crimes can be seen as natural extensions of an ideology where the urge to individualise success and profit is the preferred avenue of advancement. In this book space prevents us from paying more than cursory attention to the whole area of upper-world crime. We feel this important, however, to counterbalance the view of crime, promoted by the Conservative Party, and accepted by some on the left, as being nothing more than violence, mugging and burglary.

Obviously, fraud is a somewhat grey area, in the sense that it covers a spectrum of activities ranging from wilful bare-faced swindles to sharp business practices involving dubious accountancy. It may, for example, involve liquidation fraud, where a company voluntarily goes into liquidation to avoid its responsibilities. Encouraged by the spirit of the enterprise culture this was so prevalent by 1985 that the Insolvency Act of 1985 was set up to control liquidation fraudsters, and mainly involved asset stripping. One problem with analysing fraud is that the official statistics do not record the class or occupation of the offender, nor the detail of the offence. This means that an offence categorised as fraud, can include company crimes, minor embezzlements and major swindles, ranging from small-time scams on the street to sophisticated computer fraud. Approximately 50 years ago, the Metropolitan Police Fraud Squad was set up to deal with the then growing incidence of company fraud. Twenty years later saw the creation of provincial fraud squads. By the 1960s fraud became to be recognised as a major criminal problem, but the fraud squads were hampered by small staffing levels, and their access to an unofficial nucleus of specialist fraud lawyers was slow to develop.

In 1961 recorded fraud cases numbered 39,651 of a total of 806,900 crimes, and by 1986 this had increased by 210 per cent to 122,802 of 3,857,400 by 1986. Total recorded figures on these offences have increased by 378 per cent, but in 1981 fraud was 4.9 per cent of total crime, and in 1986 3.18 per cent of the total. It is worth emphasising again the 'dark' statistics of unreported crime, which is particularly relevant here where it has been estimated that 70 per cent of computer crime is unreported, because of the fear of loss of public confidence in the financial institutions concerned. In 1985 company fraud was calculated to cost £3 billion a year, with half of British companies being affected. Levi's survey (Levi 1986) put the figure at £1 billion losses, with recorded offences rising annually at 5 per cent, and the Confederate of British Industry estimates that computer crime runs at an annual figure of £25 to £30 million. Levi (1987) found that commercial fraud recorded by the London fraud squads represented nearly three times the total cost of all property crimes in London, and that 40 per cent of companies in the survey reported at least one fraud costing over £50,000.

WHITE-COLLAR CRIME, FRAUD AND ITS CONTROL

Corporate crime

Because of the more visible appearance, combined with several major scandals, of corporate crime, it is an area which the Thatcher Government has been forced to address. There are two aspects to corporate crime, firstly commercial crime, including fraud, and secondly a spin-off from criminal activities, the laundering of money by organised crime, in particular that involving drugs. The 1984 PACE Act, the 1987 Criminal Justice Act (which set up the Serious Fraud Office) and the Criminal Justice Act of 1988 all contained measures which strengthened legal powers to investigate fraud. The setting up of the Serious Fraud Office was an important development, as were the increased powers of the Department of Trade and Industry under the Financial Services Act 1986 and the Companies Act 1985. The political context of this is well discussed in Levi (1987, Chapters 4 and 5) who argues that with the proposed deregulation of our prime export earner, the insurance, money and securities market, Britain has to be seen by prospective investors to have the power to eliminate financial fraud. By 1986 employment in the financial service industries had increased by one-fifth since 1979, and income by one-third, in contrast to the manufacturing and construction industries where employment was down by one-quarter, whilst wages increased only one-seventh. Another area of major concern to the police and the judiciary is drug smuggling and the methods used to deal with the huge profits it generates. Previously the law was such that punishment by fines and imprisonment left the capital and income of the traffickers untouched. Consequently, this was curbed by an attack on the laundering of money earned by drug dealers, through banks, corporate ownership and securities transactions.

Under the provisions of PACE, the police now have powers to search for evidence prior to charging a suspect. This includes obtaining access through a judge, prior to charging a suspect, to bank accounts and other documentary evidence. Indeed, where the bank or other party refuses to co-operate and the offence is serious, or is likely to lead to substantial financial gain or loss to any person, the same act allows the police to search for evidence which has the intention of furthering a criminal purpose, and in such cases this provision overrides legal privilege. However as Levi points out, different official agencies use these powers in a manner which is related to the level of tolerance they expect from the media and politicians. DSS officials are far more vigorous in handling suspect benefit claimants than is the Inland Revenue in dealing with suspected tax evasion. The agencies dealing with business and corporate elites tend to employ a more co-operative mode than those dealing with the poor.

Drug profits have also been affected by provisions in the Drug Trafficking Offences Act 1986 (Section 24), which makes assisting drug trafficking an offence, and also provides immunity from breach of contract where it is disclosed to the police that funds or investments are derived from drug trafficking. Great consternation was felt in banking circles, who felt they could be implicated, and less draconian measures to deal with the matter were brought in under the CJA 1988, which allows the waiving of civil liabilities if banks inform the police of suspicions of fraud or drug trafficking in good faith. For Levi this is an indicator that:

> the state is extending its intelligence-gathering capabilities into the upper world as well as the under world and the lumpenproletariat.
>
> (Levi 1989, p.194)

There have been some dramatic prosecutions of commercial fraud, or what may be seen as criminal negligence. This includes the senior members of Morgan Grenfell, Johnson Matthey Bankers, Guinness, Lloyds and Barlow Clowes, all apparent bastions of the establishment of the City of London.

The catalogue of suspect financial deals in the 1980s included such cause celebres as the Fayed brothers, takeover of the House of Fraser, and the sale of the Rover Group to British Aerospace. Perhaps the most infamous example of the new buccaneering spirit abroad in British boardrooms was the Guinness affair. Whilst the zealous pursuit of the villains in the case is trumpeted as an indication of the Establishment's hard line on corporate criminality, it should be remembered that the conspiracy was only discovered as a result of the work of the US Securities and Exchange Commission during their investigation of the Wall Street insider dealer Ivan Boesky. The trial during the summer of 1990 of four wealthy and supposedly respectable members of the business and financial community revealed the extent of boardroom greed. In order to support the Guinness share price during its takeover of the Distillers Group criminal acts of theft, false accountancy and conspiracy were committed. The pay-offs were enormous. Gerald Ronson's Heron Group received £5 million for its illegal support of the shares whilst Anthony Barnes and Sir Jack Lyons each had £3 million paid into private Swiss bank accounts. Against these sums the sentences imposed on the defendants appear modest when compared to less successful white-collar criminals. During 1990 the Appeal Court upheld prison sentences of 6 years for a confidence trickster who raised barely £1000, 7 years for a man who obtained £36,000 using fraudulent cheques, and 12 years for a Post Office employee who defrauded his employer of £136,000 (*Guardian* 29.8.90). When dismissing Mr Ronson's appeal against his £5 million fine the judge commented that:

> Although it would seem an enormous sum to ordinary people it was a comparatively run-of-the mill sum to Mr. Ronson.
>
> (*The Times* 3.10.90)

During the original trial Ronson's defence counsel emphasised his client's integrity on several occasions, a fact which the trial judge found difficult to reconcile with his criminal behaviour concluding it must have 'been a moment of greed'. Surprisingly, for a man of such integrity, Mr Ronson appealed against the fine on the grounds that his wealth was only £10.7 million, an amount which the judge dismissed derisively as 'an artificial evaluation done for the purposes of sentencing'. Whatever one's opinions of their sentences there is no doubt that the defendants received much gentler treatment than less distinguished offenders. Ernest Saunders' organised media campaign, which included regular press briefings, would surely have brought ordinary criminals before the judge for contempt. Again the response to the violent forging through the press and public outside the court by the accused's 'minders' had they been the heavies of more traditional villains is open to speculation. The crimes of the respectable are viewed more sympathetically than those of miscreants from humbler backgrounds.

In the same week as the verdicts in the Guinness trial the Department of Trade and Industry published a report into the Lloyds' insurance market which suggested that big frauds were almost impossible to prevent:

> We recognise that when a number of intelligent and ingenious individuals in the most senior positions, but bereft of commercial morality and intent on personal gain, set out together to rob and to deceive, it is extremely difficult to ensure they will be deterred or exposed, before much damage is caused.
>
> (Department of Trade and Industry 1990)

This conclusion underlines yet again that there are wicked people, whereas a more structural analysis of this would perhaps see the behaviour as a logical extension of the search for profits.

In the words of the *Guardian*:

> The Government investigations paint a picture of decadent fraud flourishing in a climate of lax controls dating back to the 19th century and policed by professional advisors who paid insufficient attention to the task at hand.
>
> (*Guardian* 1.9.90)

The report is a remarkable admission that despite tightening of Lloyds' regulations such frauds will continue. The subjects of the investigation, the Alexander Howden and PCW frauds, together involved more than $100 million of investors' money. The offences only came to light because of an attempt to inflate profits at Alexander Howden, which was discovered by the American company Alexander and Alexander after it bought the company. The report accepted that, without this, the frauds would not have come to light and that there were probably other, undetected, offences. Although criminal proceedings were brought in the Alexander Howden case, no prosecutions have followed the PCW affair where $50 million was siphoned away from Lloyds' investors, and related underwriting losses were estimated at £230 million. The scam involved a series of bogus re-insurance deals and the DTI inspectors found:

> no mitigating circumstances to excuse or condone the systematic, dishonest and cynical plunder of the Names' (investors') premium over such a period of time and on such a scale.
>
> (Department of Trade and Industry 1990)

The Guinness case and the PCW affair are hardly calculated to inspire confidence in the notion of self-regulation for the financial and commercial world. In both cases the information which led to the discovery of wrongdoing came from outside the UK. Indeed one commentator has gone so far as to describe the DTI's performance in these cases coupled with its sloppiness in the Barlow Clowes affair and failure to press prosecution over the House of Fraser takeover as 'part of a lengthy and dishonourable supine tradition' (Alex Brummer, *Guardian*, 28.8.90).

Nor are the problems confined to the rarified atmosphere of corporate boardrooms. In August 1990, the Securities Association, the self-regulatory body covering share dealers and advisers, acted for the first time against a broker found guilty of 'churning' his clients' portfolios. This involves brokers generating income by constantly and needlessly buying and selling investments for their clients in order to collect the heavy commissions which accrue. It is virtually impossible to prove because guilty brokers tend to 'churn' the portfolios of inexperienced clients. The Security Association suggests that the responsibility for monitoring this swindle lies with the clients:

> There is no cut-off point above which 'churning' may be considered to be unacceptable, so clients have to watch their portfolios carefully.
>
> (*Money Guardian* 1.9.90)

It is not only in the world of high finance that fraud has occurred. Conservative economic policy ironically has created social conditions which have led to increased crime amongst the middle as well as working classes. The Association of British Insurers reported in September 1990 an annual increase in business fire insurance claims of 25 per cent. A sizeable proportion of these cases were suspected arson and were related to increased business failure because of high interest rates.

We can see that the Government law and order policy has been irrelevant to all crime, including upper-world crime, and indeed that its social and economic policy has caused the crime rate to rise. Box (1987) argues that crimes committed by corporations, businesses and professions are likely to increase in times of economic recession although he admits that the evidence is less strong than for 'conventional' crimes (see Chapter Four). The anti-collective, individualistic morality of the pursuit of money in the enterprise culture has led to a belief by some speculators that they can take risks which are criminal. This is either with other people's money, or with the lives and safety of the employees. Profit has been seen as more pursuable than collective concern for others.

TAX EVASION AND WELFARE FRAUD

There are 30 – 40 times more prosecutions for social security frauds than for tax offences. The Department of Social Security (DSS) considers £250 to be the amount at which prosecution becomes cost-effective. In contrast, few criminal proceedings are brought for lack of compliance or evasion in the tax world. The Inland Revenue does not need to prosecute because they have powers to exert penalties similar to a fine, and basically they want to get the money back. Levi (1987) argues that the caution exercised by the Inland Revenue is in marked contrast to the enthusiasm of the DSS, a view shared by Uglow (1988b) and Cook, (1989). Obviously the way in which powers are used by different agencies, such as the Inland Revenue, DSS or the police, depend largely to the support they feel they will receive from the media, the Government and the public. A major and highly publicised target has been the welfare 'scroungers', whether these are young people allegedly on the 'Costa del Dole', looking for seasonal casual work in seaside towns, or those who are claiming while working. 'Welfare scroungers' perform an important ideological function as symbols for those who the Welfare State has encouraged to exploit the system rather than fend for themselves. 'Scroungers' expect something for nothing from the Welfare State, rather than offering a fair day's work for a fair day's pay. As such they are seen as antithetical to the work ethic which has been such an integral part of Thatcherite political rhetoric. Young claimants who refuse demeaning or underpaid work necessarily fall into this group. They are often dealt with by a system which attempts to get them off benefit, rather than prosecute. It is often difficult to differentiate those who deliberately commit fraud from those who are confused in their claims. Welfare fraud is an ideologically emotional topic, because it is usually expressed in terms of aggregated amounts (Uglow 1988b). (£5200 over 24 months sounds far worse than £50 per week. One traditionally impoverished group – women – have become more represented in this offence than elsewhere in criminal statistics. Explained, no doubt, by Conservatives not by their drive to break the 'dependency culture', whatever the human cost, or the low levels of pay for women workers, but moral inadequacy which has led to the breakdown of families and the high incidence of single mothers.

The person who is suspected of welfare fraud is more likely to be detected, prosecuted, convicted and to receive a custodial sentence than those involved in a wide range of other forms of non-violent property offences, including fraud and tax evasion (Uglow 1988b). Welfare fraud squads have increased for example from 800 to 1,500 in the last few years, and in 1983 the regional fraud teams (10 groups of 9) were developed, saving, it was argued in 1987, £55 million. Dispatch riders, hotel workers, mini cab drivers and building trade workers were targeted (*Guardian*, 1.6.88). Throughout the 1980s there were drives to recruit more specialist fraud staff. By 1985 there were 1,512 specialist fraud officers in benefits offices, as well as another 112 officers working in the specialist claims control (SCC). The techniques were criticised, and the SCC system was replaced by regional benefit fraud teams, in 1986, when another 600 fraud staff were recruited.

On 1 June 1988 the Department of Employment (DoE) reported that during 1987–88 DoE staff had made 396,200 investigations, leading to 80,000 people withdrawing their claims to benefit (*Unemployment Bulletin* 1988) saving £55 million in the year. Behind this announcement is the political point emphasised in the February 1988 White Paper, the short-and-long term unemployed who are 'respectable' must be differentiated from the sign on and work 'unrespectable'. The same report re-announced the prosecutions of specific groups (street traders, casual workers, mini cab drivers and despatch riders in London, the South Coast, Birmingham and Scotland) with the suggestion that a larger number of claimants are involved than those who come to the courts. However, in 1987–88 only 3,960 prosecutions occurred, or 1 per cent of the total of 396,200 investigations, or 5 per cent of the total of 80,000 withdrawals from the register, and less than 0.1 per cent of the 4,390,200 claims for that year. An investigation is considered successful if the claimant signs off within 2 weeks of being contacted by an investigation officer, but it is hard to differentiate these from those who would have signed off anyway. The estimated savings are based on the claimant being 22 weeks off the register, but again some stay off for a year, and some return much sooner. The savings figure, then, is highly speculative, but it is certainly good publicity for the department.

During the same period the numbers of Inland Revenue staff were declining, by some 20 per cent to 68,000 in 1987. There are several specialist groups for business, subcontractors, large-scale tax avoidance and transfer of assets overseas. The Keith Report (1983) estimated losses due to tax evasion at 7 per cent of the Gross Domestic Product, around £15 billion, and tax loss at £4 billion, roughly 15 times the amount of welfare abuse. Interestingly, the close scrutiny of tax returns is less likely than detailed examination of supplementary benefit (now income support) claims, which of course is much simpler. The number of social security prosecutions has declined, having halved by 1984. There is an attempt often to stop illegal claiming, rather than prosecute. Prosecutions occur, as we noted above when overpayment exceeds 250. This should be compared with Customs and Excise policy to prosecute for VAT fraud when the amount exceeds £75,000 (Uglow 1988b). There were 9,487 prosecutions for welfare fraud in 1987–88, of which about 28 per cent were conducted by the police. Again prosecution is clearly aimed at the undeserving poor. Because nearly everyone pays taxes but not everyone claims welfare, there is a feeling that tax evasion is fair game. The Inland Revenue attempts to maximise revenue, and are prepared to negotiate terms with tax offenders. Tax fraud work brings in £1.6 billion p.a. but the criminal justice system is seldom used (472 in 1987).

The case against the comedian Ken Dodd in August 1989, and the earlier conviction of the former champion jockey Lester Piggott, highlighted the different public attitudes towards welfare and tax fraud. After a long deliberation by the jury, Mr Dodd was cleared of wilfully avoiding tax on the considerable sums of money he had hidden, but had to pay large amounts of tax considered owing, as well as legal costs. The affair seemed only to add to his status as folk hero.

The conviction rate for social security offences is approximately 95 per cent, mostly guilty pleas. For other frauds the rate is about 77 per cent. Again with welfare fraud, the appeal court has refused to recognise there must be dishonesty or intent to defraud (Barrass v Reeve (1980)). Welfare convictions attract longer sentences than other summary offences (Uglow 1988b). However, when tax cases do reach the courts convicted tax dodgers, such as Lester Piggott, receive relatively severe sentences even in comparison with welfare fraud convictions. The sums involved, however, are much higher, and, as we noted, the prosecutions less likely. The disparity is in the prosecution policies, not the sentencing (McEwan 1980).

HEALTH AND SAFETY REGULATIONS: 'SAFETY STANDARDS ARE BEING DICTATED BY ACCOUNTANTS'

A series of disasters involving public safety travelling or spectating at sports stadiums have occurred since 1985. In each case there were criticisms that each could have been prevented by better safety measures and checking.

At the Bradford football stadium disaster on 11 May 1985, 56 fans were killed when a stand burnt down. The Popplewell report into the disaster concluded that it could easily have been prevented. It found that the Health and Safety Executive, West Yorkshire County Council, the Fire Brigade and Bradford City football club were all aware of the fire hazard caused by years of accumulated rubbish, yet nothing was done to eliminate it.

A second major disaster at a football game occurred on 15 April 1989 at Hillsborough Stadium, Sheffield, when 95 football fans were killed and 175 badly injured, when they were unable to escape from overcrowded terracing because of the perimeter fencing. The Taylor report found some responsibility for the tragedy lay with the stadium's management, some with the fans and some with the South Yorkshire police, and suggested that senior officers had been dubious witnesses. It specifically blamed the failure of police control. Senior officers did not even visit the ground before approving the ground control plan, and the club was criticised for lack of rescue and medical equipment, and inadequate signposting to steer any latecomers away from full terraces. The Chief Constable of South Yorkshire, Peter Wright, offered to resign, but this was refused by the South Yorkshire Police Authority. The West Midlands Force were instructed to investigate the South Yorkshire Police, ironically, at a time when their own Serious Crimes Squad was the subject of an investigation.

There have been a number of tragedies involving the travelling public. At Manchester Airport on 25 August 1985, a British Airtours charter jet crashed as it prepared for take-off. The inquiry said economic pressures for more seating had impeded escape from the aircraft, and among its recommendations was to change the materials used in the construction of seats – 48 of the 55 dead were killed by smoke and toxic gases. On 21 December 1989, at Lockerbie all 259 passengers and crew on a Pan Am jumbo going to New York were killed by a bomb. This was Britain's worst air tragedy, and whilst this cannot be classified as an accident in the usual sense of the word, there were calls for greater airport security, and considerable concern over whether a warning that an attack would be made on an American airliner had not been passed onto the public because a drop in seat sales would occur. On 8 January 1989, at Kegworth, 47 people were killed when a British Midland 737 crashed while attempting an emergency landing. More than 1,500 people died in civilian air crashes throughout the world, little more than average for the decade. Pilots have complained that airlines force them to work long hours, new jets are being grounded or sent back to the manufacturers for modification, and the government has been attacked for a series of embarrassing lapses at major airports. In an increasingly competitive climate, airlines and manufacturers are under pressure to put profit ahead of safety. Official statistics indicate that the potentially dangerous near misses involving civil and military aircraft has increased from 80 in 1979 to 92 in 1988, but the risk has declined, because of the increase in volume of civil traffic. Britain's congested airline traffic has increased since 1979 from 180,000 to 655,000 per annum. Bill Brett, general secretary of the Institution of Professional Civil Servants, which includes air traffic controllers and transport safety inspectors declared his concern over the cuts in the safety inspectorate over the recent years, and growing pressure on overworked air traffic controllers coping with increased traffic. He suggested:

Public transport is less safe than it was. It is the burden of a non regulatory government which is only interested in the private sector.

(*Guardian* 22.8.89)

Rail accidents were plentiful. Four people were killed when a train plunged into a flooded Welsh river on 19 October 1987, at Glanrhyd. British Rail (BR) accepted responsibility, and the inquest jury returned a verdict of unlawful killing. The Welsh Water Authority issued a Red 2 flood warning, and BR's Swindon control centre telexed Swansea that it would be 'probably imprudent' to allow the train's departure. One hour later it crashed into the river.

At King's Cross on 18 November 1988, 31 people were killed when a fire rapidly spread through the Underground ticket hall. The Fennell inquiry said London Underground senior management had 'narrow horizons and a dangerous, blinkered self-sufficiency', being unwilling to take outside advice. Safety officers (described as voices in the wilderness) had for years reported poor electrical wiring in escalator rooms, but no action was taken. Staff were unsupervised, untrained and ill-equipped to deal with fire. It argued that outbreaks of fire in Underground stations were seen as inevitable by management, which monitored strictly financial matters, rather than safety. At Clapham on 12 December 1988, 35 people were killed in a triple train crash. An inquiry heard that the disaster was 'wholly avoidable', and BR was criticised for failing to check that proper safety measures were carried out. Technicians were criticised for defective workmanship on vital signalling equipment, lack of checks on work and lack of proper testing. A factor in this was excessive overtime with many signalmen working 7 days a week for a month. A working culture which allows excessive overtime encourages sub-standard work, and poor inspection. The Director of Public Prosecutions decided that there was insufficient evidence to prosecute BR for manslaughter or any other offence, even though the inquiry concluded that working standards and supervision had slipped to unacceptable and dangerous levels. Management had 'failed abysmally to ensure work was of the proper standard'.

At Purley on 4 March 1989, five people were killed and 87 injured after a crash, and a BR internal inquiry blamed the train driver for going through a red light. On 6 March 1989, at Glasgow, two people were killed and 40 injured when two suburban trains collided. BR suggested human error in handling signal warning systems, and the number of train drivers passing red lights had doubled to 800 a year since 1979. Again the picture seems to be slack maintenance, 60-hour working weeks, overcrowded trains (BR's response to this is to increase fares to cut passenger traffic) and cutting corners to meet financial targets. Laurie Harris, of the National Union of Railwaymen has said:

> The pendulum has swung away from safety to economics. Safety standards are being dictated by accountants.

A report by John Brown, Engineering and Constructors, leaked by *Time Out* Magazine (28.8.89) suggested 126 fire risks at Tottenham Court Road tube station. At 19 of the locations, flames could not be put out easily, if at all, because of poor access to hoses. Rush hour crowding was a serious hazard, and the station was 39 per cent understaffed. An internal document found faults on BR's £47 million new resignalling project between Liverpool Street and Colchester (*Guardian* 29.8.89). A picture emerges of declining Government support of a previously nationalised industry under privatisation which has led to intense pressure to reduce overheads and manpower with steadily deteriorating safety standards.

Accidents also occurred on the water. On 6 March 1987, the ironically named P & O ferry *Herald of Free Enterprise* capsized with the loss of 188 lives, as a result of leaving the bow doors open. It appeared that in order to cut time and costs it had become customary to close the doors after the ferries were sailing. In this case the bosun responsible was asleep. The Sheen inquiry found that the ferry company was 'infected with sloppiness from top to bottom'. The master, chief officer and assistant boatswain were directly responsible for 'errors of omission' which led to the disaster. Underlying cardinal faults were the management who failed to consider safety on the vessels and did not listen to masters' complaints. The Zeebrugge tragedy led to the prosecution of individual members of the crew of the vessel, and the board of the company concerned for unlawful killing, although they were eventually acquitted on the direction of the trial judge. The National Union of Seamen declared a strike after the tragedy, one of the major concerns being over health and safety practice and legislation at sea.

On 20 August 1989, the pleasure craft *Marchioness* was struck in the early hours of the morning on the Thames by the 2,000 ton dredger *Bowbelle* with the loss of 57 passengers and crew. The adequacy of the safety regulations, which allowed lighter craft to use the same bridge arches as heavy vessels was criticised, and immediate changes in regulations were brought. The inquiry is still under consideration. Mrs Thatcher saw this as the tragic side of a prosperous Britain, pointing out on the BBC news on 20 August 1989 when visiting the wreck, that people had more money nowadays, and seemed to be going out and enjoying themselves, which was why so many people were on board.

Seven coastguard stations have been closed since 1979, leaving 21 stations to cover 6,000 miles of coast. The demand on these has increased, with

11,132 people being aided in 1988, as opposed to 8,867 in 1987 (26 per cent). Michael Portillo, then Transport Minister, admitted in December 1989 that coastguards made up less than 1 per cent of his departmental budget, but 49 per cent of all overtime.

There are no regulations which limit the hours ships' crews work, unlike land transport workers. Derek Bond (*Guardian* 22.8.89), assistant general secretary of the sea officers union UMAST, pointed out that adequate rest periods for crews is a mere recommendation which cannot be enforced.

> The only way to compete with Third World and eastern bloc ships seems, to be to cut back on crew rest hours and leave. Since the *Spirit of Free Enterprise* disaster, the conditions on the ferries has got worse.
>
> (*Guardian* 22.8.89)

Mandatory safety checks have been increased, without an increase in resources. The Department of Transport regulates shipping safety, but UMAST and the NUS would prefer the Health and Safety Executive to do this. Jack Kinahan, spokesman for the NUS said:

> All these regulations are seen as impediments and burdens on the industry. That generates an attitude of formal control, instead of the day by day probing and checking that should be practiced.

The concern over the difficulty of finding out how many passengers were on board the Thames pleasure craft was a repeat of the problem which occurred when the Zeebrugge ferry overturned. After that for ferries, but not other classes of vessel, boarding passes were introduced.

That these were not just accidents which inevitably happen in modern travel and industry, was pointed out by the director general of the British Safety Council, James Tye:

> Many of the accidents were foreseen, there had been warnings about fires in Tubes, how quickly ferries sank, and the hazards at football grounds. Nothing was done until after these disasters. Safety depends on good procedures, good management and sufficient inspectors to carry it out. It is no use putting these accidents down to acts of God. Why does God always pick on badly managed places with sloppy practices?
>
> (*Guardian* 22.8.89)

However, the change in safety regulations and the harder line taken is not sufficient compensation for the curtailing and running down of health and safety inspections, nor the differences in health and safety regulations which exist between companies operating on land, and those, such as contractors on off-shore oil rigs who are at sea.

HEALTH AND SAFETY IN INDUSTRY

The catalogue of disasters affecting travel and sports industries has been mirrored by a steady rise in the accident rate in work places. The general standard of work place health and safety regulation has declined, partially because there are insufficient inspectors to maintain regular safety checks. In a report to the London Hazards Centre, Michael Meacher, then Shadow Employment Secretary, was quoted as saying of the Conservatives:

> This government has cut factory inspectors by nearly 20% while at the same time increasing DHSS fraud inspectors by 160%.
>
> (*Hazards* 88)

A mere 792 factory inspectors exist to protect 16 million workers in 400,000 work places and agriculture has had its inspectors reduced from 190 in 1979 to 156 in 1988 (*Guardian* 16.11.88). Whilst accidents are increasing, health and safety inspectors have been cut by 20 per cent. The Health and Safety Executive (HSE), is currently receiving more Government support in order to attempt to prevent the increase in accidents, although the time between factory visits can be up to 5 years. A leaked report (*Guardian* 27.4.90) concluded that the factory inspectorate was understaffed, with a 16 per cent shortage in the numbers of inspectors, low in morale and almost 4 years behind in its work. The Government, however, is considering removing trade-union officials from the commission controlling the HSE before 1992, when the single European market becomes operable.

Construction is a notorious trouble concerning safety. The HSE (Labour Research 1988b) analysed the deaths of 739 people killed in the construction industry between 1981–85. There was an average of two deaths a week, of which 517 could have been prevented. In 70 per cent of the cases positive action by management could have saved lives, and over 10 years the basic causes of death have not changed. Experienced workers are just as likely to be killed as trainees. The Channel Tunnel project led to the deaths of nine workers between mid–1988 and August 1990. Seven of these were on the British side, where the contractors were fined 50,000 in March 1990 after the fifth death. The injury rate on the tunnel site is 4.7 per cent of the workforce compared to a construction industry average of 1.8 per cent. Men working on the site complained of pressure to cut corners to save time on the delayed project. A safety audit in 1990 by Health and Safety Executive Inspectors pointed to:

> an underlying weakness in safety management, particularly in leadership and administration, giving rise to an inadequate safety culture.
>
> (Reported in the *Guardian* 13.7.90)

Between 1980 and 1985, 28 young people died and over 1,000 were seriously injured whilst working on Manpower Services Commission (MSC) programmes (Labour Research 1986). The post-war period of improvement in the annual death toll at work has, in recent years, come to an end. In 1985 there was a distinct rise in children killed whilst working. The Low Pay Unit found that the annual death and fatal accident averages rose from 59 per 100,000 in 1985 to 142 per 100,000 by March 1989.

There were in addition 2,735 minor accidents involving Youth Training Scheme (YTS) participants in 1988–89. Despite Government counter-claims that this increase is due to 1986 changes in definitions of accidents from minor to major and fatal categories, all the increases cannot be accounted for by the redefinition. Ministers claim that accident rates on YTS are better than for the rest of the working population in that age group. However, what actually has happened is that accidents for the 16–19-age-working groups have increased, so the comparison is hardly reassuring (*Guardian* 19.8.89). The 1989 Employment Act now removes laws protecting 18-year-olds from long hours and shift work, so that there is more likelihood of industrial accidents.

Firms employing less than 100 people have higher death and injury rates than bigger ones. During 1987 blitzes by the HSE of over 1,000 prohibition notices, which can only be served where there is a risk of 'serious personal injury' were issued, but led to only 25 prosecutions.

The issues of health and safety have been taken up by trade unions in the P & O ferries dispute, and the transport strikes of 1989. A contributory factor in the Kings Cross Underground disaster was the lack of staff training staff in fire-hazard emergencies, and the low standard of cleaning due to cutbacks. An earlier report by the Chief HMI of Factories commented that the sad record of death and injury in the quarrying industry showed no sign of reducing (July 1987).

Labour Research (1988a) suggested that the strict mining safety laws would have to be weakened if the coal industry were to be privatised. Interestingly, after September 1987 factory and mines inspectors were forbidden to speak to the press on pain of disciplinary action. However, John Howard, an official of their union commented as early as November 1985 that the HMI of Mines feared that the proposed new mining legislation would reduce the power of the HMI whilst raising the power of the colliery manager, who could decide what is 'reasonably practicable' (Labour Research 1988a). The reduction in the mining workforce (over half since 1979), has led to extra pressures on those miners remaining. Mining and quarrying are still the most dangerous industries to work in, and in 1985 mining deaths and major industries were over five times the rate for other industries, including construction. New technology has increased dust and noise levels, and current dust levels suggest that one in 20 miners may develop lung damage after a lifetime's exposure, and four-fifths according to a British Coal survey in 1983 were exposed to damaging levels of noise. Further risks are the increase in diesel fumes, back injuries, dermatitis and stress-related problems – all increasing in coal mines.

One spin-off of the miners' strike has been management's disappointment (see House of Commons Energy Committee, January 1988; comments by Sir Robert Haslam, Chairman of British Coal) with pit deputies responsible for health and safety, who are members of NACODS. Haslam had hoped to recruit them to management, but was surprised and disappointed in their industrial action, and in March 1988, British Coal trained 100 members of the United Democratic Mineworkers to do NACOD jobs, alarmed by the militancy of NACOD. This was in line with the Government's legislation aimed at preventing militancy in trade unions.

It should also be pointed out that white-collar industries have suffered from privatisation. Up to 1980 the sick leave for industrial accidents declined considerably at British Telecom (BT), but from 1981 as a run-up to privatisation, BT introduced more competition into its working methods. The accident rate rose notably from that time (Labour Research, 1987b) – a rate not helped by BT's cut in its safety officers which started in 1985.

On 6 July there was an explosion of the North Sea Piper Alpha oil rig which claimed 167 lives. The inquiry was told fire fighting equipment was 'virtually useless' for 4 months before the disaster. Several safety audits had been carried out after an earlier explosion in 1984, but Occidental, the owners, never released the findings. A lack of life jackets and portable fire extinguisher in the emergency muster area, and the role of the rig's support ship during the rescue operation were criticised. One problem is that offshore oil and gas industries have a number of bodies making regulations, but the principal inspectorate is the Department of Energy, which also has an interest in maximising production. As with the shipping industry, this is seen as a conflict of interest. In 1988 eight inspectors were responsible for the safety of 123 installations in the North Sea, including annual inspections, investigations of accidents and criminal prosecutions. The unofficial strike of oil-rig workers in 1990 had as one of its major aims an improvement in safety. A key demand was the transfer of responsibility from the Department of Energy to the Health and Safety Executive.

The general reduction in health and safety standards and inspection comes from Government cutbacks, and commercial pressure in an economy which favours profit maximisation and privatisation. Judith Church, Health and Safety Officer of the Manufacturing, Science and Finance Union summed up the government's attitude to health and safety as:

We have a get rich quick philosophy where everything is geared to maximum profits. If companies had to say how many died and were injured in their service each year, it might give the life and death of workers a higher priority.

POLLUTION

It is not just workers in industry whose health and lives are put at risk by criminal acts. The pharmaceutical industry has a record of putting the consumer at risk of which the Thalidomide and Opren cases are the most famous. The general public are also in danger from industrial pollution. For example, in August 1989 there was concern over the amount of dangerous industrial waste brought to Britain for disposal from other countries. As a result of exposure by Greenpeace, vessels were refused entry by harbourmasters and port managers. The Labour Party environmental spokesperson argued (*Evening Standard* 9.8.89) that 800,000 tons of industrial waste were annually brought to Britain to be disposed of. The same month saw growing concern over the water industry, subsequently privatised, because of the dangerously high level of nitrates and other chemicals being found in the water in some areas.

Britain has, however, constantly obstructed European Commission proposals to reduce atmospheric and water pollution, involving acid rain, control of emissions from large combustion plants, dumping of sewage sludge, disposal of titanium dioxide, and the entry of fertilisers into the water supply, according to Stanley Clinton Davis, EC Commissioner for the Environment (*Labour Party News*, April 1989). According to the House of Commons Environment Committee our waste control regulations are a 'shambles', and nothing has been done about nitrates and excessive use of pesticides and fertilizers as requested by the EC. Of the 426 chemicals cleared for use in farming, 166 are known to cause, or are suspected of links with cancer, birth defects, genetic mutations and allergies. Forty-three per cent of fruit and vegetables in the UK have detectable pesticide residues. Exemptions have been sought for EC standards concerning drinking and bathing water, whilst privatisation is implemented. Britain disposes of toxic waste at sea – something forbidden in most other EC countries.

The reason for the reluctance to act on these issues, is of course, that they would be expensive and consequently affect the competitiveness of British capital.

MINIMUM-WAGE POLICY VIOLATIONS

The Wages Act of 1986 (WA) received the Royal Assent together with the

Social Security Act in July 1986. Under the WA, young workers under 21 were removed from Wages Council protection. Young people in service industries, garment industries, catering and shops, no longer have legal minimum rights covering wages and holidays. Adults lose special rates for specific jobs, shift pay, holiday pay and unsocial hours pay. There is one basic hourly rate with a limited number of hours and a single overtime rate. Employees will no longer be able to opt out of cashless pay systems. Wages inspectors (who police Britain's minimum-wage system), have been cut by 40 per cent. Wages inspectors cover nearly half a million firms, mostly small and non-unionised, with a workforce of some two and a half million. The inspectorate in 1990 could only visit, according to the Low Pay Review, some 7 per cent of firms, which averages out at a visit every 14 years. One-third of inspections are a telephone call or a questionnaire, and the 1988 under-payment statistics suggested that 34.6 per cent of firms were underpaying their staff, and of the 9,000 firms involved only two were prosecuted. The Government argued that as the Wages Act removes rights to paid holidays, additional rates for weekend and shift work, as well as 550,000 young people losing their rights to minimum wages, these cuts are justified. This leaves each 'outdoor' inspector overseeing the wages of 31,000 workers in over 5,000 firms each year, as well as an additional 2,000 enquiries. In the North of England, nearly half of firms visited were found to be illegally underpay-ing workers.

We can now see that the law and order issue cannot be divorced from the rest of the Conservative Government's policies during the Thatcher years. In the field of welfare law, for example, the 1988 Social Security Act (SSA) upholds labour discipline, whilst developing the tradition of lesser eligibility. The 1980 Social Security Act had made the abdication of one's duty to support one's dependants a criminal offence. It altered the position of sponsored relatives for black people. Sponsors could now be liable to criminal charges if their sponsored relatives had 'recourse to public funds'. Welfare benefits paid to strikers' families, who are, of course, not on strike but certainly impoverished, were to be docked £12 on the assumption they were in receipt of strike pay. The 1988 SSA keeps benefits low and subsidises low wages. If a claimant leaves his or her job 'voluntarily' benefit is withheld for up to 6 months. The YTS scheme has forced young people into low-paid, and often dangerous work schemes, without significantly improving their employment possibilities after the 2-year term. If they refuse to join one of the schemes, they lose their benefits. Long-term unemployed claimants who work for 'Benefit Plus' receive benefits plus a top-up award for involvement on a job creation scheme, similar to the American Workfare projects.

CONCLUSION

This, then, is the other side to the Conservative notions of law and order. Encouragement has been given to individualism, free enterprise and the pursuit of profit. The struggle for intellectual domination has been supported by the use of think tanks such as the Institute of Economic Affairs, the Centre for Policy Studies and the Adam Smith Institute. These have given an appearance of academic and scientific credibility to radical Conservative policies. They have become involved in the hegemonic struggle by setting the agenda for political debate. Formally independent of the Government, they have been able to raise contentious issues under the guise of kite-flying exercises without compromising individual politicians. Intellectually central in moving privatisation into the centre-stage of policy making, and in the introduction of market economies in health and welfare they have added credibility to the enterprise culture. The dismantling of the welfare infrastructure and the encouragement of the pursuit of profit has at times taken on the mantle of a moral endeavour. While corporate crime might not be officially approved, the climate in 1991 certainly has encouraged the bending of rules and a cavalier attitude to the law amongst entrepreneurs.

The ideology of the enterprise culture through society has penetrated to a considerable degree to the young who grew up under Thatcher – 'Thatcher's children'. A 1989 MORI Poll conducted by the BBC and *The Independent* newspaper argued that the ideology of Thatcherism was reaching its target of the young. Fifteen to 28 year olds were significantly keener than their elders on private enterprise, sceptical about trade unions and a substantial minority hoped to own their own business. Privatisation was particularly valued by the young, whether it be prisons, motorways, transport or care of the elderly. Young males in particular were keener on high pay and promotion than older people, and less concerned with security or job satisfaction. They preferred to negotiate their own pay and conditions, rather than leave this to trade unions. Young working-class as much as middle-class respondents wanted home ownership, private pensions, meals out and foreign holidays. Fish and chips, council housing, State pensions and holidays at home were out for all the young. One-quarter of the sample wanted more ideologically luxurious goods, such as exotic fruit, stocks and shares, private education for their children, expensive cars and second homes. Their only fears were nuclear war and AIDs. Given the ideological success of the enterprise culture, it is hardly surprising that the Thatcherite package has been bought, although, interestingly, more by young men than young women. Of young women 66 per cent thought Britain was heading in the wrong direction, and that major changes were needed, and only 28 per cent felt things were all right the way they were. This is the cultural background against which fraud has been carried out. The ideological success of Thatcherism is that it has been adopted by many young people for the values which direct their life style.

The Government, in order to attack the notion of the Welfare State, has held it responsible for encouraging dependency, idleness and the break-up of families. The culture of dependency has to be replaced by the enterprise culture. The work of Murray (1984) who attacked welfare scroungers in the United States has influenced the policies of the British Government. There has been an attack on organised trade-union resistance, on marginalised groups, on young people, especially young black people in the name of a pragmatic economic programme. Liberty has been sacrificed for convenience, the appeal to the rising crime rate as an ideological weapon against progressive teachers and liberal social workers has strengthened the Government's hand. The only area in which this strategy is likely to come unstuck is health, where even radical supporters of Thatcherite policies have recognised that the sick cannot be held responsible for their illness. Private insurance schemes clearly do not wish to become involved with either the mentally ill or the chronically sick. They cannot be written off like other marginalised groups. The enterprise culture has, however, led to an individualism which has encouraged fraud, materialism and contempt for collective support and social responsibility.

In this chapter we have tried to give some idea of the impact of the Conservatives' economic and social policies upon those crimes which do not fit into their own view of criminality. By stressing superiority of the competitive as opposed to the collaborative, the individual as against the collective, the private as compared to the public and by elevating profitability to at times the sole criterion of success, they have created an economic framework where the survival of the fittest has in many cases come to mean the survival of those who are best at avoiding controls on their activities without being caught. Workers, clients and the general public have all been victims in this *laissez faire* environment. By allowing, in the interests of economic profitability, the financial institutions to regulate themselves, by weakening, in order to keep down industry's costs, the power of the agencies who are meant to control health and safety and pollution, the Conservatives again have revealed the ideological basis to their law and order position.

7 Inside the crisis and the crisis inside

Prisons, punishment and Conservative criminology

On 1 April 1990 prisoners took over the Strangeways Prison, Manchester in what was to become the most prolonged protest against inhuman and degrading conditions in penal institutions. It was to be 24 days before the last hard-core protestors gave themselves up. The protest sparked off disturbances in 20 other prison establishments and spotlighted yet again the overcrowding in British Prisons. The immediate response of the Government was to set up a committee of inquiry under Lord Justice Woolf to examine the events and the underlying causes. One can only assume the Government had not read the steady stream of reports from both the Chief Inspector of Prisons and various prison boards of visitors during the 1980s. The 1990 disturbances were only the latest in a series of eruptions – in 1986, 1988 and 1989, which led to injuries and damage to prison buildings and equipment. The Woolf inquiry was the fourth such in 5 years. We may anticipate its conclusions on the basis of its predecessors. Prisons are overcrowded with two or three inmates to a cell designed for one not uncommon. Most prisoners are confined to their cells for long periods of time. Sanitation is totally inadequate with the dehumanising practice of 'slopping out' still widespread. Prison visits are too short and the facilities available for them are inadequate. The general picture is of a barbaric degrading system in which the only real surprise is that violence does not break out more often. In this chapter we will attempt to examine some of the reasons for the continued use of custodial sentences. But we shall see as well that the Conservative belief, for both retributive and deterrent purposes, in punishment by incarceration, has at least had to acknowledge economic realities. The vast expense of the prison system has led to the development of various non-custodial alternatives. Punishment in the community has become the other side of Conservative penal policy. The problem is to persuade both their supporters, and the judiciary and magistracy, that it is not an easy alternative, that the guilty will still suffer, the Government is not becoming soft on crime.

PRISON OVERCROWDING

To comprehend the scale of the problem facing British prisons some statistics are necessary. In 1989 the average prison population for England and Wales stood at 48,600, a drop of some 3 per cent (1,350) over 1988. This was the first fall since 1973 and was due predominantly to reductions in the numbers of remand prisoners, due to the success of the probation service's bail information schemes, and sentenced young offenders, partly due to the stricter criteria for custodial sentences for young people required by the 1988 Criminal Justice Act, and partly to the drawing up and implementation of 'action plans' for community plans by the probation service. For adult offenders the picture showed little change from previous years and indeed the number of sentenced adult male prisoners had increased. 'Certified normal accommodation' (CNA), the official figures for the number of prisoners which the system can officially cater for without overcrowding, allowed for 45,268 prisoners. This was an increase of 2,700 over 1987 but little change (+18) from the previous year. While a welcome improvement it still meant a gap of 3,332 between CNA and average population. Worst hit were local prisons whose population on 30 June 1988, for example, exceeded CNA by 54 per cent (NACRO Briefing 1989c). The Government had to deal with this as a matter of urgency, but had to maintain its hard line on law and order. In July 1988, the Home Secretary announced an increase in the remission period, from one-third to one-half for prisoners serving short sentences. This reduced the prison population by over 3,000, and without it the figure would have been 53,000.

The 1990 Home Office projections forecast that the average daily prison population would rise to between 61,700 and 62,600 by 1998 (Home Office 1990c). This was slightly less than earlier forecasts to which the Government had responded by announcing a major prison-building programme. Even with these forecasts, the programme is the largest undertaken this century. It provides for the construction of 24 new prisons and, with extensions to existing prisons, for the provision of over 21,000 extra prison places by 1995. In 1990 the average capital cost per place in those prisons under construction, or where work was shortly due to start was 117,000.

One reason for the increase in the prison population during the 1980s was the rise in the number of remand prisoners awaiting trial or sentence. The average waiting time for trial at Crown Court was 56 days in 1989, and in that year remand prisoners made up just over one-fifth of the average prison population. Incarceration has increased as a form of punishment. In 1988 the courts imprisoned 20 per cent of adult men convicted, and 7 per cent of adult women, compared with 16 per cent of men and 3 per cent of women in 1976 (Criminal Statistics 1988). We will discuss the trends in sentencing practice in more detail below. Less than one-fifth of offenders imprisoned during 1988 had committed an offence involving sexual or physical violence (Prison Statistics 1988). Reconviction figures for prisoners released in 1985 suggest that 55 per cent of men and 34 per cent of women are reconvicted within 2 years. Given that the average cost of a keeping a person in prison is £288 per week (a staggering £14,976 per annum), the cost-effectiveness and efficacy of imprisonment is questionable. We need only to compare this to the average annual cost in 1986–87 of probation orders (£900), community service orders (£520), attendance sentence orders (£117) or even places in probation hostels (£7,174) to see why the Treasury is in danger of becoming a radical advocate of decarceration! (Probation Statistics 1987, quoted in NACRO Briefing 1989b.)

Expenditure on the prison service has also risen considerably. Between 1978–79 and 1989 the budget for the penal system has risen 36 per cent in real terms (156 per cent in cash terms), with overtime pay for prison officers rising 137 per cent between 1979 and 1985. Staff in the prison service has been increased, but the conditions of service, and the overcrowding have led to militant action by prison officers. As Fitzgerald and Sim (1982) suggested, one reason for the instability of the prison system in the 1970s and 1980s was the militancy of the rank-and-file prison officers in conflict with their own union, the Home Office, prison governors and the prisoners themselves. Since 1985, there has been action in several prisons over several demands, but perennially the amount of overtime that has to be worked. In May 1985, Leon Brittan, then Home Secretary, was booed despite his figures saying that prison officer ranks had increased since 1979 by one-fifth, and that the budget for the Prison Service had risen 85 per cent.

The poor conditions within prison led to several conflicts between prisoners and prison officers. This occurred at a time when the militancy of rank-and-file officers increased. In 1985, officers took action at Bedford, Parkhurst, and Wormwood Scrubs. Several incidents of violence became public. In April and June 1985, 316 prisoners and 135 prisoners respectively, were injured (*Guardian*, August 10 1985), and in June a demonstration occurred at Holloway by 43 women protesting about brutality inflicted upon a fellow prisoner. In April 1985, at Gartree – a long-term maximum security prison – there was a sit-in by prisoners, and in June of that year another at Parkhurst, Isle of Wight. In September the staff at Albany, another maximum security prison, voted to keep prisoners in their cells, after a confrontation between staff and prisoners. Prisoners were also involved in legal initiatives involving their civil rights. They challenged the Home Secretary's 1983 policies which effectively abolished parole for certain categories of prisoners, but did win the right, with the assistance of the European Commission for Human Rights to be legally represented at prison disciplinary hearings.

A number of support groups were involved: Radical Alternatives to Prison; National Prisoners' Movement (PROP); Women in Prison; Inquest and the Prison Reform Trust. The isolation of prisoners and their rights became less severe. The problems which had arisen for the Government were the rising prison population, and the cost of imprisonment.

The solution suggested by the State to overcrowding in prison has been to expand the prison building programme (a suggested 16 new prisons), whilst simultaneously exploring non-custodial alternatives. As early as 1973, community service orders had been introduced so that offenders could work in the community for up to 240 hours. However, this has been used mainly for those whose crimes would not have sent them to prison anyway. Alternatives to custody are more likely to pull into the system, new populations rather than reduce incarcerated ones. We shall explore this further in the next chapter. Prison security has become an issue, especially since the troubles in Northern Ireland, and it is worth noting that the 1983 report of the Chief Inspector of Prisons suggested that the lessons of the 38-prisoner-escape from the Maze could be applied to England and Wales. Internal security has been strengthened by the use of MUFTI (Minimum Use of Force Tactical Intervention Squad) and the increased training of prison officers in riot control. Segregation and control units have been used for difficult prisoners, especially in womens' prisons. New prisons are likely to be made up of self-contained units holding 50–100 prisoners, with cells opening into a central area for staff observation.

Obviously, the prison building programme is based on the fear that violent crime particularly, is out of control. Murders of policemen, child murders, and terrorism are seen as escalating, but of course these are far from the common run of prisoners – 95 per cent of crimes are relatively trivial offences against property.

Box and Hale (1982) located the prison building programme in a wider political context. They saw the growth of unemployment, related as it was to a deepening economic crisis, as being accompanied by growing state coercion. This was reflected in the rate and length of imprisonment:

> This increased use of imprisonment is not a direct response to any rise in crime, but is an ideologically motivated response to the perceived threat of crime posed by the swelling population of economically marginalised persons.

> (Box and Hale 1982, p.22)

They also indicate that for every 1,000 increase in youth unemployment, 23 additional males are incarcerated, even when the effects of crime rates and court workload are controlled for. Sentencing policies, as a result of law and order campaigns mean the prisoners are younger and more likely to be black. These campaigns are not concerned to control serious crime.

> Rather they are more concerned to instil discipline, directly and indirectly on those people who are no longer controlled by the soft discipline machine at work, and who might become growingly resentful that they are being made to pay the price of the economic recession.
>
> (Box 1987, p.119)

As Box argues:

> Not only have the total numbers and percentage of the population increased, but within this group the economically disadvantaged figure prominently.
>
> (Box 1987, p.12)

As Box reminds us, and as we discussed in Chapter Five, the arrest rate is higher for young blacks (Stevens and Willis 1979) and these cannot be accounted for entirely by differences in criminal activity. Black British youth tend to be charged for offences 'easy to prove', and appear before 'tough minded' magistrates (Cain and Sadigh 1982). As Box puts it:

> These disparities are bound to percolate through and produce a blacker prison population.
>
> (Box 1987, p.15)

Prisoners are male, and disproportionately young – a quarter of the prison population being under 21, whereas 15–20-year-olds make up only 10 per cent of the British population. Prisoners have also become younger in their age profile. By 1984 under–21s were 28 per cent of the prison population.

The prison system in England and Wales, then, is creaking and close to collapse. During 1988 in a desperate attempt to ameliorate the problem in the short term, the Government opened unused Army camps as temporary prisons. After the destruction of Strangeways prison and the dispute with the POA over conditions this option was again on the agenda in 1990. Successive Governments, of both left and right, have failed to make any impact upon the excessive use of imprisonment as a means of punishment by the judiciary. To understand the reasons for this we need to look at penal policy in a wider economic and social framework.

THE POLITICAL ECONOMY, PUNISHMENT AND IMPRISONMENT

Box and Hale (1982, 1985, 1986) and Hale (1989ab) have examined the relationship between unemployment and imprisonment since the end of the

Second World War. The general conclusion of these analyses was that unemployment and imprisonment were related, in the sense that, after controlling statistically for the level of crime and numbers convicted, an increase in the level of unemployment led, on average, to an increase in the numbers incarcerated. This needs to be seen in the context of recent trends in punishment in England and Wales, and in particular the proportionate use of imprisonment, probation and fines. For statistical reasons, they used data from England and Wales only, leaving the separate judicial systems of Northern Ireland and Scotland, while acknowledging the experimental use of control techniques in Northern Ireland, and the softening up of public opinion prior to their introduction to the mainland. Hale (1989b) argues that the long-term trend of a decrease in the proportionate use of imprisonment and a corresponding increase in the use of fines has been reversed. Since 1974, and particularly since 1979, the use of imprisonment has been increasing relatively as well as absolutely.

There may be similar trends in imprisonment in other advanced capitalist societies which face similar economic and social problems to Britain. However, as Downes (1982) shows, this is not inevitable. Between 1950 and 1975 both Britain and Holland had similar increases in crime levels, but whilst the prison population in England and Wales doubled, in the Netherlands it more than halved. Hence societies with similar modes of production can respond differently to imprisonment.

Rusche and Kirchheimer (1939) consider the relationship of changes in punishment and modes of production. They argue that every system of production tends to discover and use punishments corresponding to its productive relationships – a classical Marxist approach.

When labour surpluses became a general phenomenon, and with declining profitability, there was fiscal pressure in the nineteenth century to reduce the size of the prison population. In the relatively short period of time prior to the Industrial Revolution the function of the prison can be seen as related directly to the needs of the economy, in that labour was forced to work on specific projects to overcome labour shortages. The prison served as a means of ensuring a supply of labour. Since then there has been less of a general shortage of labour, but rather a shortfall in skilled, rather than unskilled labour. Since the late nineteenth century, the problem has been one of a surplus of labour. Quinney (1977) and Jankovic (1977) have argued that prison acts as a way of reducing the size of the reserve army of labour. This is a rather simplistic argument. It assumes that it is actually the unemployed who are being imprisoned, and, furthermore, is clearly untenable when faced with data which show the numbers unemployed in England and Wales many times greater than the numbers imprisoned.

This deterministic approach suffers by seeing the prison as existing to remove people from circulation, rather than its ideological function of social control. Crises, of which high levels of unemployment are one manifestation, involve the totality of capitalist social relations. The solution to these crises is a complex economic, political and ideological process. As Braithwaite puts it:

> during a period of economic crisis the hegemony of capitalist ideology fosters a search for alternatives to the failure of the system as an explanation for the crisis. An explanation which makes eminent sense to everyone is to blame the victims of the crisis for the crisis.
>
> (Braithwaite 1981)

While rejecting the mechanistic connection of Quinney and Jankovic, one can argue that in times of economic crisis, typified by rising levels of unemployment, imprisonment does serve an important social control function as a constant reminder to those not in work of the consequences of stepping out of line. This approach, however, is open to charges of functionalism and presumes a conspiracy between judiciary and government.

Evidence for an association between unemployment and imprisonment has, however, been presented in various studies from different countries (Braithwaite 1980; Inverarity and Grattet 1987; Inverarity and McCarthy 1988; Montgomery 1985; Laffargue and Godefroy 1987) and has been most strongly supported by time series data analysed using some variant of least squares regression. The advantage of this method is that it is a multivariate technique which allows an analysis of the relationship between unemployment and imprisonment to be examined after controlling for other factors such as crime levels, numbers of convictions, and age structure of the population, which might affect the rate of incarceration.

The results of Box and Hale show that for post-war England and Wales, unemployment and imprisonment were positively related even after allowing for variations in other factors. However, the disadvantage is that the use of regression analysis seduces its users into a causality which may not always be appropriate. It would not follow that the recent decline in unemployment rates in England and Wales would lead to reductions in the numbers imprisoned after taking crime rates into account. Unemployment is one indicator of underlying economic problems, and how a state chooses to deal with a crisis will have important implications for its social policies in general, and of course this includes policies on imprisonment. Overall, however, the work done by Box and Hale for England and Wales suggests that after controlling for other relevant variables, rising levels of unemployment have been associated with the increased use of imprisonment. The relationship between unemployment and imprisonment has persisted throughout the post-war period, intensifying since 1974 (Hale 1989b).

TRENDS IN THE USE OF PUNISHMENT IN ENGLAND AND WALES

In September 1986, the prison population of the United Kingdom was, in absolute numbers, the highest of the member states of the Council of Europe – 53,971 or 95.3 per 100,000 of the population. Only Austria with 102.5 per 100,000 and Turkey with 102.3 had higher proportions of their populations in prison. By 1988, the United Kingdom had risen to top position in both absolute and relative terms. In September of that year 55,457 people or 97.4 per 100,000 of the population were imprisoned. This compares with relative figures of 95.6 for Turkey, 84.9 for West Germany, 75.8 for Spain, 44.0 for Greece and 40.0 for the Netherlands (NACRO Briefing 1990a, Council of Europe 1989). A similar picture emerges when prison admissions are considered, with the United Kingdom in 1987 imprisoning 347.9 people per 100,000, the highest for any major member state of the Council.

The average size of the sentenced prison population has been increasing steadily since the Second World War. In 1948 it was 19,765 and by 1988, 38,500 – of which 1,286 were female. Crime rates have risen even more dramatically over the same period: from 522,684 indictable crimes recorded by the police in 1948, to 1,407,774 in 1968, and by 1988 to 3,715,800. It does not follow that increases in crime accompanied by increased numbers of convictions necessarily entails more people being incarcerated. If we wish to discuss changes in punishment it is perhaps more helpful to look at the percentage of those found guilty receiving different types of sentence.

Until 1974 in England and Wales the probability of receiving a custodial sentence upon conviction had been declining steadily. Bottoms (1983) examines data from 1938, 1959 and 1980 and shows that for all adult indictable offenders the percentage of custodial sentences drops from 33.3 in 1938 to 29.1 in 1959 to 14.8 in 1980. The penalty which had the greatest proportional increase over this period was the fine, roughly doubling in its proportionate use from 27 per cent to 53 per cent while probation also declined from 15 per cent of all sentences to 7 per cent (Bottoms 1983; see Table 7.1). Since Bottoms wrote his essay however, this trend has gone into reverse, as he himself reports in a later work (Bottoms 1987), and as can be seen from the figures given in Table 7.1 (updated from Bottoms (1987) using Criminal Statistics (1988)).

Table 7.1   Sentencing trends (%) in England and Wales for adult male convicted of indictable offences 1968–88

	Prison*	Prob.	Fines	CSO	SS	Disch.	Other
1968	18	7	48	–	17	8	1
1969	18	7	49	–	16	9	1
1970	19	6	50	–	15	8	1
1971	19	7	51	–	14	9	1
1972	18	7	52	–	14	9	1
1973	16	7	55	–	12	9	2
1974	15	6	56	–	12	9	1
1975	16	6	55	1	13	9	1
1976	16	5	53	2	13	9	1
1977	17	5	55	2	13	8	1
1978	17	4	54	3	12	7	1
1979	17	5	54	3	12	7	1
1980	17	5	52	4	12	7	1
1981	18	6	49	5	12	8	1
1982	19	6	47	6	12	8	1
1983	20	6	47	7	11	9	1
1984	20	7	45	7	11	9	2
1985	21	7	43	7	12	9	1
1986	21	7	41	7	12	10	1
1987	21	8	41	7	12	10	1
1988	20	8	42	7	12	10	1

Source: Bottoms 1987

Note: *Includes partially suspended sentences after 1982. CSO = Community Service Order. SS = suspended sentence. The figures for 1977 and subsequent years are not strictly comparable with those earlier due to alterations in the definition of indictable offences and the introduction of new counting procedure. These changes did not affect the underlying trend

The downward trend in the proportionate use of imprisonment which had begun in the early 1950s halted in the mid–1970s. In fact the turning point can be located quite clearly in 1974. In that year the proportion of convicted adult males given a custodial sentence had reached a low of 15 per cent. Subsequently this figure began to increase steadily and by 1988, the latest year for which figures are available, it was 20 per cent. (The corresponding figures for adult females were 2 per cent and 7 per cent and again 1974 marked the low point in the proportionate use of imprisonment.) Over the same period there was an accompanying shift away from the use of fines. By 1974 they were used in 56 per cent of guilty cases for adult males but subsequently their proportionate use declined and by 1988 the figure was 42 per cent. In other words between 1974 and 1988 there had been a 25 per cent reduction in the proportionate use of fines and a corresponding 25 per cent increase in the proportionate use of imprisonment. What is also clear from Table 7.1 is that these changes were most pronounced after 1979. Since 1974 not only have the absolute numbers being sent to prison increased but the courts have become more punitive in the sense that they are sending a higher proportion of those convicted to prison. Since their election victory in 1979 the Tories have followed a two-pronged penal policy. While exhorting the judiciary to use custodial sentences only for the really wicked, who commit serious offences, they have refused to compromise the supposed independence of the judiciary by interfering directly in the judicial process. Instead, they have on the one hand embarked upon the biggest programme of prison building this century, whilst on the other searching for alternative punishments to prison. In the 1989 statement on Government expenditure they announced that the Home Office was to receive yet another increase in money to enable it to build two extra prisons, to set up 30 day centres for parole on probation, to recruit 300 more police officers in provincial forces, to employ an additional 1,300 civilians in the police forces and to make the Immigration and Nationality Department more efficient. The day centres are clearly part of a campaign to make probation a 'tougher' option for the courts. The two new prisons were in addition to the eight new ones opened since 1985 and another 18 at various stages of completion. They will bring the total of new places available by 1991 to 10,000 and the programme will provide 20,000 new places in all by the mid–1990s. Prior to the announcement of the additional two it had been estimated that the total capital cost of the 26 new prisons would be £870 million at an average cost per place of 69,200. The Government has also increased the manpower in the prison service. Between 1982 and 1987 the average annual numbers of prison officers have increased by around 12 per cent per annum. The long-term trend has been to reduce the number of inmates per officer. Forty years ago there were about six inmates for each officer. In 1986–87 there were approximately two and a half inmates to one officer.

The principle of least eligibility, notwithstanding the massive prison building programme, seems to operating with some vengeance. We noted earlier that in 1989 the certified normal occupation (CNA) of the prison system had reached 45,286. The average prison population of 48,600 thus represented an average overcrowding of 8 per cent. The situation is particularly acute in remand centres and local prisons. There are 28 local prisons in England and Wales housing over one-third of the prison population. They are used to hold the least dangerous categories of prisoner, including those waiting to be tried or sentenced (remand prisoners), fine defaulters, those serving short sentences and prisoners awaiting reallocation to training prisons. Table 7.2 shows the extent of overcrowding in the ten worst local prisons in March 1990. The average overcrowding in male local prisons in

1989 was 29 per cent. Many of the prisoners are locked up in their cells for most of the 24 hours in the day. The problem of remand prisoners, is particularly acute. On 28 February 1990 10,228 prisoners were awaiting trial or sentence in penal establishments. This constituted 22 per cent of the total prison population. In addition, more remand prisoners were held in police or court cells. If 1988 is any guideline only 60 per cent of these remand prisoners will eventually receive custodial sentences. Perhaps the simplest way to conclude this section is to quote the words of Her Majesty's Chief Inspector of Prisons who wrote in his annual report for 1986:

> The physical conditions in which many prisoners had to live continued, therefore, in many cases, to border on the intolerable. For remand prisoners in particular, whose numbers increased sharply during the year, conditions were particularly poor. Overcrowding, coupled with the lack of in-cell sanitation and the sharing of limited and inadequate facilities on landings, represented much human misery. Many inmates in the local prisons spent almost all day locked up, two or three men to a cell intended for one, with no integral sanitation and little to do.

Table 7.2   Prison overcrowding: the ten worst prisons on 31 March 1990

	CNA	Population	% overcrowded
Leeds	627	1223	95
Bedford	171	322	88
Birmingham	571	998	75
Leicester	205	353	72
Manchester	997	1646	65
Hull	402	641	59
Shrewsbury	176	276	57
Chelmsford	244	373	53
Reading	178	269	51
Lincoln	391	590	51

Source: NACRO Briefing (1990b)
Note: CNA = Certified Normal Accommodation

IDEOLOGY, IMPRISONMENT AND RECESSION

Melossi (1985) discusses how social discourses change with the various stages of what he calls the political business cycle. In the upswing this discourse is characterised by energy and hectic frenzy. As he notes they are 'not a time for punishment'. Melossi discusses the 'roaring twenties' and notes that 'an attitude of leniency, indulgence and experimentation with newer methods and reforms permeated the whole society'. His description could well apply to the 1960s in the UK, with the proviso perhaps that social changes lagged behind the business cycle somewhat. The sixties, however, certainly marked the end of the era of post-war austerity and a time when the belief that the State could solve most economic problems was strong. It was a period when the newly (re)found sense of idealism and hope led to great expectations of the rehabilitative force of prison and its alternatives. Hudson (1984, 1987) has catalogued how the reforming penal language of the 1960s became replaced with that of justice and punishment during the 1970s. Here we will consider the reasons for this change in language and consider how Melossi's 'vocabulary of motives' helps us to understand changes in England and Wales since 1974.

For Melossi it's the discourses which count:

> For this reason in the downswing of the cycle, the sources for an increase in severity of punishment should not be sought either in specific 'economic' functions, such as the control of an increasing mass of the unemployed, or in specific motives of individual agents of social control, such as the common belief that unemployment causes crime. Although such motives can be found in individuals, they, like the punishment rate itself, are associated with the general 'moral climate' that develops in hard times.
>
> (Melossi 1985, p. 183)

Melossi contends that earlier attempts by Box and Hale to use an argument based upon the 'unintended consequences of purposive social action' are limited. In this section we will consider review this argument and develop it using the work of Box (1987). We believe that the argument is strengthened by linking it to Melossi's 'discursive chain of discourse' and by showing how this discourse changed in the 1970s. The climate which developed in this period in Britain was one in which the prejudices of the judiciary were reinforced by a media campaign supportive of the Tory Party's ideas on moral decay and over-dependence upon the state.

It is no coincidence that 1974, the year in England and Wales which saw the end of the decline the proportionate use of imprisonment, and the beginning of a major economic crisis during which the numbers of male unemployed more than doubled by 1976 and increased by a factor of 5 by 1984, also marked the beginning of the end of the welfarist consensus.

As we discussed on p.5 the Labour Party responded to the economic crisis with a programme of public expenditure cuts. At the same time it launched an ideological offensive launched to justify this approach to solving the crisis. This offensive had other faces and one of the major targets of the media was the power of the unions which had been used to protect, more or less successfully, the interests of the workers and to maintain the Welfare State. The celebrations surrounding the 25th anniversary of the accession of the

Queen were used as means of playing down class differences and uniting the country around slogans like 'coats off for Britain'. At the same time a campaign against welfare scroungers was launched to make unemployment financially and socially undesirable. Law and order became increasingly to be used as symbol for the moral and economic decay of the country and this was reinforced by the use of the latent racism of the working class in the publicity given to muggers which was presented at least implicitly as a black crime (see Hall *et al.*1978). The popular press was also to play the racist card in attacks on the social security system with lurid reports of Asian families staying in luxury hotels on welfare payments. Perhaps most crucial, however, was the transformation of trade unionists from harmless cart-horses into mindless, vicious thugs. The problem for the Labour Party, of course, was that playing this propaganda card was always likely to backfire since its natural constituency should have been the very groups it was attacking.

The Tory Party meanwhile had no such problems. As we saw in Chapter Three it was able to give voice to the fears of many concerning the supposed breakdown in moral standards, they equated economic decline with moral weakness and established hegemonic control by focusing on the breakdown of law and order. The Tory Party had a clear mission which was to break the power of the unions, and the way that it did this was by using the law. It successfully portrayed itself as having the solution to Britain's economic problems which it saw as being due to excessive State intervention in every sphere, and to the dependance mentality which this produced. It committed itself, as we have seen, to a radical restructuring of the British economy at the expense of the working class, and integral to this programme was an attack upon trade-union 'power' and the dismantling of the welfare-state.

Union power had to be broken, and this was achieved by linking it with the breakdown in law and order. By implication, the Labour Party was seen as supporting unions, and thus having no respect for the rule of law. The period prior to the 1979 election was one of acute crisis – Callaghan's 'winter of discontent', economic chaos, and a general feeling of malaise.

The Conservatives successfully mounted a campaign which linked welfare scroungers, individualism, anti-collectivism, breaking the dependency culture and replacing it with the enterprise culture, trade unionists as criminals, moral decline, the need for personal responsibility and personal discipline. The collectivist welfarist society was presented as being a central part of the moral decline. The social security scrounger, seriously curtailed in the restructuring of income support systems in 1988, joined industrial pickets, single-parent families, youths and gays in the Tory gallery of folk devils. Taylor (1987) argued that the Tories were aided in this by:

organisations of people carrying out crucial authority functions, within the English bourgeois state, in particular local magistrates, local police chiefs, police federation representatives and senior traditional school-masters.

(Taylor 1987, p.312)

In the early years of the 1970s each of these groups was involved through their professional organisations in a campaign against what they saw as the damaging consequences of the 1960s liberalism. The Magistrates Association mounted a successful campaign against the 1969 Children and Young Persons Act which sought to replace courtroom hearings for young people with 'welfare dispositions'. The National Association of Schoolmasters (NAS) concentrated upon attacking the comprehensive school system and importantly, was involved in public campaigns around the level of violence in schools (Taylor op. cit.). The violent, dangerous and delinquent youth of the magistrates and NAS were also present in the statements of individual Chief Constables and representatives of the Police Federation who articulated publicly their own theories on the causes of crime in a manner which would have been thought unthinkable a few years previously. We have discussed this in more detail in Chapter Three where we saw how the parameters of this debate as set out in these campaigns were seized upon by the Tory Party with little or no response from the Labour Party who seemed unable to cope with the authoritarian drift. 'Law and order', 'respect for the law', 'moral degeneracy', 'the burgeoning crime levels' became the catch phrases of the moment. What was needed, of course, was a return to discipline both at work and in society. Since industrial anarchy was nothing other than the other side of the coin of the rapidly rising crime levels, both would be defeated by tough measures which would restore to the citizen a feeling of security and freedom. Furthermore, the Welfare State had encouraged moral decline and negated individual responsibility for individual actions. The growing army of unemployed was the consequence of years of trade-union power and restrictive practices and the first step in the restructuring of the economy would be to criminalise many of the traditional weapons used by the working class to defend their interests.

The most disturbing threat to our freedom and security is the growing disrespect for the rule of law. In government as in opposition Labour have undermined it.

(Conservative Party Manifesto 1979)

The number of crimes in England and Wales is nearly half as much again as it was in 1973. The next Conservative Government will spend more on fighting crime even while we economise elsewhere.

(Conservative Party Manifesto 1979)

The Conservatives won the 1979 election at least in part on a law and order programme. An Independent Television News Research survey reported on election night after the closure of the polls indicated that 23 per cent of voters who switched allegiance did so on law and order and that 22 per cent were concerned with the role of trade unions. As Clarke and Taylor (1980) and Clarke *et al*. (1982) show, the coverage of the Law and Order issue by the media was dominated by the agenda set out by the Tory Party aided by the magistracy, the NAS and certain sections of the police.

We find, then, in the discourses of crucial sectors of the bourgeoisie in this period precisely that change in the general moral climate described by Melossi:

in periods of economic decline, a 'discursive chain' of punitiveness and severity spreads across society.

(Melossi 1985, p.183)

Central to their economic strategy was a commitment to reduce public expenditure (except for the law and order budget) and the breaking of the power of the trade unions. The two were of course linked. Strong trade unions, especially in the public sector, had successfully resisted attacks on the Welfare State in the past, and so needed to be defeated if the Tories' solution to what they saw as the major problem – inflation – were to be successful. At the same time the huge increases in unemployment, which were the corollary of the expenditure cuts and non-interventionist market-oriented economic policy, undermined the resistance and the strength of the unions. It was within this ideological framework which was always present but as outlined above became to be more and more publicly articulated by the Tories prior to 1979 that the operations of the justice system in England and Wales need to be considered. The Courts have responded to perceived growing crime rates during this period by increasing the use of prison sentences and reducing the use of non-supervisory sentences such as fines or unconditional discharges. The outcome has been the imposition of more sentences at the higher end of the punishment tariff over and above the changes in the volume of crime. As Box and Hale (1982, 1985, 1986) have argued, this response is not merely a mechanical response due to the in-creased workload but is due to a sufficiently large proportion of judges and magistrates responding to deteriorating economic conditions by resorting more frequently to the use of imprisonment. This is made easier by the shift in the ideological climate discussed earlier, since to be too soft on those convicted would be to prolong the permissive trend which had led to the high crime levels and the chronic economic problems. The judiciary and magistrates are of course drawn predominantly from the middle and upper classes (see Box 1987, p.134–135) and as such can be expected to reflect the beliefs and prejudices of their class. Their natural constituency is 'conservative' and especially the preservation of private property. Consequently, rises in the level of unemployment are likely to be a source of deep anxiety to them since they *believe* that the unemployed are weak and amoral and therefore more likely to be criminal. Add to this their desire to protect private property and to end the moral decline which has crippled the country and a potent brew is produced. As Box argues, when this is combined with:

> the 'knowledge' that 'crime is getting worse' and that 'fear of crime' is becoming a major social problem – messages that politicians, via the media, communicate – then the judiciary are bound to become more sensitised to the dangers that lurk in high levels of unemployment.
>
> (Box 1987: 135)

And so they are bound to respond in a more punitive manner. Hence we do not need to argue that the judiciary are in any sense part of a gigantic conspiracy; they merely act according to their beliefs which inevitably reflect their class interests. Furthermore, as Box succinctly puts it:

> given the 'Constitutional Independence' (but political reliability) of the judiciary, there will be no concerted effort to prevent or curtail the steady drift towards more frequent use of severe penal sanctions whenever many judges and magistrates react to their perceptions of growing or potential disruption resulting from the upsurge in the volume of unemployment and an intensification of class conflict in general.
>
> (ibid, pp.135–136)

TOO MUCH LAW AND ORDER? THE PROBLEM – OVERCROWDED PRISONS: THE SOLUTION – PUNISHMENT IN THE COMMUNITY?

The proponents of a Conservative approach to criminology in the United Kingdom are faced with the contradictions inherent in the Manifesto pledges of the 1979 Election. They have to deal with not only a still increasing level of crime, but also, because of a judiciary which shares their belief in the efficacy of toughness and hence is over-enthusiastic in the use of custodial sentences, the consequent overcrowding and appalling conditions of prisons.

As we noted earlier the Conservative Government has followed two major policies in an attempt to deal with this penal crisis: firstly, simply to build more prisons; and secondly, to reduce the numbers receiving custodial sentences. Integral to the second policy is the need to extend custody into the community. In this concluding section we will examine this strategy in more detail. Successive governments have stressed that imprisonment should be used only as a last resort yet, as we have seen, its use increased during the 1980s. The recent history of Government attempts to reduce the prison population is a history of 'tinkering'. Each Home Secretary has in turn drawn back from taking the most obvious and practical steps with the excuse that they cannot legislate for the judiciary – its independence is inviolable:

> It is not for the Home Secretary, government or the House to lay down to the courts how many people they send to prison. It is our job to provide places for them.
>
> (Douglas Hurd, *Hansard*, 5 November 1987, Column 1055)

The judiciary can be encouraged, exhorted, informed, reasoned with, but it can never be instructed. The result has been that major reforms are completely avoided and every minor reform is weakened or sabotaged. The principle of judicial independence is so prized by judges that Lord Lane, the Lord Chief Justice, has refused even to meet Home Secretaries to discuss sentencing policies. The nearest the Government came to bringing the judges and magistrates 'within the disciplines of efficiency and cost effectiveness' (*Guardian* 1.10.90), was to circulate to all courts details of the full costs of their sentencing decisions. The Magistrates Association's immediate response was that its members already had this information and would continue to pass the sentence they considered appropriate to the offence. For a more extensive discussion of earlier failures to reduce the prison population see Box and Hale (1986).

In the late 1980s the Government began yet another attempt to reduce prison overcrowding. In line with its notions of community crime prevention it saw the way forward to be shifting the emphasis from custodial institutions to punishment in the community. To do this it had to gain the support, both of the judiciary and the public, for its new measures. It began an attempt to do this in several policy documents. The 1988 Green Paper (Home Office 1988b) announced its concern over the numbers of offenders sentenced to custody. It stated that the Government's intention was to increase court and public confidence in the effectiveness of community-based penalties. It argued that these were not soft options but properly applied would be tough penalties which aided the battle to reduce crime. The paper emphasised the diversion of offenders from custody, noting the success of intermediate treatment programmes and the increased use of cautions for juveniles. A major theme was that of reparation; offenders would recompense the community, and where possible, the individual victim for their crimes.

More use was to be made of day centres and community service. The guilty offender's freedom was still to be curtailed but outside of institutions. Drug and alcohol abuse were raised as issues which, because of their connection with crime, needed to be part of a programme for offenders. To pacify the law and order lobby, a distinct difference was recognised, between property offences (95 per cent of all crime), viewed as amenable to punishment in the community, and crimes of violence which need to be punished more severely in order to protect the public.

The role of the probation service became clear when the Home Office published, in 1988c, *Tackling Offending – An Action Plan*', a document setting out how these proposals could be put into practice. It suggested that probation services took the lead in drawing up local initiatives for young adult offenders at risk of custodial sentences. The probation service was seen as central to organising punishment in the community. Tracking, curfews, electronic monitoring and weekend restrictions were suggested for use with new supervision and restriction orders. In the early stages after sentencing, supervision would be strict, and because of this would have an effect upon the probation officers' traditional caring function, emphasising instead a more custodial role.

One problem recognised in the paper is the question of whether the magistracy and judiciary would be prepared to substitute this form of sentence for those previously receiving a custodial sentence. What has tended to happen historically, with earlier attempts to provide alternatives to custody, is that instead of moving offenders currently receiving a sentence of imprisonment down-tariff, in this case to some form of punishment in the community, down-tariff offenders – those who formerly were dealt with by a fine or conditional discharge – have been given the new sentence. The sentencers have used the new powers, not to reduce the numbers being sent to prison, but as a way of substituting a tougher penalty for petty offenders. The original motivation for the new measures – to reduce the prison intake – thus has been thwarted.

The implication of shifting the role of the probation officer from the rehabilitative ideal of 'befriending the prisoner' to being more centrally involved in punishment, surveillance and control means that:

> the new order would contain additional elements of control which some members of the probation service might perceive as inimical to their approach to working with offenders.
>
> (Home Office 1988b, p.17)

but should this happen, the probation service could:

contract with other services, and private and voluntary organisations to obtain some of the components of punishment in the community.

(ibid)

The probation service would supervise the order, 'but would not itself be responsible for providing all the elements'. The role of a multi-agency, market-oriented provision emerges. The implied threat to a non-co-operating probation service is that a new organisation could be created:

to take responsibility for the arrangements for punishment in the community and providing services through contracts with other organisations.

(ibid, p.18)

Overcrowding in custody is to be prevented by extending control to community custody, using a mixture of existing and contracted services. The main disadvantages emphasised are not humanistic or rehabilitative objections, but financial ones. A new service would have to be funded by the Exchequer, not local government using existing services.

In response, the probation service agreed to set up Intensive Probation Programmes, and in April 1989 national standards were announced for community service orders:

Their purpose is to ensure that community service orders are tough and demanding; that they are managed consistently and with discipline and thus that the public and sentencers can have confidence in them.

(Home Office, 1990b).

The 1989 Audit Commission report on the probation service noted considerable variations in hours of attendance required at day centres, in breach of procedures for failure to attend the centres, in the frequency of visits offenders received whilst on probation and in unit costs. These would have to be standardised, but with some local flexibility according to the offence.

In 1990, David Waddington, the then Home Secretary, presented proposals which included reducing standard sentence remission from two-thirds to half the initial sentence. This 'hard line strategy' reveals yet again the contradictions inherent in the Conservatives' law and order policy. The move argued against the notion of reducing custodial sentences, clearly signalling to the judiciary a more cavalier attitude to the problems of prison overcrowding. These recommendations are part of the 1990 Government White Paper (Home Office 1990a), which claimed to set out a coherent, legislative framework for sentencing, matching punishment to the seriousness of the crime, and making the distinction between violent and non-violent crime. A hard line was to be maintained for violent and sexual offences with provisions for longer sentences, and Crown Courts were to be given the powers to impose heavier sentences than the individual offence justified, to persistent offenders deemed to be a public risk. A sharp distinction was made between these crimes and property crimes which could be subject to a community-focused punishment, involving a mixture of community service, probation, and curfews. A major theme of the paper was that punishment should fit the crime not the criminal, that vandals, thieves, and burglars should not be jailed for persistent offending.

The White Paper placed great emphasis on probation reports, to which attention would have to be paid before a custodial sentence is recommended. Increased use of financial penalties were also advocated. In addition to the changes in remission it was proposed to allow parole to be removed for prisoners serving over 4 years if it was felt that their release would put the public at risk. A post-imprisonment supervision was to be introduced for those serving more than one year, and wider powers given to the courts to make parents take responsibility for their children's offences.

The White Paper recognised that since 1981 the number of juveniles under 17 given custodial sentences, had fallen by more than 50 per cent, and there is no evidence that the reduction in custodial sentences has increased juvenile crime (174,000 known juvenile offenders was reduced to 119,000 in 1988). Females under 18 years of age were recommended as particularly suitable for non-custodial sentences, and attention was drawn to the strengthening of supervision orders for juveniles in the Children's Act of 1989. A new youth court was proposed to deal with the 14–16-year-old group – the largest group of juvenile offenders – whilst under-14-year-olds were to be dealt with increasingly by non-court procedures.

The White Paper put forward punishment in the community as an attempt to reduce custodial sentencing and to save on expenditure. The probation service and voluntary agencies were to be funded to provide an alternative form of punishment for the less serious offender. In line with the Green Paper which preceded it, it advocated an increased use of curfew orders, day centres, community service, bail hostels, electronic monitoring, financial penalties, and combinations of financial penalties, and community punishment.

The success of the Criminal Justice Bill stemming from the White Paper ultimately depends on the judiciary and the magistracy changing their sentencing strategies. This can happen, as local initiatives with magistrates have shown but the prognosis for major change on a national level is, judging from the history of earlier attempts, gloomy. This will require the Court of Appeal to extend its work on guideline sentences to more relatively minor crimes. This is a gamble, and there are indications that the Court of Appeal may refuse, seeing this as political interference with the judiciary. There were already signs of the difficulties ahead in May 1990 when it was reported that in order to avert a row with judges and magistrates the Home Secretary was contemplating watering down the principle that punishment should fit the crime not the criminal. Given that:

> Judges, magistrates and justices' clerks believe they must keep custody as a deterrent against frequent offenders and 'to give society a rest'.
>
> (*Guardian* 25.6.90)

Mr Waddington was apparently considering allowing them to take into account the need to protect the public from even quite minor offences. This attempted compromise will not help the Government in persuading the probation service to alter its traditional role and manage punishment in the community. A major argument put forward by the Home Office was that the proposed tougher community punishments would be an alternative to custody for persistent petty offenders. Harry Fletcher, the Assistant General Secretary of the National Association of Probation Officers (NAPO), commented that the move was:

> fudging the principle, and the result will be a flawed strategy which will increase the prison population.
>
> (*Guardian* 25.6.90)

since he now feared, that as with previous alternatives to custody, the new measures would be used instead for people who would previously have avoided jail. Financially, the programme depends on savings gained from reducing the prison population. Consequently, if the judiciary fail to reduce their proclivities or custodial sentences, and hence the savings fail to materialise, the alternative system will be under great strain.

At the same time as the White Paper the Government published a Green Paper (Home Office 1990b) on the reorganization of the probation service. This argued it was necessary to create a 'new model probation officer' with less emphasis on social work, but with the right balance between care and control. Probation should in no sense be seen as a soft option by the judiciary. The Green Paper considered in detail how the working practices of probation officers would have to change, reminding the probation service that it is a criminal justice agency, in obvious anticipation opposition from NAPO. The paper emphasised the need to protect the public from serious offenders punished in the community, and noted that crime prevention initiatives with offenders: 'involves firm and constructive work'.

These moves will also mean that the probation service has to stop seeing itself as the exclusive provider of services and facilities: it is suggested that other voluntary or private sectors may make better provision. Assessment, rather like the Griffiths report for community care and health is to become a primary intervention task, so as to plan and manage suitable programmes for offenders. Planning, social inquiry reports and enforcing court orders are to be the future task of probation, with an emphasis on the new task of the management and organisation of time, resources and workloads. Funding is to be centralised and Home Office policy on contracting out is to be followed. Some local areas will be amalgamated to improve their economics and management. The Green Paper makes clear the future direction of probation, through comments on the training of probation officers. It takes note of the Coleman Report (1989), which recommends removing Home Office sponsorship from sub-standard courses. Davies (1989) sees these as being those courses which pay insufficient attention to practical probation issues, such as resource management, penology, criminology, criminal law, principles of sentencing and other issues. The emphasis is clearly on the probation officer as part of the criminal justice system with a managerial role in supervising punishment.

Implicit in the Green Paper is the notion that generic social work principles are not paramount, and that probation courses will be brought to heel over their curriculum and orientation. The training of probation officers could continue and be included in the Certificate of Qualification in Social Work and the Diploma in Social Work courses, but if these do not measure up to required standards, they will be replaced with a new training syllabus put out to tender in the educational market place. A new more punitive role is envisaged for the probation service, which is threatened by being replaced by a new executive service.

Faced with the financial consequences of its commitment to a hard law and order policy the Government has attempted a conjuring trick. It has proposed a community-based programme of punishment but in order to sell this to both the judiciary and its supporters it has constructed around it a rhetoric of toughness. Question marks are already being raised over its proposed new measures. NAPO believes that rather than reducing the jail population the prison numbers will rise. It argues that the stricter probation conditions proposed will lead to more breaches of the orders, and at present a large proportion of those who breach go straight to prison. The history of previous attempts to reduce the prison population by introducing alternative punishments suggest that NAPO is likely to be proved right.

8 Is Conservative criminology here to stay?

CONSERVATIVE CRIMINOLOGY, IDEOLOGY AND THE STATE

As we have seen, conservative criminology is distinctly linked to other conservative social policy. The problem with New Right Conservatism is that it has to claim to be reducing the influence of the State in the field of welfare, health, income support and education, but has to maintain the strong State in the arena of law and order. Mrs Thatcher saw State control as central to socialism:

> Communism is the left foot of socialism, and Fascism is the right foot, using socialism in the sense that it is total regimentation and control by the state.
>
> *(The Times,* 29.8.77)

A major part of the Conservative agenda has been to undermine socialism and develop a contemporary form of *laissez-faire* market economics, to move Britain from a culture of dependency to the enterprise culture. This has had to be done in the context of a strong State – a State which will keep the streets safe, preserve the 'British' way of life, and protect property. The belief has grown that somewhere in the urban jungles, there lurk the dangerous classes who will, if not closely surveyed and controlled, challenge the peace of the streets. Without a strong State, this underclass will erupt into fragmented resistance, indicated in social disorder. In a strange way, this is a truth believed in by both the left and right criminology, as well as in British society at large.

There is a classical thread running through sociology which wants to argue (see for example, Giddens 1973; Rex and Tomlinson 1979) for the existence of an underclass, composed of underemployed, unskilled people – a significant number of them black. This lumpenproletariat has fared badly, hit by the increasing market competitiveness for jobs, housing, education and hence, decent incomes and good health. For Rex and Tomlinson, black people have become 'a separate under-privileged class' (Rex and Tomlinson 1979, p. 275). This group's inferior class position is linked to their families' origins as immigrants, and is compounded by poor incomes and racism. We see that the origins of racism lie embedded within the relations of capital, and are reinforced by institutions which historically regulated the flow of black labour. Hence immigration, and that attitudinal spin-off from immigration, the view that black people are all 'immigrants'. The sectional interests of the white working class and trade unions all indicate that divisive and sectional class interests are not just cultural phenomena.

Sivanandan (1982) engages in a dialogue with racist ideology, by seeing the relationship between racism and capitalism as essentially instrumental. Racial struggle is linked to class struggle, and racism fractures both the political superstructure and economic base. Field (1989), in his discussion of the underclass, leaves out the racial dimension and emphasises the economic aspects. He produces evidence to show how the poor have fallen behind the better-off sections of the British class system. The better off have, in many ways, forgotten the underclasses, yet they live indirectly off their misery. This group or sub-class has been detached from the rest of the British population, and is composed of the longer-term unemployed, single parents and elderly pensioners. It suffers from current economic policy, with the holding down and restructuring of welfare benefits in the context of rising inflation. Whilst Field does not emphasise an ethnic dimension to this underclass, it is clear that public fears are focused not on the elderly, sick or female, but on the young, especially young men – and particularly young black men. Most sociological writing on the underclass has suggested that it has a potential for what Giddens calls 'hostile outbursts' – that is, riots or mass violence and public disorder. This is a view shared by the general public, and by politicians.

Scruton (1984) has argued that freedom for conservatives is only possible when subordinated to an organisation or arrangement which defines the individual's aim. The value of individual liberty is not absolute, but is subject to the authority of established government. People need congenial government:

> It is through an ideal of authority that the conservative experiences the political world.
>
> (Scruton 1984, p.19)

This is why social consciousness in the form of patriotism, for example, is important to Scruton. It also helps us understand the ethnocentric and ruling-class view of much conservative criminology. Nationalism is not only acknowledged, but is a virtue. Even the National Front are only an extension of a marked allegiance to patriotism, authority and the Government. Scruton offers us an articulate perspective on the attractions of conservatism for those who, fearing social change and the future, try to hold firmly onto the past. For all its brave talk of radicalism, the New Right depends emotionally on the attractions of the familiar and the known, constructing a romantic view of a mythical past to bolster up its attack on collectivism. Legal change becomes prioritised and justified through expediency; opposition becomes reduced – an irritation to the smooth flow of economic policy.

We begin to see why, as Scraton and Chadwick (1987) remind us, sexism, racism and class hatred are so deeply institutionalised in the British State. They allow the marginalisation of identifiable groups, who are the product of a surplus population suffering the enforced unemployment necessary to stabilise the long recessions of capitalism. As sections of the working class become sectionalised, so their reputations become criminalised. Scraton and Chadwick correctly identify the politics of marginalisation as an integral part of the operation of criminal justice, just as Hall *et al*. (1978) showed us it was part of policing the crisis.

The politics of marginalisation are essential in the smooth operating of a set of social and economic policies intended to reform radically a welfare state, maintain unemployment and to deal with the consequences that therefore manifest themselves in social problems such as public disorder, addictions, inner city riots and rebellious fractions of communities. This means that a necessary emphasis has to be made on respectability, hard work, thrift and respect for law, so that marginalisation can become extended into criminalisation. Sir Kenneth Newman, then Commissioner of the Metropolitan Police commented:

> Throughout London there are locations where unemployed youth – often black youth – congregate; where the sale and purchase of drugs, the exchange of stolen property and illegal drinking and gaming is not uncommon. The youths regard these locations as their territory. Police are viewed as intruders, the symbol of authority – largely white authority – in a society that is responsible for all their grievances about unemployment, prejudice and discrimination. They equate closely with the criminal rookeries of Dickensian London.
>
> (Newman, 1983 'Policing London: post Scarman'. The 1983 Sir George Bean Memorial Lecture 24.10.83.)

Black youth, then, assumes symbolic importance by being equated with the inability of the police to maintain public order, a feature which encourages law breaking elsewhere and reinforces the phenomenon of urban decay.

We may bring some theoretical light on this by considering discussions of ideological formations in a culture of authoritarianism populism, called

'Thatcherism'. For the Conservative Government to maintain any level of legitimation in ideological or cultural spheres, they have had to construct a definition of common sense which reinforces their definition of the social order. The cultural and ideological influence of the Conservative government since 1979 has been considerable, articulated most clearly in the utterances of Mrs Thatcher. Discursive themes such as nation, self-help, respectability, have been constructed and related to class subjectivity.

Hall (1988), in particular, has argued that the power of that brand of New-Right Conservatism known as Thatcherism consists largely of the skilful way in which it has disconnected a number of themes – self-help, anti-statism, public order, anti-trade unionism, nationalism, share ownership – from the basically bourgeois discourse in which they have been tradition-ally lodged. They have then been re-articulated into a discourse of popular common sense and respectability. Thatcherism's new discourse has had consequent effects on the construction of subjectivity and consciousness. This common sense has affected not only Conservatism's traditional adher-ents, but has had an effect upon that Conservatism latent in working-class respectability. To develop hegemonic gain the Conservative Party has con-structed itself as the party which will bring prosperity, reconstruct traditional values, end dependency, encourage work and oppose the threats of progress-iveness, ethnic groups and cultures, and 'loony left' policies in local government. Hence law and order, the maintenance and control of the dangerous classes and the preservation of public order have been ideologi-cally central to its construction of consensual support. Where this fails, a legitimation crisis occurs.

On the level of ideology the Conservative Government has attempted to tackle not only a crisis of legitimation but also of motivation. This has been done by an emphasis on individualism, self-help, hard work and thrift, whilst at the same time there has been an attack on collectivism and socialism as repressive and unwordly values.

Gramsci (1978) has suggested:

> The methodological criterion on which our own study must be based is the following; that the supremacy of a social group manifests itself in two ways, as 'domination' and as 'intellectual and moral leadership'.
>
> (Gramsci 1978, p.57)

He argues that in the historical process of conflict and compromises, one fundamental class emerges as dominant and directive, not only in the eco-nomic sphere, but also in the moral and intellectual spheres. The State is the unifier and arbitrator of differing interests and conflicts. Hegemony evolves in an extensive but temporary form, equilibrium is only relative. When hegemony begins to come apart, the dominant class resorts to coercion, leading to a 'crisis of authority'. However, it is through popular beliefs that the mass of the people and the leading groups in society connect. Ideas are material forces for Gramsci, and hence consciousness is not spontaneous but structured in certain ways, which correspond to the general structure of society. For Gramsci:

> Philosophy cannot be separated from the history of philosophy, nor can culture from the history of culture.... One's conception of the world is a response to certain specific problems posed by reality, which are quite specific and 'original' in their immediate relevance.
>
> (Gramsci 1978, p.424)

Common sense is central for Gramsci, pervasive yet unsystematic. It has a basis in popular experience, but unlike philosophy does not present a unified conception of the world:

> Every social stratum has its own 'common sense' and its own 'good sense' which are basically the most widespread conception of life and man.... 'Common sense' is the folklore of philosophy, and is always halfway between folklore properly speaking and the philosophy, science and economics of the specialists.
>
> (Gramsci 1978, p.326)

We can see then, that as conscious subjects, we may draw upon common sense as explanation, and that there is a struggle for the definition of this *vis-à-vis* the State. The force of law is that it becomes part of common sense, and makes 'common sense' prescriptions about public order, theft and hard work. The State then operates as an educational function, as Gramsci suggests, in this case, to educate us as to the worthy and the unworthy, the deserving and the undeserving. For Gramsci, law reflects economic relations, and it is eternally and generally a weapon of class domination, a classical Marxist position. However, the link with common sense is put well by his biographer, Fiori:

> Gramsci's originality as a Marxist lay partly in his conception of the nature of bourgeois rule (and indeed of any previous established social order), in his argument that the system's real strength does not lie in the violence of the ruling class, or the coercive power of its state apparatus, but in the acceptance by the ruled of a 'conception of the world' which belongs to the rulers. The philosophy of the ruling class passes through a whole tissue of complex vulgarizations to merge as a 'common sense' that is the philosophy of the masses, who accept the morality, customs, the institutionalised rules of behaviour of the society they live in.
>
> (Fiori 1970, p.238)

The law for Gramsci exists both in political society or the State, and civil society – private organisations outside the State. The State exercises coercion, but civil society performs the function of maintaining hegemony, or domination by consent. The legal apparatus operates coercively to maintain hegemony, particularly in periods of political and ideological crisis. Law educates and adapts the mass of the people to the goals of civil society, defined through ruling class, notions of morality and custom. The general function of law – that is the dynamic of the legal system or the 'juridical problems' as Gramsci called it – is to render the ruling group homogeneous:

> creating a social conformism which is useful to the ruling groups' line of development.

> (Gramsci 1971)

For Gramsci law unifies fractions of the ruling class, as well as concealing the reality of the social structures for the masses. Ideological mystification obtained through legal devices has to be won so that political propaganda, political party speeches, definitions of marginalised and criminalised groups such as militant trade unionists and black youth, are vital in the construction of conformity and mystifying legal enactments. Hegemony has to be won and is central to maintaining the status quo in legal enactment. The State teaches us how to view the world:

> In reality, the state must be conceived of as an 'educator', in as much as it tends precisely to create a new type of civilisation.... The law is the repressive and negative aspect of the entire, positive, civilising activity undertaken by the state. The 'prize given' activities of individuals and groups must be also incorporated in the conception of the law.

> (Gramsci 1971, p.247)

The practice of politicians and intellectuals is central to understanding law as a key apparatus maintaining hegemony. Hunt (1976, pp.178–187) has developed some of these ideas in his consideration of law as an instrument of ideological domination, which legitimises and mystifies class rule. The effectiveness of such a legal system depends upon its ability to express the rights, powers and interests of subordinate classes. Sumner (1979), makes the point that law depends upon its ideological encapsulation of a consensus constructed outside itself, in other economic, political and cultural practices. Any legal system has to have an ideological base which represents an ideological alliance between the ruling class and other classes and class fractions. Progressive legislation is fought for and gained by organised resistance, often on a class base, though this may be concealed. However, the problem with law is that it can be radically re-ordered through political institutions. Its relationship with justice varies considerably from State to State, depending on the degree of coercion necessary.

For Sumner, law embodies the appearance of reality produced by social relations, so that, for example, an employment contract appears as a consensual contract between equals (a point also made by Hunt), but it also embodies those appearances as they have been seen and interpreted by classes and groups who make laws. An employment contract not only individualises what is essentially a class relation, but it individualises it in such a way that it expresses the dominance of the employers and their ideological grasp of the apparent relations between individuals. The ideological grasp of the employees is subordinated and does not appear in the legal document which ensues. Whilst the examples used come from civil law, we can see that the ideological grasp of those subject to criminal law is removed totally, because 'common sense' would not allow it a voice. One could not maintain the criminal justice system otherwise. That is not to say that miscarriage of justice, or reform of criminal law does not occur. This can be expressed through disputes between high-bourgeois individuals, themselves acceptable to the legal system as with the Guildford Four, who, partly as a result of international pressure, had highly placed clerics and members of the judiciary supporting their release.

Alternatively, it can be the result of a public campaign, as with the repeal of the 'sus' law which was repealed because of public pressure, but allowed public order to be maintained through other laws. Law can be seen as a public ideological front, which conceals the workings of a social formation, Sumner (1979) reminds us. This reveals law as a politically constructed, ideologically formulated institution, which has an educative process. Gramsci (1978) has pointed out that once a mode of production is established, with corresponding modes of political and cultural discourse, then law is developed to regulate that particular social formation. Legalisation and legal process respond to social problems, and are not unilaterally constructed. At different levels and in a very real sense, it is 'the law of the land'.

The Conservative Government has won important victories in ideological consent. It has had to rewrite aspects of law and order in order to gain support for its economic policies. It has played on the fears of rising crime, unsafe streets, unemployed youth, in order to develop common-sense notions of criminal justice. This has not occurred in a simplistic or deterministic manner, as can be seen from the retention of the abolition of the death penalty. However, as a Party it has managed to project itself as the supporter of law and order, and simultaneously to construct the parties of opposition as the supporters of disorder, misrule and irresponsibility. The differing strata of the working class have shifted in their forms of work, in the divisions created by long-term unemployment, by generational differences, and by ethnic composition. Because of this, culture and identification have also shifted in terms of the sites in which subjectivity is constructed. Many forms of political resistance and consciousness, feminist, gay, ecological and pacifist, have developed outside of party politics, and have developed analyses and strategies which go beyond traditional class politics.

Class is only one site in which subjectivity is constructed. Opposition to conservatism has relied too much on traditional class subjectivity, only recently reading its divisions and movement. The strategies for the modernisation of the British economy has meant that strategies to undergo this, operate as modes of both economic and social regulation. Hence, there is a necessary attempt, in order to bring in economic regulation, to construct a conservative recomposition of social and moral life. This is why the themes current in Conservative criminology are so important. This is not to deny the force of economistic elements in capitalism, but to indicate how certain ideological and moral themes assist in the maintenance of economic control.

Hence the extent to which Conservative criminology is here to stay depends on more than mere changes of political parties. It is closely related to the regulation of a particular form of social formation and is intimately linked with political and economic forces, and the consequent social problems which emerge. In order to gain any consensual alliance in the area of law and order a State has to take note of the emerging social formations, class fractions, cultures and consciousnesses of a multi-ethnic, gender-conscious society. It has to respond to the emerging consciousness of the black community, gay people, feminists by marginalising them and delegitimating their claims. By making such groups irrelevant, the State can write off the progressive movements of the last 20 years.

We have seen in this account the rise and legitimation of Conservative criminology for a government elected on a law and order issue. What has become a matter of concern is that as society becomes more complex, and as the common coin of politics moves away from socialism – and indeed social democracy – it becomes important to preserve and develop those rights which have come to be considered fundamental. Those rights which have been established, need to be defended, and therefore access to effective legal resource is indispensable. Without this, the rule of law becomes supplanted by the law of power. It is essential for the powerless and the poor to have access to as large a range of legal services and skills as those at the disposal of the authorities. The Critical Lawyers Group has suggested the establishment of a Public Law Project which would provide assistance in matters relating to public law to people who have little or no access to such assistance, due to their social disadvantage or lack of income. Britain has been considered to have fundamental, but uncodified rights. These include fair and open government, ready access to justice, as well as expectations about a home, an adequate income, a full education and employment. However, as there is a shift away from the concept of the State as a provider, and more towards the private sector making provision on a market basis, there arises an alteration in the balance of social power. The Public Law Project is seen by radical lawyers as essential in being able to offer a range of legal skills to the disadvantaged. This pays particular attention to the body of law which has attempted to redress abuse of power by central and local government, and other organisations. The Public Law Project would undertake specialist legal work in relation to public and administrative law, including legislation and public policy. The aim would be to provide specialist research, advice and information, to agencies on the 'front line' and to provide legal services to the disadvantaged in public law issues.

In some ways this move is paralleled by the development of Charter 88, set up in November 1988 on the anniversary of the revolution of 1688. It aims at bringing about a Bill of Rights, a fair electoral system, proper devolution and a written constitution that ensures government is subject to the rule of law. This was a response to a widespread belief that the concept of an unwritten constitution could mean the erosion of civil liberties. Scotland is governed like a province, Northern Ireland is a colony and the Government has eroded such traditional civil liberties, such as habeas corpus, peaceful assembly, the freedom of information and expression, trade-union member-ship, freedom of movement and freedom of local government. An important ideological feature here is that the erosion of freedom in each of these areas is seen as an individual issue, systematically lessening the sum of these curtailments of freedom. The issue central to the analysis of Charter 88 is that:

> Being unwritten, the constitution also encourages a piecemeal approach to politics; an approach that gives little protection against a determined, authoritarian state.

The Charter considers that civil rights, because of their unformulated nature, are conditional upon the goodwill of the Government and the compassion of bureaucracy. It calls for a new constitutional settlement which enshrines civil rights in a Bill of Rights, and places the executive under the power of a democratically renewed Parliament, and all State agencies under the rule of law. It wants the independence of a reformed judiciary, and the provision of legal remedies for all abuse of power by the state and its officials. Given the move towards a common European community with common citizenship and agreed rights, this is a well-selected moment to press for this radical reform.

This suggestion was, not surprisingly, refused by Mrs Thatcher, who, despite the fact that her Government used the guillotine in Parliament to ensure a jury can no longer have a say in the public interest, as they had in the trial of Clive Ponting, declared in a written reply to Baroness Ewart Biggs, that:

> The government consider that our present constitutional arrangements continue to serve us well and that the citizen of this country enjoys the greatest degree of liberty that is compatible with the rights of others and the vital interests of the State.... Some of the most oppressive states in the world have written constitutions.

However, whether Mrs Thatcher meant by 'us', the British, the Government, or whether she was using again the royal 'we', is not clear. What is clear is that current constitutional arrangements do suit an authoritarian government well. Such a state can manipulate ideologically and legally the vagaries and anomalies of an unwritten constitution. The Charter has considerable social democratic support (as Ken Livingstone pointed out, *Tribune*, 13.1.89), but this is mainly directed at its hint of a Lib–Lab alliance.

The British constitution, by being unwritten, lacks fundamental protection for its citizens. For example, it lacks a law such as the American Fifth Amendment, which protects a defendant being compelled to 'be a witness against himself'. That means that the British Government could, as it did in September 1988, simply decree that the courts can take a negative view of any defendant who chooses not to co-operate with the police, or take the stand in his or her own defence, as in the changes in the right to silence rules. There is no Sixth Amendment guaranteeing the right to 'a speedy and public trial, by an impartial jury', which would have prevented the trials without jury which have existed in Northern Ireland since the 1970s.

When considering the right to silence it is salutary to examine the case of Clintom McCurbin who, in October 1988, died while being arrested in a Next clothes shop on a case of alleged credit card fraud. McCurbin died of asphyxiation from pressure applied to the neck, but the police who arrested him said that they thought he was faking as he struggled for life. The coroner's jury brought in death by misadventure, on advice by the coroner. Detective Chief Superintendent Cole, the final witness at the inquest, said he was unable to interview the two arresting constables, as they had been advised by their solicitors not to answer questions. In contrast, when, in the same month, three terrorists were charged with conspiracy to murder Tom King, former Secretary for Northern Ireland, armed not with weapons but with a magazine article on sniping, it was announced in mid-trial that significant changes were to be made to a suspect's right to silence.

All three were sentenced to 25 years, although Martina Shanahan had served 200 days virtually of solitary confinement at Risley whilst on remand and was said to be losing her mind by the time the trial began. Subsequently, the three were to be released on the grounds that the statements of King and others had prejudiced their case. Interestingly, *The Times* reported at the time that not enough professional people served on juries, and that manual workers and the unemployed did not 'represent a cross section of society' made up by juries. Letters followed from various retired judges and lawyers agreeing that juries performed better when they were 'middle aged, middle class and male'.

Whilst the Charter can be regarded with suspicion because of its association with political pacts, and therefore a drift to centrist politics, it does nevertheless raise important issues about legislative reform. It could stop the erosion of rights catalogued throughout this book, and for this reason such a document needs to be considered seriously by the socialist opposition in Britain, and not written off as mere attempts at electoral reform when instead it should be developing a radical heart along democratic socialist lines.

What is illustrated by these attempts to introduce a written constitution – an unlikely event in modern times – is that there is considerable concern over the ambiguities and lack of clear codification in an unwritten constitution. A determined and authoritarian State can prepare ideologically the ground for repressive legislation by constructing certain forms of criminal personality and behaviour as necessarily outside of reason, and outside of ordinary law. We have seen that this can be used to monitor communities seen as rebellious and 'un-British', be they black or Irish, non-familial groups such as gay communities, militant trade unionists, alleged terrorists, the poor, single parents and the unemployed. Once defined as unrespectable or dangerous, they are subject to legal prosecution, often by semi-legal and dubious methods. The danger is that this form of prosecution and monitoring becomes accepted by the parties of opposition as realistic. The difficult thing is to defend those who are unpopular or anti-social defendants. This is to confuse their civil rights with their activities. Once the feeling arises that a strict law and order has to be maintained defined by the Government, deviant and oppositional groups become no longer worthy of fair trial and due procedures of justice.

One theme which has occurred throughout this book, is that law and order, and indeed Conservative criminology, has developed in response to social anxieties felt by 'respectable' elements of British society about a Britain which has difficulties in coming to terms with its position in a changing world. It is no longer possible to maintain a Little England attitude in the new European community. Contemporary Britain is a multi-ethnic, multi-racial, culturally diverse society.

It is no longer dominated by established tradition, or established religious beliefs; it has new populations with new sets of consciousness. In order to gain hegemonic support, the Conservative Government had to establish a moral position which sought to comfort those sections of the British electorate concerned about the changing political and moral climate. In its economic sphere, commercial interests needed to emphasise consumerism, which meant the developments of new leisure interests, life styles, and the liberalisation of sexuality. Even a cursory examination of television advertising styles reveals young people, usually male, depicted in styles which are not the traditional collective uniforms of the youth cultures of the 1970s, but mixed to combine street style with street creditability. The individualised young men and women in the advertisements are single, and hence available, but could be any class, even classless. Their occupation is not clear (they might even be unemployed) but they are linked by consumerism and by success. The young men struggle alone through dark urban streets, radiating glamour and style, the message is clear you are never alone with a flexible friend.

However, this necessarily locks out the unemployed, who are the dark side of this culture. Against the changing world envisaged by the consumer-oriented enterprise, there are the new poor, the new urban beggars. Consequently, there is a nostalgia for traditional values, and it is to the socially threatened lower middle class, and to the respectable working class that the Conservative Party has made a moral appeal. It has to counteract its won message of self-centred pursuit of affluence, the enterprising go-getting individual, so central to its enterprise culture, by positing the safe world of clear, responsible morality. We have seen since the early 1980s appeals to the family, attacks on the 'moaning Minnies' and 'whingers' who cannot make it, and counteractions to permissiveness. Since recessive threats to the money markets occurred in the 'big bangs' of the 1980s, the enterprise culture has shown it can remove jobs as quickly as it creates them. It is vulnerable to wider world economic forces, and stability is then to be found in respectable family life and firmly grounded morality. Pressure groups have arisen against permissiveness, single-action campaigns against abortion, homosexuality and 'loose' sexuality. Outrage has been expressed against crime, trade-union activities and public disorder, often linked with outrages concerning terrorism in popular rhetoric. The moral terrain of the right has taken a strong line with football hooliganism, under-age drinking, heroin addiction, welfare scroungers, young criminals and the unemployed and homeless youth. Even the school curriculum has been closely scrutinised in its national form. English Christianity is preferred to multi-ethnic religion and British heroes of history, not the interpretation of political events, are emphasised.

We can see that the economic aims of Thatcherism have been contradictory to its moral postures. What these moral stances have done successfully, is to define the Labour Party as progressive, which has become synonymous with irresponsibility and permissiveness. This is particularly emphasised in progressive municipal boroughs, whose opposition is written off as the insanity of the 'loony left', to the extent that the Labour Party itself seems nervous of suggesting anything socialist or progressive for fear of losing the middle ground. Traditional political concerns such as class war, or class exploitation have become muted.

Obviously the ideological appeal to Thatcherism is across a broad spectrum of social locations. Taylor (1987) has interestingly suggested that the key roles played by organisations in the law and order debate, were those with crucial authority functions within the British State. These include magistrates, police chiefs, police federation representatives and senior traditional schoolteachers. Noticeably absent from this list are senior members of social services departments.

Drawn from a more liberal tradition, they are seen as part of the permissive professions who encourage the delinquent and the feckless. They are perceived as unlikely to take an authoritarian line, yet they have remained politically uncritical of Government policy, during the attacks on their departments made by the media during the child abuse, and transnational adoption controversies. Never once have they suggested that cuts and understaffing have tragic consequences, a view put forward by their colleagues in the health professions. The groups mentioned by Taylor, he suggests, were concerned with the falling legitimacy of moral authority in Britain. It was to this group that the moral and cultural rhetoric of the right was addressed. This rhetoric was offered to make sense of a changing society, which by the mid-1980s resulted from Conservative economic policy. Its appeal was, however, beyond this group, but it offered the prioritisation of authority, patriotism and family values. Obviously this contained its own contradictions; the patriotism of the football hooligan had to be tempered by the authority of the law. The central theme of Conservative morality and order was that of public order. The streets and public spaces had to be seen to be safe, from both criminals and demonstrators. Traditional values had to be re-established, and it is this which may be the heritage of Conservative law and order.

While we have charted the moves away from the more strident outpourings of the 1979 campaign, within the Conservatives' law and order strategy over the last decade, it should not be assumed that they will not revert to this rhetoric if the need arises. Lagging in the opinion-poll ratings in the early months of 1990 they seized upon the Anti-Poll Tax campaign as a means of once more attacking the Labour Party. After the demonstration against the Poll Tax on 30 March 1990, the Home Secretary accused Labour MPs of exhorting people to break the law. In the House of Commons he responded to Tony Benn's comment that 'despair and a sense of social injustice have often lain at the roots of civil disturbance', by suggesting that Mr Benn was selective about which laws people ought to obey and went on to provide another explanation:

> I think one can identify quite easily the cause of this violence: sheer wickedness.

> (*Guardian* 4.4.90)

However, this attempt to once more equate opposition to their policies with criminality, and hence deflect attention from the real issues, was thwarted somewhat by the Strangeways riot the next day.

CONCLUSION

In this book we have tried to indicate the ways in which a law and order policy informed by a conservative criminology emerged before and since Mrs Thatcher came to power in Britain in 1979. In order to pursue its economic policies, the Conservatives had to construct an ideological climate which justified its unpicking of the Welfare State. This it did by demanding a return to the family and Victorian values. Yet it replaced the philanthropic and rehabilitative ideas the Victorians had towards the 'dangerous classes' with the notion of evil individuals. Conservative criminology is part of the ideological background of economic liberalism. A moral climate has been created in which collective responsibility has become unfashionable. Instead, we have the enterprise society where profit at any cost has become the holy grail. Ironically, with its determined attempt to restructure the British economy at the expense of the working class, and by taking such a hard line on scroungers and loungers, the Conservative Government has created the very social conditions which have led to the intensification of the very crime wave it was elected to end. To retain its hegemonic dominance it criminalised the inner city uprisings of disenchanted youth, marginalised the youth of the black communities and removed trade-union struggles from the field of civil law to the arena of public disorder. When expedient justification for a more centralised and militaristic policing was required British citizens were presented with the spectre of Northern Ireland, the colony over the water, its 'special case' justifying its separate code of judicial practice. Under Conservative rule civil liberty became seriously eroded. Any support, whether financial or political for those outside the enterprise culture – the poor, the homeless, the unemployed – has been written off as the unrealistic and dangerous machinations of the 'loony left'.

We have seen the ways in which a law and order policy, informed by a Conservative criminology, constructs oppositional subjects to the State against which it then acts. The ideological and political levels are closely related to the economic. Ultimately, the legal system in this form of social structure defends the economic planning of the State. Market forces remain free because of public imagery about the feckless, the idle and the deviant. The great danger is that this will not be reconstructed when there is a change from an authoritarian State to one more committed to socialism or social democracy. Having lost the ideological battle for being the party of law and order, will the next Labour Government want to show that it, too, can take a firm line over public order, fraud, social monitoring and industrial militancy.

The aims of the Conservative discourse, we have argued, have been to develop a law and order society. This was the only area in which a strong State was encouraged. Taking as its bench mark the fears and anxieties of the lower middle classes, discipline and thrift were encouraged, safe streets promised and firm action taken against militants, trade unionists, terrorists and other folk devils. As we have seen, this approach became less dominant in the second half of the 1980s, although it is still there as a card to be played should political problems necessitate it. We need look no further than the police handling of the Poll Tax demonstrators in March 1990 and the subsequent attempt by the then Home Secretary to turn this into an issue of law and order. This occurred at a time when the Government support in the opinion polls was at one of its lowest ebbs and seemed a desperate attempt to create an atmosphere in which opposition to the Poll Tax became synonymous with criminality. Nevertheless by the mid–1980s there was a move away from the idea that the strong State and its criminal justice institutions could stop crime to an emphasis on the need to involve the active citizen. The iron hand of the Conservative administration's first 5 years gave way to sermons on personal responsibility. This served two purposes. Firstly, it allowed the Government a potential escape route from the escalating costs of its apparently futile tough tactics. Secondly, it allowed them to make virtue out of a necessity by pushing law and order once more ideologically centre-stage as another area where the individual could do more than the State. Crime prevention has becomes the responsibility of the private citizen. This has taken either a commercial form, for example, the encouragement of better security for private housing, or a voluntary form, such as neighbourhood-watch schemes. The basis of morality and law-abiding behaviour has become the family and it follows that parents must be made responsible for their children's misdemeanors. A major sub-theme is privatisation, seen in the plans to put electronic surveillance out to tender, and the running of certain penal institutions such as bail hostels by private firms. After the Strangeways disturbances the problem of prison overcrowding became more immediate and the need to encourage more use of community-based punishments more urgent.

The tensions between toughness and value for money persisted, however, and against a background of large increases in the crime figures, David

Waddington faced, in October 1990, the annual ordeal for Home Secretaries of addressing the Conservative Party Conference. He received a standing ovation for his comments on retribution from violent offenders, on his personal belief in the deterrent effect of capital punishment and for his promise that 'life imprisonment in the worst cases will mean life'. Changes in the parole system were promised so that serious offenders would serve a longer proportion of their time in jail. He also announced in the same speech the Government's first considered response to Strangeways; they would introduce a new offence of prison mutiny with a maximum penalty of 10 years. He commented on the riot:

> It was a disgraceful affair and over the past few years there have been far too many riots in our prisons. We have all had enough.

(The Times 11.10.90)

His speech was redolent with phrases designed to warm the hearts of the rank and file. He pledged to 'sweep the drunken louts off the streets'. He announced that courts would be given powers to bind parents over for the good behaviour of their children so that they could be 'brought face to face with their neglect'. In line with the wide-spread Conservative emphasis on family virtues the central message of the speech was that the starting point of the fight against crime was the family. The importance of punishment in the community was restated but in such a way that electronic tagging was seen as a tough option. The Home Secretary was not about to be seen as going soft on the petty criminal. No word was given, however, on how the Government's social policies had worsened the plight of the poorest families already suffering under the economic consequences of Conservative rule. No discussion was initiated on how the climate of rampant economic individualism might have coloured the moral climate of society. No considered view was offered on the underlying problems of prison conditions that had triggered the riots. The speech underlined the fact that the self-proclaimed party of law and order, despite 11 years of holding the reins of power and massive investment in the criminal justice system had no long-term solutions to the problems.

Bibliography

Amnesty International (1977) *Report of Allegations of Ill Treatment in Northern Ireland*, London: Amnesty International.

Atkins, F. (1986) 'Thatcherism, populist authoritarianism and the search for a new left political stategy', *Capital and Class*, 28, 25–48.

Asmal, K. (1985) *Shoot to Kill: International Lawyers' Inquiry into the Lethal Use of Firearms by the Security Forces in Northern Ireland*, Dublin: Mercier Press.

Audit Commission (1989) *The Probation Service – Promoting Value for Money*.

Barrass v Reeve (1980) 3 All ER 705.

Bennett, T. (1987) *An Evaluation of Two Neighbourhood Watch Schemes in London*, Report to the Home Office, Cambridge: Institute of Criminology.

—— (1988) 'An assessment of the design, implementation and effectiveness of neighbourhood watch in London', *Howard Journal of Criminal Justice*, 27, 241–255.

—— (1989a) 'The Neighbourhood Watch Experiment', in R. Morgan and D.J. Smith (eds) *Coming to Terms with Policing: Perspectives on Policy*, London: Routledge, Chapter 8.

—— (1989b) 'Factors related to participation in neighbourhood watch schemes,' *British Journal of Criminology*, 10, 207–218.

Bottoms, A.E. (1983) 'Neglected features of contemporary penal systems', in D. Garland and P. Young (eds) *The Power to Punish*, London: Heinemann.

—— (1987) 'Limiting prison use: experience in England and Wales', *The Howard Journal*, 26, 177–202.

Bowden, T. (1978) *Beyond the Limits of the Law*, Harmondsworth: Penguin.

Box, S. (1987) *Recession, Crime and Punishment*, Macmillan: London.

Box, S. and Hale, C. (1982) 'Economic crisis and the rising prisoner population', *Crime and Social Justice*, 17, 20 –35.

—— (1984) 'Liberation/emancipation, economic marginalisation, or less chivalry', *Criminology*, 22, 473–97.

—— (1985) 'Unemployment, imprisonment and prison overcrowding', *Contemporary Crisis*, 9, 209–228.

—— (1986) 'Unemployment, crime and imprisonment and the enduring problem of prison overcrowding', in R. Matthews and J. Young (eds) *Confronting Crime*, London: Sage, Chapter 4.

Box, S., Hale, C. and Andrews, G. (1988) 'Explaining fear of crime', *British Journal of Criminology*, 28, 340–356.

Boyson, R. (1983) *Down with the Poor*, London: Britannia.

Braithwaite, J. (1980) 'The political economy of punishment', in E.L. Wheelwright and K. Buckley (eds) *Essays in the Political Economy of Australian Capitalism*, Sydney: ANZ Books.

—— (1982) 'Challenging just deserts: punishing white-collar criminals', *Journal of Criminal Law and Criminology*, 723–763.

—— (1987) 'The mesomorphs strike back', *Australian and New Zealand Journal of Criminology*, 20, 45–53.

Brake, M. and Hale, C. (1989) 'Law and order', in R. Sparks and P. Brown, (eds) *Beyond Thatcherism*, Milton Keynes: Open University Press, Chapter 10.

Brockington, N. and Shaw, M. (1986) 'Tracking the trackers', *Home Office Research Bulletin*, 27, 37–40.

Brogden, M. (1983) *The Police, Autonomy and Consent*, London: Academic Press.

Bunyan, T. (1977) *The Political Police in Britain*, London: Quartet.

Burrows, J. and Tarling, R. (1987) 'The investigation of crime in England and Wales', *British Journal of Criminology*, 27, 229–251.

Cain, M. and Sadigh, S. (1982) 'Racism, the police and community policing', *Journal of Law and Society*, 9, 87–102.

Campbell, D. (1989) 'Carrying on spying or dying', *New Statesman and Society*, 20 October 1989.

Carr-Hill, R.A. and Stern, N.H. (1979) *Crime, the Police and Criminal Statistics*, New York: Academic Press.

Cavadino, P. (1985) 'Clearer law', *Community Care*, November.

CIPFA (1990) *Police Statistics 1988–89 Actuals*, London: The Chartered Institute of Public Finance and Accountancy.

Clarke, A. and Taylor, I. (1980) 'Vandals, pickets and muggers: television coverage of law and order in the 1979 Election', *Screen Education*, 38, 99–111.

Clarke, A., Taylor, I. and Wren-Lewis, J. (1982) 'Inequality of access to political television: the case of the General Election of 1979', in D. Robbins *et al.* (eds) *Rethinking Social Inequality*, London: Gower.

Clarke, R. and Hough, M. (1980) *The Effectiveness of Policing*, Farnborough: Gower.

—— (1984) *Crime and Police Effectiveness*, London: Home Office Research and Planning Unit.

Coleman, D. (1989) *Review of Probation Training*, London: Home Office.

Compton Committee (1971) *Report of the Enquiry into Allegations against the Security Forces of Physical Brutality in Northern Ireland Arising out of Events on 9 August 1979*, Cmnd 4283, London: HMSO.

Conservative Party (1979) *Conservative Party Manifesto*, London: Conservative Central Office.

—— (1987) *Conservative Party Manifesto*, London: Conservative Central Office.

Cook, D. (1989) *Rich Law, Poor Law*, Milton Keynes: Open University Press.

Coulter, J., Miller, S. and Walker, M. (1985) *A State of Siege*, London: Canary Press.

Council of Europe (1989) *Prison Information Bulletin*, Strasbourg: Council of Europe.

Cowell, D., Edwards, S. and Lees, R. (1986) *The Police Response to Domestic Violence in London*, Polytechnic of Central London.

Crawford, A., Jones, T., Woodhouse, T. and Young, J. (1990) *The Second Islington Crime Survey*, London: Centre for Criminology, Middlesex Polytechnic.

Cressey, D.R. (1982) 'Criminology in the 1980s', *Criminal News*, Newsletter of the Criminology Section, American Sociological Association.

Criminal Statistics England and Wales 1988, Cm 847, London: HMSO.

Currie, E. (1985) *Confronting Crime: An American Challenge*, New York: Pantheon Books.

Dale, D. (1984) 'The politics of crime', *Salisbury Review*, 17–19.

Dahrendorf, R. (1986) *Law and Order*, London: Stevens.

Davies, M. (1989) *The Nature of Probation Today*, London: Home Office.

Department of Trade and Industry (1990) *Inspectors' Report in the Minutes of WDM Underwriting*, London: DTI.

Downes, D. (1982) 'The origins and consequences of Dutch penal policy since 1945: a preliminary analysis', *British Journal of Criminology*, 22, 325–357.

—— (1983) *Law and Order: Theft of an Issue*, Fabian Tract 490, London: Fabian Society.

Downes, D. and Young, J. (1987) 'Crime and government', *New Society*, May 21.

Dworkin, R. (1985) *A Matter of Principle*, Cambridge: Harvard University Press.

Ely, P. (1985) 'Delinquency and Disillusion', in N. Manning (ed.) *Social Problems and Welfare Ideology*, Aldershot: Gower, Chapter 5.

Ely, P., Swift, A. and Sutherland, A. (1987) *The Medway Close Support Unit*, Edinburgh: Scottish Academic Press.

Farrell, M. (1983) *Arming the Protestants*, London: Pluto.

Farrington, D.P. and Dowds, E.A. (1985) 'Disentangling criminal behaviour and police reaction', in P.D. Farrington and J. Gunn (eds) *Reactions to Crime, the Public, the Police, Court and Prisons*, Chichester: John Wiley.

Farrington, D.P., Gallagher, B., Morley, L., St. Ledger, R.J. and West, D.J. (1986) 'Unemployment, school leaving and crime', *British Journal of Criminology*, 26, 335–356.

Field, F. (1989) *Losing Out: the Emergence of Britain's Underclass*, Oxford: Basil Blackwell.

Field, S. (1990) 'Trends in crime and their interpretation: a study of recorded crime in post-war England and Wales', *Home Office Research Study No.119*, London: HMSO.

Fiori, A. (1970) *Antonio Gramsci*, London: New Left Books.

Fitzgerald, M. and Sim, J. (1982) *British Prisons*, Oxford: Basil Blackwell.

Fludger, N. (1981) *Ethnic Minorities in Borstal*, London: Prison Department, Home Office.

Gamble, A. (1983) 'The 1982 Budget', *Capital and Class*, 17, 5–16.

Giddens, A. (1973) *The Class Structure of Advanced Societies*, London: Hutchinson.

Gifford (1986) *The Broadwater Farm Enquiry*, London: Borough of Haringey.

Gill, P. (1987) 'Clearing up crime: the big con', *Journal of Law and Society*, 14, 254–265.

Gilroy, P. (1987) 'The myth of black criminality' in P. Scraton (ed.) *Law Order and the Authoritarian State*, Milton Keynes: Open University Press, chapter 3.

Gilroy, P. and Sim, J. (1985) 'Law, order and the state of the Left', *Capital and Class*, 25, 15–51.

Gordon, P. (1983) *White Law*, London: Pluto Press.

—— (1984) 'Community policing: towards the local police state', *Critical Social Policy*, 10, 39–58.

Gough, I. 'Thatcher and the Welfare State', in S. Hall and M. Jaques (eds) *The Politics of Thatcherism*, London: Lawrence & Wishart, pp. 148–168.

Graef, R. (1990) 'What's gone wrong with the police?' *Independent on Sunday* 18 March.

Grahl, J. (1983) 'Restructuring in Western European industry', *Capital and Class*, 19, 118–142.

Gramsci, A. (1978) *Selections from the Prison Notebooks 1921–26*, translated and edited by Q. Hoare and G. Nowell-Smith, London: Lawrence & Wishart.

Green, C., Haseler, J., Hester, R. and Turnbull, A. (1987) *The North London Custody Study*.

Hakim, C. (1982) 'The social consequences of high unemployment', *Journal of Social Policy*, 11, 433–67.

Hale, C. (1989a) 'Unemployment, imprisonment and the stability of punishment hypothesis: some results using cointegration and error correction models', *Journal of Quantitative Criminology*, 169–186.

—— (1989b) 'Economy, punishment and imprisonment', *Contemporary Crises*, 13, 327–349.

Hall, R. (1985) *Ask Any Woman*, Bristol: Falling Wall Press.

Hall, S. (1979) *Drifting Into a Law and Order Society*, London: Cobden Trust.

—— (1982) *The Scarman Report*, Critical Social Policy, 2, 66–72.

—— (1985) 'Authoritarian populism', *New Left Review*, 151, 115–124.

—— (1988) 'The hard road to renewal: Thatcherism and the crisis of the left', *Marxism Today*, pp. 20–30, March.

Hall, S., Critcher, C., Jefferson, T., Clark, J. and Roberts, B. (1978) *Policing the Crisis: Mugging, the State and Law and Order*, London: Macmillan.

Harman, H. and Griffith, J. (1979) *Justice Deserted: the Subversion of the Jury*, London: National Council of Civil Liberties.

Hayek, F. von (1982) *Law, Legislation and Liberty*, London: Routledge & Kegan Paul.

Hillyard, P. (1987) 'The normalisation of special powers; from Northern Ireland to Britain', in P. Scraton (1987) (ed.) *Law, Order and the Authoritarian State*, Milton Keynes: Open University Press.

Hirshi, T. (1983) 'Crime and family policy', *Journal of Contemporary Studies*, 6, 10–13.

Hirst, J. (1988) 'The power of the watch', *New Statesman and Society*, 1(3), 26–27.

HMSO (1984) *Tougher Regimes in Detention Centres*, Home Office Young Offenders Psychology Unit, London: HMSO.

Holdaway, S. (1983) *Inside the British Police*, Oxford: Basil Blackwell.

Home Office (1984) *Working Paper on Criminal Justice*, London: Home Office.

—— (1986) *The Ethnic Origin of Prisoners: the Prison Population to 30 June 1985 and Persons Received July 1984-March 1985*, Home Office Statistical Bulletin, 17/86, London: Home Office.

—— (1988a) *The Prison Population in 1987*, Home Office Statistical Bulletin 8/88, London: Home Office.

—— (1988b) *Punishment, Custody and the Community*, Cm.424, London: HMSO.

—— (1988c) *Training Offenders – An Action Report*. London: Home Office Criminal Justice and Constitutional Department.

—— (1989a) *Practical Ways to Crack Crime*, London: HMSO.

—— (1989b) *Safer Cities Progress Report, 1988–1989*, London: HMSO.

—— (1989c) *The Ethnic Group of Those Proceeded Against or Sentenced by the Courts in the Metropolitan District in 1984 and 1985*, Home Office Statistical Bulletin 6/89. London: Home Office.

—— (1990a) *Crime, Justice and Protecting the Public*, Cm. 965, London: HMSO.

—— (1990b) *Supervision and Punishment in the Community: A Framework for Action*, Cm. 966, London: HMSO.

—— (1990c) *Projections of the Long Term Trends in the Prison Population to 1998*, Home Office Statistical Bulletin 13/90. London: Home Office.

Hope, T. (1988) 'Support for neighbourhood watch: a British crime survey analysis', in T. Hope and M. Shaw (eds) *Communities and Crime Reduction*, London: HMSO, Chapter 9.

Hope, T. and Shaw M. (1988) 'Community approaches to reducing crime', in T. Hope and M. Shaw (eds) *Communities and Crime Reduction*, London: HMSO, Chapter 1.

Hough, M. and Mayhew, P. (1983) 'The British crime survey: first report', *Home Office Research Study No.76*, London: HMSO.

Hough, M. and Mayhew, P. (1985) 'Taking account of crime: findings from the second British crime survey', *Home Office Research Study No.85*, London: HMSO.

Hudson, B. (1984) 'The rising use of imprisonment: the impact of "Decarceration" policies', *Critical Social Policy*, 11, 46–59.

—— (1987) *Justice through Punishment: a Critique of the 'Justice' Model of Corrections*, London: Macmillan.

Hunt, A. (1976) 'Law, state and class struggle', *Marxism Today*, 20(6).

Hymans, R. (1987) 'Trade unions and the law: papering over the cracks?', *Capital and Class*, 31, 93–114.

Inverarity, J. and Grattet, R. (1987) 'Institutional responses to unemployment: a comparative analysis of US trends, 1948–1984', Paper presented to the 39th Annual Meeting of the American Criminological Society, Montreal, November.

Inverarity, J. and McCarthy, J. (1988) 'Punishment and social structure revisited: unemployment and imprisonment in the US 1948–1984', *Sociological Quarterly*, 29, 263–279.

Jankovic, I. (1977) 'Labour market and imprisonment', *Crime and Social Justice*, 9, 17–31.

Jennings, A. (1989) *Justice Under Fire – The Abuse of Civil Liberties in Northern Ireland*, London: Unwin Hyman.

Johnston, P. (1982) 'Family re-union', *Observer*, 10 October.

Jones, T., MacLean, B.D. and Young, J. (1986) *The Islington Crime Survey*, London: Gower.

Junger-Tass, J. and Blok, R. (1984) *Juvenile Delinquency in the Netherlands*, Amsterdam: Amstelveent Kinglee.

Keith Report (1983) *Report of the Committee on Enforcement Powers of the Revenue Departments*, Cmd 8822; London: HMSO.

Kettle, M. (1980) 'The politics of the police and the policing of politics', in P. Hain (ed.) *Policing the Police 2*, London: Calder.

—— (1982) 'The police and the left', *New Society*, 70, 366–7.

—— (1983) 'The drift to law and order', in Hall, S. and Jacques, M. *The Politics of Thatcherism*, London: Lawrence and Wishart.

King, M. (1987) 'Crime prevention in France', *Home Office Research Bulletin No. 24*, London: HMSO.

—— (1989) 'Social crime prevention à la Thatcher', *The Howard Journal of Criminal Justice*, 28, 291–312.

Kinsey, R., (1985) *Merseyside Crime and Police Surveys: Final Report*, Merseyside: County Council.

Kinsey, R., Lea, J. and Young, J. (1986) *Losing the Fight Against Crime*, Oxford: Basil Blackwell.

Kolenzo, E. (1984) 'Police in schools', *Challenging Racism*, London Teachers Against Racism.

Labour Research (1986), 75 (7) London: Labour Research Department.

―― (1987a) 76 (5) London: Labour Research Department.

―― (1987b) 76 (11) London: Labour Research Department.

―― (1988a) 77 (6) London: Labour Research Department.

―― (1988b) 77 (8) London: Labour Research Department.

Laffargue, B. and Godefroy, T. (1987) 'Economic cycles and punishment: unemployment and imprisonment', Paper presented to the 39th Annual Meeting of the American Criminological Society, Montreal, November.

Landau, H. (1981) 'Juveniles and the police', *British Journal of Criminology*, 21, 143–72.

Landau, H. and Nathan, G. (1983) 'Discrimination in the Criminal Justice System', *British Journal of Criminology*, 23, 128–49.

Laycock, G. and Heal, K. (1989) 'Crime prevention: the British experience', in D.J. Evans and D.T. Shaw (eds) *The Geography of Crime*, London: Routledge, Chapter 15.

Lewis, H. and Mo, J. (1986) *Burglary Insurance: Findings from the British Crime Survey*, Research Bulletin No. 22. London: Home Office Research and Planning Unit.

Lea, J. (1986), 'Police racism: some theories and their policy implications', in R. Matthews and J. Young (eds) *Confronting Crime*, London: Sage, Chapter 7.

Lea, J. and Young, J. (1984) *What is to be Done about Law and Order?*, Harmondsworth: Penguin.

Levi, M. (1987) *Regulating Fraud*, London: Tavistock.

―― (1989) 'Policing developments in the 80s', in M. Brenton and C. Ungerson *Social Policy Review*, London: Longman.

―― (1986) 'The incidence, reporting and prevention of commercial fraud', unpublished monograph prepared for the Home Office Crime Prevention Unit.

Liddelow, P. (1990) 'Are crime rates increasing? A study of the impact of demographic shifts on crime rates in England and Wales, 1974–1987', University of Kent BA Dissertation.

London Strategic Policy Unit (1986) 'Police response to domestic violence', *Police Monitoring and Research Unit Briefing Paper 1*, London: London Strategic Policy Unit.

―― (1988) 'Policing Wapping' *Police Monitoring and Research Unit Briefing Paper*, London: London Strategic Policy Unit.

Loveday, B. (1986) 'Central co-ordination: police authorities and the miners' strike', *Political Quarterly*, 57.

McDonnell, K. (1978) 'Ideology, crisis and the cuts', *Capital and Class*, 4, 34–70.

McEwan, P. (1980) 'Tax evasion; is it treated too leniently?' *The Conveyancer*, p.114.

McGuffin, J. (1973) *Internment*, Kerry: Anvil Press.

Mark, R. (1977) *Policing a Perplexed Society*, London: Allen & Unwin.

―― (1978) *In the Office of Constable*, London: Collins.

―― (1979) *Security Gazette*, May.

Matthews, R. (1987) 'Taking realist criminology seriously', *Contemporary Crises*, 11, 371–401.

Mayhew, P., Elliott, D. and Dowds, L. (1989) *The 1988 British Crime Survey*, Home Office Research Study no. 111. London: HMSO.

Maxfield, M. (1987) *Explaining Fear of Crime: Evidence from the 1984 British Crime Survey*, Reseach and Planning Unit Paper 43, London: Home Office.

Maynard, G. (1988) *The Economy under Mrs Thatcher*, Oxford: Basil Blackwell.

Melossi, D. (1985) 'Punishment and social action: changing vocabularies of punitive motive within a political business cycle', *Current Perspectives in Social Theory*,6, 169–197.

Menter, I. (1988) 'The long arm of education: a review of recent documents on police/school liaison', *Critical Social Policy*, 21, 68–77.

Metropolitan Police (1983) *Police Order 24: Crime Prevention – Neighbourhood Watch and Property Marking Schemes*, London: Metropolitan Police.

Metropolitan Police Commissioner (1984) *Annual Report of the Metropolitan Police Commissioner*, Cmnd 9541, London: HMSO.

Montgomery, R. (1985) 'Time series analysis of imprisonment in the context of the conflict–consensus debate on social control', *Criminometrica*, 1, 49–73.

Morgan, P. (1978) *Delinquent Fantasies*, London: Temple Smith.

Morris, P. and Heal, K. (1981) *Crime Control and the Police*, London: Home Office Research Unit.

Murray, C. (1984) *Losing Ground, American Social Policy – 1950–8*, New York: Basic Books, Chapter 6.

NACRO Briefing (1989a) *Some Facts and Findings about Black People in the Criminal Justice System* (77) May, London: National Association for the Care and Resettlement of Offenders.

—— (1989b) *The Cost of Penal Measures* (23) July, London: National Association for the Care and Resettlement of Offenders.

—— (1989c) *The Prison Population in 1988* (29) September, London: National Association for the Care and Resettlement of Offenders.

—— (1990a) *Imprisonment in Western Europe: Some Facts and Figures* (25) January, London: National Association for the Care and Resettlement of Offenders.

—— (1990b) *Prison Overcrowding: Some Facts and Figures* (28) June, London: National Association for the Care and Resettlement of Offenders.

Newman, K. (1983) *Policing London: Post Scarman*, The 1983 Sir George Bean Memorial Lecture.

Northam, G. (1988) *Shooting in the Dark: Riot Police In Britain*, London: Faber & Faber.

O'Brien, R. (1987) 'The interracial nature of violent crimes, a re-examination', *American Journal Of Sociology*, 92, 817–35.

Policing London (1984) *Miners' Strike*. London: Strategic Police Monitoring and Research Group, Chapter 4.

Pearce, F. (1976) *Crimes of the Powerful*, London: Pluto Press.

Pearson, G. (1983) *Hooligan: a History of Respectable Fears*, London: Macmillan.

Politics Today, (1988) No.2. London: Conservative Party Research Department.

Pratt, J. (1980) *Mugging as a Social Problem*, London: Routledge.

—— (1985) 'Delinquency as a scarce resource', *The Howard Journal*, 24, 19–37.

Prison Statistics, England and Wales 1988, Cm 825; London: HMSO.

Probation Statistics, England and Wales 1987, London: Home Office.

Pitts, J. (1986) 'Black young people and crime: some unanswered questions', in R. Matthews and J. Young (eds) *Confronting Crime*, London: Sage, Chapter 6.

—— (1988) *The Politics of Juvenile Crime*, London: Sage.

Pyle, D.J. (1982) 'Property crime in England and Wales', University of Leicester Economics Department.

—— (1987) 'The fight against crime', *Social Studies Review*,2. 17–21.

—— (1989) 'The economics of crime in Britain', *Economic Affairs*, 6–9.

Quinney, R. (1977) *State, Class and Crime*, New York: McKay.

Reiner, R. (1985) *The Politics of the Police*, Brighton: Wheatsheaf.

—— (1987) 'Four books on crime', *Critical Social Policy*, 20, 103–106.

—— (1989) 'Where the buck stops: Chief Constables' views on police accountability', in R. Morgan and D.J. Smith (eds) *Coming to Terms with Policing: Perspectives on Policy*, London: Routledge, Chapter 11.

Rex J. and Tomlinson S. (1979) *Colonial Immigrants in a British City*, London: Routledge & Kegan Paul.

Rosenbaum, D.P. (1988) 'A critical eye on neighbourhood watch; does it reduce crime and fear?' in T. Hope and M. Shaw (eds) *Communities and Crime Reduction*, London: HMSO, Chapter 8.

Ross, S. (1984) 'The sacred cow of IT', *Community Care*, pp. 25–27, 16 February.

Royal Commission (1962) *Report of the Royal Commission on the Police*, Cmnd 1728, London: HMSO.

—— (1981) *Report of the Royal Commission on Criminal Procedure*, Cmnd 8092, London: HMSO.

Rusche, G. and Kirchheimer, O. (1939) *Punishment and Social Structure*, New York: Russell & Russell.

Rutter, M. (1978) 'Family, area and school influences in the genesis of conduct disorders', in L.A. Hersov and M. Berger (eds) *Aggression and Anti-Social Behaviour in Childhood and Adolescence*, Oxford: Pergamon Press.

Sampson, R.J. and Wooldredge, J.D. (1987) 'Linking the micro and macro levels of lifestyle – routine activity and opportunity models of predatory victimization', *Journal of Quantitative Criminology*, 3, 371–393.

Scarman, Lord (1982) *The Scarman Report: the Brixton Disorder 10–12 April 1981*, London: Penguin.

Scraton, P. (1985) *The State of the Police*, London: Pluto Press.

Scraton, P. and Chadwick, K. (1987), in P. Scraton (ed.) *Law Order and the Authoritarian State*, Milton Keynes, Open University Press, Chapter 7.

Scruton, R. (1984) *The Meaning of Conservatism*, London: Macmillan.

Shaw, C.R. and McKay, H.D. (1942) *Juvenile Delinquency and Urban Areas*, Chicago: University of Chicago Press.

Sim, J., Scraton, P. and Gordon, P. 'Introduction: crime, the State and critical analysis', in P. Scraton (ed.) *Law, Order and the Authoritarian State*, Milton Keynes: Open University Press.

Shaw, S. (1987) 'Whatever happened to the short sharp shock?', *The Guardian*, 2 September.

Sivanandan, A, (1982) *A Different Hunger*, London: Pluto Press.

Smith, D. (1984) 'Law and order, arguments for what?', *Critical Social Policy*, 11.

Smith, D. and Gray, J. (1983) *Police and People in London* Vol.IV, London: Policy Studies Institute.

Smith, L.J.F. (1989) 'Domestic violence: an overview of the literature', *Home Office Research Study No.107*, London: HMSO.

Stalker, J. (1988) *Stalker*, London: Harrap.

Steffensmeier, D. and Harer, M. (1987) 'Is the crime rate really falling? An "Aging"

US population and its impact on the nations' crime rate', *Journal of Research in Crime and Delinquency*, 24, 24–48.

Stevens, P. and Willis, C.F. (1979) 'Race, crime and arrests', *Home Office Research Study No.58*, London: HMSO.

Sumner, C. (1979) *Reading Ideologies: an Investigation into the Marxist Theory of Ideology and Law*, London: Academic Press.

Taylor, I. (1981) *Law and Order, Arguments for Socialism*, London: Macmillan.

—— (1982) 'Against crime and for socialism', *Crime and Social Justice*, 18, 4–15.

—— (1987) 'Law and order, moral order: the changing rhetorics of the Thatcher Government', *Socialist Register 1987*, London: Merlin Press, pp.297–331.

Taylor, P. (1980) *Beating the Terrorists – Interrogation in Omagh, Gough and Castlereagh*, Harmondsworth: Penguin.

Taylor, W. (1982) 'Black youth, white man's justice', *Youth and Society*, November.

Tipler, J. (1986) *Juvenile Justice in Hackney*, London: Research, Development and Programming section, Hackney Social Services Directorate.

Thompson, J. (1981) *et al, Employment and Crime: a Review of Theories and Research*, Washington DC: National Institute of Justice.

Tuck, M. and Southgate, P. (1981) 'Ethnic minorities, crime and policing: a survey of the experience of West Indians and whites' *Home Office Research Study No.70*, London: HMSO.

Turner, B.M.W. and Barker, P.J. (1983) *Study Tour of the USA: 7th–21st March 1983*, 2 vols, London: Metropolitan Police.

Uglow, S. (1988a) *Policing Liberal Society*, Oxford: Oxford University Press.

—— (1988b) 'The welfare defendant in the criminal process', University of Keele, Dept. of Criminology.

Unemployment Bulletin (1988), 27. London: Unemployment Unit.

Walker, H. and Beaumont, B. (1981) *Probation Work, Critical Theory and Socialist Practice*, Oxford: Basil Blackwell.

Walker, M.A. (1987) 'Note: ethnic origins of prisoners', *British Journal of Criminology*, 27, 202–206.

—— (1988) 'The court disposal of young males, by race in London in 1983', *British Journal of Criminology*, 28, 441–451.

Walklate, S. (1989) *Victimology: the Victim and the Criminal Justice Process*, London: Unwin & Hyman.

Walsh, D. (1983) *The Use and Abuse of Emergency Legislation in Northern Ireland*, London: Cobden Trust.

Whitehead, P. and MacMillan, J. (1985) 'Checks or blank cheque?' *Probation Journal*, September.

Willis, C. (1983) 'The use, effectiveness and impact of police stop and search powers', *Home Office Research and Planning Unit Papers No.15*, London: Home Office.

Wilson, J.Q. (1975) *Thinking About Crime*, New York: Basic Books.

—— (1977) 'Crime and punishment in England', in R.E. Tyrell Jr (ed.) *The Future That Doesn't Work: Social Democracy's Failures in Britain*, Garden City, NY: Doubleday.

—— (1983) *Thinking About Crime*. Revised edn, New York: Basic Books.

Wilson, J.Q. and Herrnstein, R.J. (1985) *Crime and Human Nature*, New York: Simon & Schuster.

Worrall, A. and Pease, K. (1986) 'Personal crime against women: evidence from the 1982 British Crime Survey', *The Howard Journal*, 25, 118–124.

Young, H. and Sioman, A. (1981) *The Thatcher Phenomenon*, Harmondsworth: Penguin.

Young, J. (1979) 'Left idealism, reformism and beyond: from new criminology to Marxism', in *Capitalism and the Rule of Law*, London: Hutchinson.

—— (1986) 'The failure of criminology: the need for a radical realism', in R. Matthews and J. Young (eds) *Confronting Crime*, London: Sage, Chapter 1.

—— (1987) 'The tasks facing a realist criminology', *Contemporary Crises*, 11.

—— (1988) 'Risk of crime and fear of crime: a realist critique of survey-based assumptions', in M. Maguire and J. Pointing (eds) *Victims of Crime: A New Deal?*, Milton Keynes: Open University Press, 159–83.

Younger Report (1974) *Young Adult Offenders*, London: HMSO.

Zander, M. (1983) 'The Police and Criminal Evidence Bill – Amendments', *New Law Journal*, 654–5.

Name index

Anderton, J. 55–6
Asmal, K. 63
Atkins, F. 3

Barker, P.J. 81
Barrass v Reeve 124
Beaumont, B. 72
Benn, T. 170–1
Bennett, T. 82–3
Blok, R. 71
Bottoms, A.E. 143
Bowden, T. 44
Box, S. 82, 112, 116, 121, 139–40, 147, 150–2
Boyson, R. 27
Braithwaite, J. 23, 142
Brittan, L. 72, 78, 138
Brockington, N. 74
Brogden, M. 38
Bunyan, T. 45
Burrows, J. 94, 97

Cain, M. 140
Campbell, D. 67
Carr-Hill, R.A. 112
Cavadino, P. 72
Chadwick, K. 160
Clarke, A. 2, 150
Clarke, R. 69
Coleman, D. 157
Cook, D. 122
Coulter, J. 53
Cowell, D. 104
Crawford, A. 84
Cressey, D.R. 20
Currie, E. 21

Dahrendorf, R. 30
Dale, D. 27
Davies, M. 157
Dowds, E.A. 98
Downes, D. 16, 95, 141
Dworkin, R. 36

Edwards, S. 104
Ely, P. 74

Farrell, M. 60
Farrington, D.P. 98, 112
Field, F. 159
Field, S. 114
Fiori, A. 162
Fitzgerald, M. 138
Fludger, N. 106
Friedman, M. 17

Gamble, A. 3, 6
Giddens, A. 158
Gifford, 52
Gill, P. 97
Gilroy, P. 35, 38–40, 51–2, 68, 109
Godefroy, T. 142
Gordon, P. 47, 77, 91
Gough, 7
Graef, R. 1
Grahl, J. 3
Gramsci, A. 35, 40, 162–4
Grattet, R. 142
Gray, J. 108, 110
Green, C. 109
Griffith, J. 67

Hakim, C. 112–13

Hale, C. 112, 139–41, 143, 150, 152
Hall, R. 103
Hall, S. 35–8, 40, 46–7, 78, 148, 160–1
Harer, M. 96
Harman, H. 67
Hayek, F. von 17, 36
Heal, K. 69, 80–1
Herrnstein, R.J. 22–6
Hillyard, P. 58–9, 63, 65–7
Hirshi, T. 21
Hirst, J. 83
Holdaway, S. 39
Hope, T. 69, 75–6, 78, 80, 82, 85
Hough, M. 69, 99–100, 104
Hudson, B. 146
Hurd, D. 51, 86–8, 152
Hunt, A. 163
Hymans, R. 3

Inverarity, J. 142

Jankovic, I. 141
Jennings, A. 59, 63–5
Johnston, P. 24
Jones, T. 101–4
Jones, V. 43
Junger-Tass, J. 71

Kettle, M. 35, 37, 46, 106
King, M. 84–5
Kinsey, R. 84, 100–3
Kirchheimer, O. 141
Kolenzo, E. 77

Laffargue, B. 142
Landau, H. 107–8
Laycock, G. 80–1
Lea, J. 91, 105, 110
Lees, R. 104
Levi, M. 43, 44, 117–19, 122
Lewis, H. 96
Liddelow, P. 96
Loveday, B. 54

McCarthy, J. 142
McDonnell, K. 3–4
McEwan, P. 124
McGuffin, J. 61
McKay, H.D. 80
MacMillan, J. 72

Mark, Sir Robert, and the SPG 44, 59; and trade unions 32, 56
Matthews, R. 105
Maxfield, M. 100
Mayhew, P. 82–3, 96, 99–100, 104–5
Maynard, G. 3
Melossi, D. 146, 150
Menter, I. 77
Metropolitan Police Commissioner 76
Miller, S. 53
Mo, J. 96
Montgomery, R. 142
Morgan, P. 26–7
Morris, P. 69
Murray, C. 135

Nathan, G. 108
Newman, Sir Kenneth, and multi-agency policing 75–6; on marginalisation 160; and the RUC 66
Northam, G. 66, 68

O'Brien, R. 105
Oxford, Sir Kenneth, on inner city riots 49

Patten, John, and the active citizen 78; and the correlates of crime 114; and neighbourhood watch 82
Pearce, F. 116
Pearson, G. 38
Pease, K. 104
Pitts, J. 70, 91, 106, 107
Pratt, J. 108
Pyle, D.J. 112

Quinney, R. 141

Reiner, R. 41, 45, 54, 75
Rex, J. 158–9
Rosenbaum, D.P. 83
Ross, S. 74
Rusche, G. 141
Rutter, M. 25

Sadigh, S. 140
Sampson, R.J. 112
Scarman, Lord 49–50, 113
Scraton, P. 44, 91, 160

Scruton, R. 28–30, 159
Shaw, C.R. 80
Shaw, M. 69, 75–6, 78, 80, 85
Shaw, S. 72
Sim, J. 35, 38–40, 51–2, 91, 138
Sioman, A. 49
Sivanandan, A. 110, 159
Smith, D. 39, 108, 110
Smith, D. 70
Smith, L.J.F. 104
Southgate, P. 104
Stalker, J. 64
Steffensmeier, D. 96
Stern, N.H. 112
Stevens, P. 106, 164
Sumner, C. 163

Tarling, R. 94, 97
Taylor, I. 2, 7, 27–8, 32, 46, 96, 111,
    148–9, 150, 170
Taylor, P. 62, 64
Taylor, W. 106–7
Tebbit, N., on the problems of inner
    city life 14
Thatcher, Margaret: 'barrier of steel'
    speech 2; on crime prevention
    79–80, 86, 89; equating industrial
    pickets with muggers 15; failure of
    law and order policies under
    94–115; on the family 28, 89; on the
    fight against crime 15, 79; as the
    firm parent 29; on the impact of
    social conditions upon crime 21; on
    the individual's responsibility for
    crime 9, 86; the influence of von

Hayek on 36; on the *Marchioness*
    disaster 127; on moral values 24–5,
    36; on progressive excuses for

criminals 9, 87–8; on socialism and
    totalitarianism 13, 158; on
    unemployment as an excuse for
    crime 49
Thompson, J. 18
Tipler, J. 108
Tomlinson, S. 158–9
Tuck, M. 104
Turner, B.M.W. 81

Uglow, S. 42, 44–6, 54, 77, 122–4

Waddington, D. 154, 156, 173
Walker, H. 72
Walker, M. 53
Walker, M.A. 108
Walklate, S. 79, 82, 103
Walsh, D. 62
Whitehead, P. 72
Whitelaw, W. 78, 113
Willis, C. 106, 140
Wilson, J.Q. 18–26, 31
Woodhouse, T. 84
Wooldredge, J.D. 112
Worrall, A. 104

Young, H. 49
Young, J. 31, 90–1, 95, 99, 105,
    114–55

Zander, M. 41

Subject index

accidents at work, and Youth Training Schemes 130; construction industry 129; mining and quarrying 130; *see also* health and safety regulations
active citizen 78–85, 86, 90, 172
Amnesty International 61–2
Audit Commission 154
authoritarian populism 35, 160–1

bail information schemes 137
'barrier of steel' 2, 33
beanfield, battle of the 43
Brixton 49–51, 75, 113
Broadwater Farm 50–1

Charter 88, 166–9
Chief Police Officers, Association of (ACPO) 53–6, 83; and National Recording Centre 53; and PACE 41–2; politicisation of 55–6; quotations from 53–6
Children and Young Persons Act, 1969 70
CIPFA 95
civil liberties: threats to 10, 30, 33, 65, 92, 94, 166
community: breakdown and crime 19; crime prevention 78–85; punishment in 151–7
community policing 69–93
Community Service Orders 71
Compton Committee 62
Confait case 41
Conservative criminology 8–12, 30, 31, 116; context of 17–18; as control culture 35–68; definition of

8; ideology and state 158–73; legitimation of 32–4; under Thatcher 94–115
control culture 35–68, 47
corporate crime 117–21
Council of Europe 143
crime: and the family *see* family; fear of 100; individualisation of 21, 26–32; prevention of 8, 10–11, 14, 19, 31, 69, 78–85, 136, 172; and the school 1, 9, 21–2, 26, 28, 76–7, 79, 86; Wilson on 20–2; and unemployment *see* unemployment
crime surveys: British 98–102, 105, 112; growth industry in 94; Islington 1985 101, 102; Islington 1989 102; Merseyside 1985 100–1
Criminal Justice Acts: 1948 38; 1967 38–9; 1982 33, 70, 71; 1986 33
Criminal Law Act 1977 39
Criminal Procedure, Royal Commission on 1981 41
criminal statistics: and clear-up rates 97–8; and crime rates 94–6
Criminal Trespass Act 1975 43

dangerous classes 30
delinquency 71, 76; syndrome 26
dependency culture 10, 13, 36–7, 74, 115, 122, 135, 148, 158, 161
Diplock courts 61–2
domestic violence 16, 92, 98, 103–4
drug trafficking 118–19, 160

economic liberalism 13–35
economy, British 3–8

Education Act 1987, 33, 77
electronic tagging 11, 73, 153, 155, 173
Employment Acts 7, 33, 52, 130
enterprise culture 10, 13–14, 37, 117,
    122, 134–5, 148, 158, 169

family 3, 7, 9, 11, 14, 24–9, 78, 87, 89,
    169–73
Fisher Report 41
fraud 116–35; broadroom 119–22; and
    its control 117–22; statistics of 117;
    welfare 122–4, 133

gay people 16–17, 39, 43, 98, 148,
    165, 169
Gibraltar shootings 63–4
Grunwick 2, 16, 51
Guinness affair 8, 119–22

health and safety regulations 124–9;
    industrial 129–32; Piper Alpha 131
hegemony 3, 9, 36–7, 40, 47, 142, 148,
    161–4, 168, 172
hippy convoys 43
Home Office 41, 81, 84, 108–9, 137,
    152–4, 156
Home Office Research and Planning
    Unit 80
Hunt Committee 60, 63

ideology 40; Conservative 16, 17, 36,
    38, 47, 69; and State 158–173
imprisonment and recession 146–51
inner city uprisings 48–51
intermediate treatment 71, 74, 153,
    107
internment 61–2

juvenile bureau 76, 108
juvenile crime 70–6
juvenile liaison department 76

Keith Report 122

Labour cabinet and picketing 2
Labour Party 1, 38–9, 46, 48, 91–2;
    and community crime prevention
    81; and the economy 4–7; and law
    and order 147–9; and local crime
    surveys 98; and Northern Ireland

62; and permissiveness 15, 17; and
    rising crime rates 95
Labour Research 56–7, 129–31
law and order 2; as party political issue
    15–17, 168; politics of 14–35;
    reclaiming the issue of 85–90;
    responses to 90–3; society 35–69;
    and youth 70–8
left realism *see* realist criminology
London Strategic Policy Unit 104
'loony left' 17, 170–1

market, and democracy 37
miners' strikes 51–3
minimum wage policy violations 132–3
monetarism 36, 37
moral values 25, 27, 28, 33, 36, 87, 89
    see also Victorian values
mugging 40, 104; and moral panics
    47–8; as a symbol of moral and
    economic decline 15
multi-agency policing *see* policing

NACRO 108–9, 137–8, 143, 146
national recording centre 53–4
National Front 32, 48, 159
neighbourhood watch 11, 14, 77–8,
    81–5, 89, 172
new conservatism 17
new realism 30, 39
New Right 14, 36
NGA 57
Northern Ireland 33, 44, 58–68
Northern Ireland (Emergency
    Provisions) Act (EPA) 1973 61
Notting Hill carnival 43

penal policy 21; crisis in 136–52; in
    the Netherlands 141; new initiatives
    in 152–7
Police, Royal Commission on 1962 45
Police Act 1964 44–6, 54
Police and Criminal Evidence Act 11,
    33, 35, 41–2, 59, 62, 67, 118
police authorities 42, 44–6
Police Federation 2, 32, 88, 113, 149
Police Support Units 44, 54 *see also*
    Special Patrol Groups
policing: accountability 42, 45–6; and
    black communities 47–8;

centralisation of 38; and class 47; community 69–93; culture of 39; and expenditure 1, 94–5; 'fire-brigade' 16; and industrial disputes 51–3; influence of Northern Ireland on 65; key moments in 44–58; multi–agency 69–93; paramilitary 35, 38; and race 47, 48, 51, 77, 160; reactive 16; subculture of 39–40, 43
Policy Studies Institute 39, 108, 110
political economy, punishment and imprisonment 140–3
poll tax demonstration 1990 170, 172
pollution 132
Prevention of Terrorism Act 39, 62–3
priority estates project 81
prisoners: demonstrations by 136, 138; ethnic composition of 108–9; special status (Northern Ireland) 63, *see also* prisons
prisons 136–57; costs of 138; expenditure 139; overcrowding 137–40, 151–7; population of 21, 136–57; statistics of 143–6; and unemployment 140–3, 146–51
privatisation: and crime control 74, 79; of criminal justice 172; and health and safety 127, 131; and pollution 132; young people's attitudes towards 134
probation orders: costs of 138; relative use of 143–5
probation service 15, 72–4, 107, 137, 145, 153–7
public order 11, 14, 17, 33–4, 43–4, 46
Public Order Act 1936 53; 1986 33, 35, 41, 43–4
punishment: trends in 143–6; in the community 151–7

race 159, and crime 91, 104–11; and prison 108–9; and probation 109; and unemployment 113; and young prisoners 140
racism 12, 23, 25–6, 29, 47–8, 51, 73, 91, 160
realist criminology 90–3; and local crime surveys 101–4; and race 110–11

safety problems: airports 125; football in Bradford 125; *Marchioness* 127; rail 126; sea, *Herald of Free Enterprise* 127; Sheffield 124
Saltley coke depot 53
Scarman Report 49–50, 75, 113
'shoot to kill' 62–5
social contract 30
social crime prevention *see* crime, prevention of
social security fraud *see* fraud
SOGAT 57
Special Patrol Groups 38, 44, 48, 54, 57, 59, 110
Special Powers Act, 60
special powers (Northern Ireland): development of 59–68; normalisation of 58–9
Stalker affair 64–6
State: the exceptional 47–8; and ideology 40, 158–73; power of 29, 33; and society 24, 28, 36, 40, 158–73; von Hayek's views on the role of 36; and welfare problems 28
Strangeways Prison, riot 8, 136, 140, 171, 173
supergrasses 62–5
'sus' 164

task force 44 *see also* Special Patrol Groups
tax evasion 122–4
territorial support units 38, 44 *see also* Special Patrol Groups
Terrorist Broadcast Ban 59
Thatcher Government: and corporate crime 117–18; as decisive break with the past 35
Thatcherism (Thatcherite): as anti-statism 40; as authoritarian populism 161; the ideological appeal of 170; and lack of social progress 87; on social security 'scroungers' and the work ethic 122; and value for money and law and order 79; views of the children of 134
Toxteth 51
tracking 51, 74, 153
Trade Union Act 1984, 52

trade unions: breaking the power of 2, 7, 153; and civil servants' rights 33; and health and safety 126–30; and industrial action 52–8; and the Labour Party 3–5, 48

Ulsterisation 62–5
Unemployment: and crime 81, 111–15; and imprisonment 140–3, 146–51
United States crime rates 19, 96, 104, 114

victimisation: 'invisible' 16; risk of 80; surveys *see* crime surveys
victims: blaming the 26, 80; and gender 102–4; and non-reporting of crime 98–100; race of 50, 104–5
Victorian values 28, 36–7, 171

Vietnam war: demonstrations against 46

Wapping, and the News International strike 57–8
welfare fraud *see* fraud
welfare state 2, 26, 40, 135, 147, 150, 160, 171; attack on 7, 13, 17, 37; dismantling of 33; failure of 23, 27; and 'scroungers' 122–3
white-collar crime 116–22; J. Q. Wilson's dismissal of 18, 22
women, as crime victims 102–4
Woolf Inquiry 136

Younger Report 72
youth, law and order and 70–8
youth 'riots' 32, 44, 47–51